the
legacy
of
logical
positivism

the
legacy
of
logical
positivism

STUDIES IN
THE PHILOSOPHY OF SCIENCE

edited by Peter Achinstein
and Stephen F. Barker

THE JOHNS HOPKINS PRESS
BALTIMORE

preface

The philosophical movement known as logical positivism began as the Vienna Circle during the 1920's and spread throughout much of the world during the 1930's. It was a revolutionary force in philosophy, for it stigmatized metaphysical, theological, and ethical pronouncements as devoid of cognitive meaning and advocated a radical reconstruction of philosophical thinking which should give pride of place to the methods of physical science and mathematical logic. Logical positivism had a dynamic impact upon all areas of philosophy, but nowhere was its influence stronger than in the philosophy of science, for this the logical positivists regarded as their especial domain. Today logical positivism no longer exists as a distinct movement, yet its effects, direct and indirect, recognized and unrecognized, continue to be felt. The time now seems ripe for an appraisal of the significance of logical positivism and its legacy for the philosophy of science. The perspective of several decades should enable us to look backward dispassionately at this movement, to characterize and examine its distinctive theses, to trace their influences upon present philosophical thinking about the sciences, and to decide what has been intellectually beneficial in logical positivism and to criticize what has been harmful.

The essays of this volume attempt to provide such an evalua-
tion. They treat various aspects of the philosophy of science in
relation to logical positivism, and they do so from various view-
points. Some contributors are strongly sympathetic toward logical
positivism: indeed, Professors Feigl and Hempel belonged to the
movement and have remained closely identified with its ideas.
The other contributors, although they find valuable elements in
logical positivism, are critical of its philosophy of science in varying degrees and in various ways—Dr. Hesse and Professor Hanson
of its conception of scientific theory, Professors Scriven and Putnam of its orientation in psychology and social science, Professors Toulmin and Shapere of its basic methodology in the
philosophy of science, and the editors in their supplementary
contributions.

Not long after his essay had been submitted, there came the
tragic news of Professor Hanson's death in the crash of his air-
plane. All who had been privileged to know him received this
news with a grave sense of personal and intellectual loss, realiz-
ing that the philosophy of science suffers by his absence.

This volume constitutes the second in the series of "Johns
Hopkins Seminars in Philosophy," the first of which was *Phenom-
enology and Existentialism,* edited by Edward Lee and Maurice
Mandelbaum. Each of the essays in this volume (except for the
last two) originated as a lecture at Johns Hopkins. While visiting the university each lecturer also conducted a discussion seminar on his topic, and these lively and enlightening sessions
proved rewarding to all who attended. For some of those who
heard them the lectures and discussions served as an introduction
to logical positivism and to the philosophy of science; for others
they provided an opportunity to extend their critical understanding of these matters. The editors hope that the essays presented
here will prove informative and stimulating to new readers, just
as they were to the original audience.

The editors warmly thank Miss Helen Longino for her help
with the proofreading and for making the index.

P. A.
S. F. B.

contents

contents

contributors

HERBERT FEIGL was a member of the Vienna Circle from its beginning and came to the United States as one of the earliest emissaries of logical positivism. He taught first at the State University of Iowa and then at the University of Minnesota, where he has held the title of Regents' Professor of Philosophy and has been Director of the Minnesota Center for Philosophy of Science. He is author of *Theorie und Erfahrung in der Physik* and *The 'Mental' and the 'Physical,'* and is co-editor of a number of books, including *Readings in Philosophical Analysis, Readings in the Philosophy of Science,* and *Minnesota Studies in the Philosophy of Science.*

STEPHEN E. TOULMIN is Professor of Philosophy at Brandeis University, previously having taught at Oxford and Leeds. He is author of *The Place of Reason in Ethics, Philosophy of Science, The Uses of Argument,* and is co-author of *The Fabric of the Heavens, The Architecture of Matter,* and *The Discovery of Time.*

MARY B. HESSE, Reader in Philosophy of Science at Cambridge University, is author of *Forces and Fields* and *Models* and *Analogies in Science*. She has served as editor of the *British Journal for the Philosophy of Science*.

NORWOOD R. HANSON was Professor of Philosophy at Yale University before his untimely death in 1967. Prior to that he taught at Cambridge University and Indiana University. He is author of *Patterns of Discovery* and *The Concept of the Positron*.

DUDLEY SHAPERE is Professor of Philosophy at the University of Chicago. He is the editor of *Philosophical Problems of Natural Science* and has written a number of articles on the philosophy of science.

CARL G. HEMPEL is Stuart Professor of Philosophy at Princeton University. His publications include *Fundamentals of Concept Formation in Empirical Science, Aspects of Scientific Explanation,* and *Philosophy of Natural Science*.

MICHAEL SCRIVEN, Professor of Philosophy at the University of California at Berkeley, previously taught at the University of Minnesota, Swarthmore College, and Indiana University. He is author of *Primary Philosophy* and a co-editor of *Minnesota Studies in the Philosophy of Science*.

HILARY PUTNAM, Professor of Philosophy at Harvard University, previously taught at Princeton. He is co-editor of *Philosophy of Mathematics* and has written numerous articles on philosophy and mathematical logic.

STEPHEN F. BARKER is Professor of Philosophy at The Johns Hopkins University. He has taught at the University of Southern California, the University of Virginia, and Ohio State University. He is author of *Induction and Hypothesis, Philosophy of Mathematics,* and *Elements of Logic*.

PETER ACHINSTEIN is Professor of Philosophy at The Johns Hopkins University. He is author of *Concepts of Science* and of various articles on the philosophy of science.

development
of
the
movement

HERBERT FEIGL

the origin and spirit of logical positivism

Logical positivism began to form a fairly definite outlook in philosophy about forty years ago. As is well known, it was primarily the influence of Ludwig Wittgenstein and Rudolf Carnap that initiated the early phase of this—then new and radical—departure from the traditional ways of philosophizing. To be sure, some aspects of logical positivism are derived historically from Hume and Comte; but, in contrast, especially to Mill's positivism, a new conception of logic (having its origins in Leibniz, Frege, and Russell) was united with the empiricism of Hume, Mach, and the early Einstein.

The Vienna Circle consisted mainly of scientifically trained philosophers and philosophically interested mathematicians and scientists. Most of the members were tough-minded thinkers, *Weltzugewandt* (as Hans Hahn put it), "this-worldly" rather than "other-worldly." They were radically opposed to metaphysical speculation, especially of the a priori and transcendent types. Since the development of the Vienna Circle is by now a familiar chapter in the history of recent philosophy, I propose, after dealing with some of the antimetaphysical doctrines of logical positivism, to concentrate on some of the aspects that are not as well known. I shall refer particularly to the work of Moritz Schlick, the founder and leader of the Vienna Circle. Schlick's early work anticipated a good deal of what in more precise formulations was later developed by Carnap, Reichenbach, and others. In his *Allgemeine Erkenntnislehre* (first edition, 1918; second edition, 1925) there were also anticipations of some of the central tenets of Wittgenstein's *Tractatus Logico-Philosophicus*. I think it was Schlick's extremely unassuming character, his great modesty and kindliness, and his deep personal devotion to Wittgenstein that made him forget or suppress the great extent to which his views, independently developed and quite differently stated, already contained very important arguments and conclusions regarding the nature of logical and analytic validity; the semantic explication of the concept of truth; the difference between pure experience (*Erleben*), acquaintance (*Kennen*), and genuine knowledge (*Erkennen*), etc. Indeed, so deeply impressed was Schlick with Wittgenstein's genius that he attributed to him profound philosophical insights which he had formulated much more lucidly long before he succumbed to Wittgenstein's almost hypnotic spell.

In the first flush of enthusiasm of the late 1920's, the Vienna Circle proclaimed its outlook as a philosophy to end all philosophies; as a decisive turn toward a new form of enlightenment. The pamphlet *Wissenschaftliche Weltauffassung: Der Wiener Kreis*, published in 1929, was our declaration of independence from traditional school philosophy. This slender brochure, composed collaboratively by Carnap, Hahn, and Neurath (aided by Waismann and myself), was presented to Schlick upon his return from his visiting appointment at Stanford University. As I remember only too well, Schlick, while appreciative of this token of friendship and admiration, was deeply disturbed by the idea of having originated another "school of thought." He was a philosophical individualist; although he promoted group colloquy and believed in the fruitfulness of mutual criticism and searching discussion, he was profoundly convinced that everyone should think for himself. The idea of a united front of philosophical attack was abhorrent to Schlick—notwithstanding the fact that he himself promulgated the Viennese point of view in many of his lectures, in Europe and also in the United States.

Logical positivism became noted, as well as notorious, through its critique and complete rejection of metaphysics. In the spirit of Hume and Comte, but equipped with more fully developed logical tools, the Vienna Circle declared any question (and any answers) of a transempirical sort to be factually meaningless. The original formulations of the criterion of meaningfulness were somewhat brash and careless. The motivation, however, was fairly obvious. Just as Hume considered significant only statements about the relations of ideas (i.e., logic and mathematics) or matters of fact (the empirical sciences), so the logical positivists were adamant in excluding as *nonsensical* any question that, in the light of logical analysis, revealed itself to be absolutely unanswerable. Always granting, and even emphasizing, that pure logic and pure mathematics have standards of meaningfulness and validity of their own, the meaning criterion was designed to separate factual questions and propositions from metaphysical pseudoproblems and pseudosolutions of such problems.

It was only some years later that the Viennese positivists realized their kinship of outlook with that of the American pragmatists, especially C. S. Peirce, and with the operationalist approach of P. W. Bridgman. The pragmatists declared a proposition meaningless if there was no difference that *made* a difference between asserting it and denying it. The difference that Peirce referred to was a difference with respect to observable consequences. Bridgman considered a concept to be genuinely meaningful only if it could be defined by specifiable, observational, mensurational, or experimental procedures. Under the influence of Wittgenstein's and Carnap's early work, Schlick maintained that the factual meaning of empirical statements consists in "the method of their verification." Taken literally, this was a regrettably inadequate formulation. No wonder that sharp criticisms from many sides were raised against this slogan. But a closer reading of Schlick's and Carnap's formulations of the late twenties and early thirties clearly shows that they were concerned with testability rather than verifiability. As I recall it, the early discussions with Hans Reichenbach, and a little later with Karl Popper,[1] engendered the more tolerant formulation of the meaning criterion in terms of testability (later, confirmability or disconfirmability). Popper quite rightly pointed out that there can be no conclusive verification of scientific hypotheses or theories. Inasmuch as these are expressed in universally quantified propositions, they are at best falsifiable, that is, refutable. (Popper himself used falsifiability, not as a criterion of meaningfulness— he rejected any and all attempts to formulate meaning criteria —but as a criterion of demarcation enabling us to distinguish between empirical and non-empirical assertions.) In any case, Carnap, as early as 1928, spoke of *"Prüfbarkeit"* or *"Nachprüfbarkeit"* in the sense of *testability,* which he later elaborated in a new and original way in his essay "Testability and Meaning" (1936).

The essential antimetaphysical attitude of the Vienna Circle is perhaps best understood in terms of a distinction between two major functions of language: the cognitive (or informative) function; and the non-cognitive (or emotive) function. In his monograph *Pseudoproblems in Philosophy* (1928) Carnap differentiated sharply between the cognitive content or knowledge claim conveyed by a linguistic utterance, and the accompanying imagery or emotions. This was the origin of the much-discussed distinction between the cognitive meaning and the emotive (i.e., expressive and/or evocative) significance of words or sentences. In transcendent-metaphysical utterances, the emotive significance was seen to masquerade for genuinely cognitive meaning. In this manner the theologians' talk of an inscrutable deity, the vitalists' talk of entelechies, and the metaphysicians' talk of the absolute (absolute substance, truth, reality, absolute space and time, or the "Absolute" of the Hegelians) were diagnosed as pieces of verbal magic or as verbal sedatives, devoid not only of any explanatory power but of all cognitive significance. The vital forces or entelechies still defended by the notable biologist-

---

1. Popper was not a member of the Vienna Circle but had intensive interchanges with, and offered incisive criticisms to, Schlick, Carnap, and myself in the early thirties.

philosopher Hans Driesch were explicitly conceived of as being "not in space" but as "acting into space," unknowable before they produce their marvelous effects but somehow inferrible *ex post facto*. Hume's analysis of the concept of causality was endorsed in that the regularity in the sequence of events was recognized as the only testable cognitive content of the principle of causality. Any introjection of "intrinsic necessity" was branded as a confusion either of logical entailment (which holds only between propositions) or of the psychological feeling of compulsion (which is all too anthropomorphic) with the objectively confirmable order of natural events. To put it in the manner of the pragmatists: There is no difference that makes a difference (in the testable consequences) between the statement "*A* is always followed by *B*" and the statement "*A* is always *and necessarily* followed by *B*." There is no testable surplus meaning in the second statement, over and above the first.

In a similar spirit the Vienna Circle accepted the relational view of space and time, and the kinematic relativity of motion. This nowadays obvious conceptual clarification was achieved by Leibniz in the seventeenth century (in his famous correspondence with Samuel Clarke in which he criticized the absolutism of Newton's conceptions). Once (in 1920) I heard a disciple of Franz Brentano's—Oskar Kraus at the University of Prague—debate Einstein with great excitement. He maintained that the following was a synthetic a priori truth: "If two bodies move relatively to each other, then at least one of them moves with respect to absolute space." This illustrates beautifully the intrusion of the pictorial appeal of the Platonic "receptacle" notion of space or a confusion of a purely definitional truth (regarding three coordinate systems) with genuinely factual and empirically testable statements regarding the motion of bodies. These are obvious matters, of course, and are quite elementary and unquestionable presuppositions of Einstein's special and general theories of relativity.

More impressive and influential in the days of the Vienna Circle was the critique of the ether concept in Einstein's special theory. The ether theory, in its final stage of defense, appeared to us to be a typical instance of a theory made proof against disproof. The hypotheses of Lorentz and Fitzgerald regarding contraction and "local time" made the ether hypothesis immune to any conceivable test. There was no difference that could conceivably make a difference in the outcome of any mechanical, optical, or electromagnetic experiment by which one might determine the velocity of a body with respect to the ether. The problem that confronted the physicists at the time was not to be solved by further *ad hoc* hypotheses but, as Einstein's genius perceived it, by a critical revision of the concept of simultaneity and, in consequence of it, a revision of the concepts of distance and duration. Einstein solved the problem by transforming the puzzle of the constancy of the speed of light into a postulate of the theory. By choosing appropriate definitions of congruence for space and time, he made the ether hypothesis not only superfluous but demonstrably devoid of empirical content or significance in the theory of Lorentz and Fitzgerald.

In his critique of the pseudoproblems of philosophy, Carnap applied the same criterion of meaningfulness to the traditional problems of realism versus idealism. The so-called problems of "the existence of the external world" and of the "reality of other minds" were shown to stem from confusions of the perfectly legitimate (because testable) ascriptions of empirical reality with some intuitive or emotive (and untestable) notions of reality. Carnap, throughout all his pronouncements (including his most recent ones), has rejected the metaphysical doctrines—of both realism *and* idealism—as being cognitively meaningless; but he has come to endorse the conceptual framework of an *empirically* realistic physicalism as a preferable reconstruction of common sense and especially of science. This seems to be essentially the same position as that taken by Wittgenstein in the *Tractatus*: (5.62) "what the solipsist *means* is quite correct; only it cannot be said, but it makes itself manifest"; and (5.64) "it can be seen that solipsism, when its implications are followed out strictly, coincides with pure realism. The self of solipsism shrinks to a point without extension, and there remains the reality co-ordinate with it."

Carnap's and Ernest Nagel's recent pronouncements on realistic versus phenomenalistic or instrumentalistic interpretations of physical theories appear to me to be essentially similar to the antimetaphysical (or ametaphysical) position of the Vienna Circle. Both Carnap and Nagel maintain that there is no factually or logically decidable issue here, and that the difference between these interpretations is merely one of preference for one *language* or another. I shall return to this controversial matter when I discuss Schlick's early critical realism and his subsequent positivism.

In regard also to other problems of philosophy, especially the philosophy of science, the attitude of the Vienna Circle was clearly empiricist. Those of us concerned with induction and probability strongly favored the frequency interpretation. We rejected all notions of probability based on a priori intuition, such as the classical one with its "principle of insufficient reason," and J. M. Keynes's version with its unanalyzable relation between the supporting evidence and the hypothesis that is probable in relation to it. It was the theory of Richard von Mises, especially as elaborated later by Hans Reichenbach, that we found most attractive. I suppose our preference for the frequency interpretation was motivated by the same reasons that C. S. Peirce advanced for his views on probability. The relative frequency of events within a given reference class seemed obviously susceptible to empirical determination. But soon enough (in my own case, as early as 1924) it dawned on us that the talk of "limits of frequencies" involved a conception radically different from the limits of infinite sequences or series in pure mathematics. There, one could always prove the existence of a limit in the light of criteria of convergence. But in the empirically given statistical ratios this is impossible.

I think I was the first of the Viennese to see quite clearly the dilemma of the frequency interpretations: To speak of a limit of statistical frequency is either to say that that limit is somewhere in the closed interval between zero and one (and that is a tautology, and hence devoid of factual information) or, if one states a limit in terms of a definite relation of n (the ordinal number of elements in a sequence) and ϵ (as used in genuine convergence criteria), to say something that is almost bound to be false. In the language of symbolic logic, the statement of genuine convergence is triply quantified. Thus, for heads or tails, for example, the limit of the frequency $\frac{1}{2}$ would be formulated by:

$$(\epsilon)\,(\exists N)\,(n)\,[(n > N) \supset (\,|\,f_n - \tfrac{1}{2}\,| < \epsilon)]$$

It is evident that because of the universal quantifiers such statements cannot be conclusively verified and that because of the existential quantifier they can never be conclusively refuted—as long as no specific function of n relating it to ϵ is stipulated. A little later, F. Waismann, influenced mainly by the scanty pronouncements on probability in Wittgenstein's *Tractatus*, attempted a purely logical definition of the probability concept in terms of the ranges (to be determined by appropriate measure functions) of the hypothesis and its relevant evidence. But it was only in the early forties that Carnap, starting from this suggestive idea, began to develop his system of inductive logic involving a definition of degree of confirmation, that is, the degree of probability bestowed upon a hypothesis by the supporting evidence. Because Carnap considered statements of degree of confirmation to be analytically or purely logically true (in virtue of his definition of probability), no synthetic a priori presuppositions seemed required. But just this point has remained controversial, and the dispute between the defenders of the subjective, the logical, and the frequency interpretations still continues. There is only one point of general agreement of all these schools of thought with the early position of the Vienna Circle: the calculus of probabilities as such is a branch of pure mathematics. It can do no more than calculate, that is, derive, deductively, the probability of complex events on the basis of given (or assumed) probabilities of elementary events. What is called, with objectionable ambiguity, the "law of large numbers" is either the theorem of Bernoulli (and that is a purely mathematical truth based on combinatorial analysis and the addition and multiplication theorems of the probability calculus) or an empirical statement about the statistical frequencies "in the long run," and as such is a logically problematic, but practically useful, conclusion of inductive inference.

The more general philosophical import of the forgoing discussion is that the so-called problem of induction (i.e., Hume's problem of the justification of non-demonstrative inferences) cannot be solved with the help of either the logical or the statistical concept of probability. Some logical positivists have therefore declared it to be a pseudoproblem; others (especially Reichenbach, myself, and, more recently, Wesley Salmon) have attempted a pragmatic solution of the old puzzle. In my own view this rests on a distinction between the justification of knowledge-claims within the framework of certain guiding principles and the practical justification of these very principles. I have tried to settle this by distinguishing between "validation" and "vindication." This is to say that the credibility of empirical hypotheses (e.g., predictions) can be validated in the light of the principles of inductive logic. But these very principles (while, of course, not open to validation) can be vindicated: their adoption can be justified pragmatically as means that are necessary (but surely never provably sufficient) for the success of scientific research, that is, for the discovery of reliable regularities. As I recall my conversations with Schlick (in 1935, one year before his untimely death), he favored this sort of approach. But I am no longer sure that it really solves the basic problem of induction.

On many occasions the logical positivists of Vienna (before and after their "diaspora") discussed the program and goals of their "reform of philosophy," especially in regard to the philosophy of science. Influenced and inspired by the ideas and achievements of Helmholtz, Mach, Poincaré, the early Bertrand Russell, and Hilbert, it was Moritz Schlick who blazed the trail for a new and synoptic approach. In his *General Theory of Knowledge*[2] he proposed as a genuine task of philosophy the clarification of the basic logical and methodological concepts and principles of the sciences. While admitting that the scientific specialist may well produce important results without being aware of, or particularly interested in, those fundamental concepts and principles, Schlick stressed again and again that a full understanding of science is possible only through reflection upon its foundations.

2. This book appeared in its first edition in 1918 as the first volume of a distinguished series of monographs and textbooks of the natural sciences.

To make these basic principles fully explicit, to specify the meaning of the pivotal concepts of science, is, according to Schlick, a proper and worthwhile job for the philosopher. Of course, this is not a new idea; at least from Aristotle down to Kant and the scientist-philosophers of the nineteenth century, it has been an acknowledged aim of philosophy. But renewed emphasis was urgently needed, especially in the German countries that had not yet recovered from the intellectual debaucheries of the post-Kantian romantic metaphysicians and the naïve agnosticism (the "ignorabimus" of Dubois-Reymond) and the equally naïve dogmatism of Ernst Haeckel (*The Riddles of the Universe!*). Much of the iconoclastic and, indeed, negativistic spirit of the Viennese positivists may be understood as a reaction against the high-flown, pretentious verbiage of metaphysical speculation. Along the lines of Bertrand Russell, Hans Hahn, the great mathematician, in a pamphlet *Überflüssige Wesenheiten* (Superfluous Entities), advocated the use of "Ockham's Razor" toward the elimination of all metaphysical, ethical, and political "absolutes."

It was Schlick's merit to have set an example of sober, lucid, and scientifically well-informed philosophical analysis. While his approach was mostly informal, he showed his appreciation of the tools of modern logic in his courses at the University of Vienna. I think it is fair to say that he conceived of the philosophy of science as a task of logical reconstruction. He distinguished quite clearly between a psychological (or sociopsychological) account of scientific discovery and a logical analysis of scientific concepts and principles. In his *General Epistemology* he dealt with the nature of scientific explanation as a prime example of cognition. He maintained that all genuine knowledge consists of a reduction of one kind of entities to another, or, of what is tantamount, the derivation of more specific propositions from more general (lawlike) ones. Thus he repeatedly used such illustrative cases as the identification of light with electromagnetic waves or the identification of the chemical bond with electromagnetic forces. Even for the level of the knowledge-claims of everyday life, he made it clear that genuine cognition amounts to the subsumption of a particular item under a class, as in recognizing a perceived thing as an elm tree.

Schlick drew a distinction (to which he ascribed fundamental philosophical importance) between *Erleben* (or *Kennen*), on the one hand, and *Erkennen,* on the other. This can be rendered in English by the distinction between *acquaintance* (or knowledge by acquaintance) and *knowledge proper* (knowledge by description). Bertrand Russell, who also recognized this indispensable distinction, used the English terms just mentioned. Thus, the mere having, that is, the undergoing (e.g., enjoying or suffering), of an immediate experience, and the ability to recognize and affix consistently the same predicates to the same qualities of immediate experience, may be called, respectively, *acquaintance* and *knowledge by acquaintance.* Both Schlick and Russell considered these to be the ultimate basis for the testing of all scientific (intersubjective, public) knowledge-claims, although they are initially subjective and private.

There are several other features of Schlick's epistemology (developed from about 1908 to 1918) which are very similar to Russell's, particularly the view contained in Russell's final systematically philosophical book, *Human Knowledge* (1948). Both consider genuine knowledge to be essentially *propositional,* that is, intersubjectively communicable by means of language. Propositions are taken to be the meanings of sentences, no matter in what language, notation, or symbolism the sentences are formulated. Thus we find in Schlick's early work important contributions to the philosophy of linguistic communication. In one of these contributions he came very close to anticipating the by now well-known *semantic* definition of *truth.* This definition, developed more systematically and precisely by Tarski (1936) and Carnap (1942), was at least adumbrated in Schlick's early articles and was fully formulated in his *General Epistemology* (1918). According to Schlick's analysis, the truth of factual statements consists in a one-to-one (or at least a many-to-one) correspondence of the words (names, predicates) of a sentence to the objects and properties or relations denoted by these words. Falsity, no matter how it may arise, ultimately consists in the equivocal use of words through which a one-to-many correspondence results between them and what they denote. Thus, if I call a given tree an oak when it actually is an elm, I am using the word "oak" ambiguously in that it would then be assigned to both kinds of tree. Schlick rejected any sort of picture view of representative language. All that seemed to matter for him was the abstract relation of correspondence (in German, *Zuordnung*). (Perhaps this is also one possible interpretation of the cryptic pronouncements on language and truth in Wittgenstein's *Tractatus*.)

Schlick realized, of course, that a direct checking of the correspondence of statements to matters of fact is possible only within the narrow scope of the perceptually given. He, like the later Russell, was therefore confronted with the problem of the meaning of truth in regard to scientific statements, most of which transcend by far the limits of immediate perception. It is interesting to note that both Schlick (from 1910 to 1925) and Russell (by 1948, at any rate) were critical realists and thus had to come to grips with the problems of transcendence. And, while they differed sharply in their views on probability and induction,[3] they argued essentially inductively for the existence of entities beyond the scope of the narrow domain of immediate experience. Both Schlick and Russell thus liberalized the radical empiricism of Hume,[4] namely, by asserting the existence of a world of *knowable* things-in-themselves—be they such objects of common life as sticks or stones, rivers or mountains, or be they the fields and particles of modern physics. It was only under the impact of Carnap's and Wittgenstein's ideas and criticisms that Schlick withdrew to what he conceived of as a neutral, non-metaphysical position. Nevertheless, he retained an *empirically* realistic view in that all specific assertions of existence—as of the atoms and electrons in physics, of the genes in biology (and perhaps also of the unconscious motives, etc., assumed in psychoanalytic theory)—were at least susceptible to *indirect* tests.

In his profoundly searching essay *Erleben, Erkennen, und Metaphysik* (1926) (as well as in his London lectures on *Form*

---

3. In 1948, contrary to his earlier empiricist views, Russell found synthetic a priori postulates indispensable for the justification of inductive and analogical inference, such as he deemed necessary also for beliefs, for instance, in the existence of the external world and of other minds.

4. Or its modernized versions as in Mach, Avenarius, in one phase of William James, and in the early phase of Russell's doctrine of neutral monism.

and Content [1932; published in 1938]) Schlick clarified the distinction between empirically testable assertions of reality and empirically untestable ones. The latter, according to Schlick, are at the very core of traditional metaphysics in that they use an intuitive and "ineffable" notion of reality. This notion could not possibly furnish a surplus of meaning to the cognitive, scientific concept of existence, but belonged to the expressive-evocative function of language. Such expression and evocation, Schlick averred, is not part of scientific knowledge-claims, but belongs to life itself and is best utilized in poetry, music, and the arts in general. It was the mistake of the traditional metaphysician to confuse (or conflate?) the cognitively meaningful and legitimate concept of existence with the intuitive, "ineffable" notion of reality.

As a consequence of this outlook, both Schlick and Russell (and there are also some hints of this in the early Carnap) maintained that knowledge proper can concern only the *structural* features of the world, and must necessarily remain silent as regards its purely qualitative *contents*. Schlick was aware of the difficulties and the dangers of this formulation. He certainly wished to avoid any type of metaphysics or mysticism regarding the "ineffable." Perhaps he did not quite succeed. Nevertheless, this kind of view, especially of physical knowledge, seems defensible. Schlick's view was in agreement not only with the epistemology developed much later (and independently) by Russell but also with the views of the brilliant but all too harshly criticized Eddington;[5] it was a view adumbrated even earlier in the writings of Poincaré. There are also traces of this kind of view in C. I. Lewis' early book *Mind and the World Order.*

How, then, did Schlick specifically interpret the logical edifice and the empirical foundations of scientific theories? Here, I think, he was chronologically the first to recognize clearly how fruitful and illuminating a reconstruction can be if it proceeds in terms of implicit definitions and correspondence rules. Schlick main-

5. See L. S. Stebbing, *Philosophy and the Physicists* (New York, 1937; republished in 1958). This is a deceptively clever positivistic critique of Eddington.

tained that the *structural* knowledge of the world provided by physical theories, for example, can be understood best by the kind of axiomatization that Hilbert had produced for geometry. The axioms (or postulates) link together a number of at first undefined and uninterpreted concepts (the so-called primitives). To this extent an axiom system—if it fulfills the necessary requirement of consistency (and to the extent that it has the desirable features of completeness and independence)—is no more than a purely logicomathematical structure (at least in the sense of Hilbert's strictly formalistic philosophy of mathematics). It is easily seen that the postulates so conceived do not convey any information whatsoever about the real world. The postulates cannot even be conceived of as definitions in the ordinary sense.[6] For they merely provide, as it were, the rules (and an initial position) in a game played with uninterpreted symbols. Viewed as definitions, they are circular in that the postulates stipulate a system of symbols related only to one another—and to nothing outside of that network. As C. I. Lewis put it so nicely: "a circle is the less vicious the bigger it is." The bon mot no doubt referred to the remarkable "fertility" of certain types of axiom systems, such as that of Peano for arithmetic, and that of Hilbert for geometry: An infinity of theorems (many of them non-trivial) can be derived deductively from sets of axioms rich enough in their initial intrinsic network connections.[7] In Schlick's picturesque account the entire deductive system, that is, the

6. Carnap was the first to see this quite clearly, and consequently distinguished "proper" concepts from "quasi" concepts in his early article, "Eigentliche und uneigentliche Begriffe," *Symposion*, 1 (1927).

7. Space does not allow more than a brief reference to the philosophy of mathematics prevalent in the Vienna Circle: We were all duly impressed with Hilbert's formalism; we found Brouwer's intuitionism intriguing and challenging, but not necessarily acceptable. Schlick, Carnap, and Hahn were clearly logicists along the lines of Frege, Russell, and Whitehead. Kurt Gödel's famous proof of his undecidability theorem ("Über formal unentscheidbar Sätze," *Monatshefte für Mathematik und Physik*, 38 [1931]) was perhaps the most exciting achievement in the Viennese philosophy of mathematics. It resulted from an arithmetization of the syntactical metalanguage of mathematics and thus utilized Carnap's important studies in the *Logical Syntax of Language* (New York, 1937). Gödel's findings were discussed in that early work of Carnap's.

postulates (implicit definitions), together with explicit definitions of equally uninterpreted, purely formal concepts (as well as all derivable theorems), form a "free-floating" structure. If this structure is to be given empirical significance, it must be anchored by "coordinative definitions" (Reichenbach's term) or "correspondence rules" (Carnap's term) to some data on the level of observation.[8] These rules of interpretation are viewed by Carnap as semantic designation rules. They are attached to some—but by no means necessarily all—of the erstwhile only implicitly defined concepts of the pure-postulate system (or to purely formal concepts that are explicitly defined in terms of the "primitives"). Carnap and Hempel have therefore spoken of a "partial interpretation" of the pure-postulate system. But they maintain that the concepts of theoretical physics can be understood adequately in terms of their empirical significance in view of this sort of logical reconstruction. In picturesque language it is the "upward seepage of the empirical juice" which provides a meaning for the otherwise altogether unvisualizable (non-intuitive) concepts of theoretical physics.

It must be kept in mind that all this is a *logical* reconstruction. It was never intended to be an account of the origin and development of scientific theories. (This is a task for psychologists, sociologists, and historians of science.) The value of the seemingly very artificial *logical* reconstruction consists in the distinction that it allows us to make between logicomathematical and empirical questions that may be asked regarding scientific theories. It is

8. This view was anticipated in an early form by N. R. Campbell in his book *Physics: The Elements* (Cambridge, 1920); it was independently and briefly expounded by Carnap in his essay "Über die Aufgabe der Physik," *Kantstudien,* 28 (1923), by H. Reichenbach in his *Axiomatik der relativistischen Raum-Zeit-Lehre* (Brunswick, 1924), and has been presented also by the American philosophers of science H. Margenau, in *The Nature of Physical Reality* (New York, 1950), and F. S. C. Northrop, in *The Logic of the Sciences and the Humanities* (New York, 1947), who speak of "epistemic correlations" or "correspondence rules" as the connecting links between the formal system and its empirical foundation. In Carnap's most recent publication, *Philosophical Foundations of Physics* (New York–London, 1966), as well as in some of his earlier essays, he too uses the term "correspondence rule"; see also C. G. Hempel's *Aspects of Scientific Explanation* (New York–London, 1965) and *Philosophy of Natural Science* (Englewood Cliffs, N.J., 1966).

clearly one thing to ask about the consistency of the postulates or the conclusiveness (validity) of the derivation of theorems; it is quite another matter to ask about the empirical significance of theoretical concepts or about the evidential support of a theory.

As I understand the intentions of Schlick, Carnap, and Reichenbach, they were especially interested in providing an adequate account not only of the logical structure of theories but also of their empirical confirmation (or disconfirmation). Schlick, Reichenbach, and Carnap, though highly impressed with Poincaré's genius, repudiated his conventionalism. This doctrine held that the postulates of the physical sciences (including physical geometry) are "disguised definitions," and that, therefore, such principles as the law of the conservation of energy are basically tautological and hence empirically neither confirmable nor disconfirmable. Schlick repeatedly referred to the clarification of this first law of thermodynamics given by Max Planck, according to which it is not at all a mere convention but the formulation of a most pervasive regularity of nature. Continuing along similar lines, Reichenbach opposed the views of Poincaré and Duhem, according to which experimental tests always concern theories as entireties (i.e., the postulate systems in their totality). Reichenbach, of course, admitted that in testing some postulates others are unquestioningly presupposed. But he also pointed out that it is possible to formulate the postulates of physical theory in such a manner that there is at least some degree of independent testability for each of them. He showed that scientific procedures usually consist in the successive securing (by experimental confirmation) of some postulates which then can be used as presuppositions for the testing of more problematic assumptions. Thus, for example, the geometrical optics of telescopes (or microscopes) can safely be presupposed when it comes to the testing of astrophysical (or biological) hypotheses. Quite generally, what seemed correct to the logical positivists in the views of Poincaré and Duhem, is no more than the obvious logical truth that, given a theory in the form of a conjunction of postulates, and an empirically refuted consequence of that conjunction, any (or even all) members of the conjunction may be false (at least one must be false). But it is precisely the virtue of ingenious experiments to pinpoint the "culprit" (or "culprits"), as it were, that is, to identify, and finally to eliminate, those postulates which are responsible for the empirically refuted conclusion.

In the light of the forgoing account of the nature of scientific theories, we may say that the meaning of theoretical concepts consists in the rules according to which they (or rather the symbols representing the concepts) are used. These rules are of at least two radically different types. We have, first, the implicit definitions and, second, the rules of correspondence. (Usually there are also explicit definitions.) If anything is to be retained of the original empiricist criterion of factual meaningfulness, then it is at least the requirement that the purely formal concepts of the postulate system (the "pure calculus," in Carnap's terminology) be connected by correspondence rules with the concepts of observable things or features.[9] Just what is to be taken as observable is a matter of pragmatic decision in a given reconstruction. Carnap long ago preferred the observables of common life (roughly the objects and their properties and relations as directly perceived) to the sense-data basis of the earlier positivists (including his own position in *Der Logische Aufbau der Welt* [1928]).

It was in view of this outlook that Carnap (in the early thirties) formulated his two famous theses of the "unity of science." Retrospectively, I am inclined to think that the *first* of these theses is relatively obvious, if not trivial, for it amounts to no more than the assertion of a certain unity of the *language* of the factual sciences. This unity of the natural and social sciences is to be understood in terms of the same confirmation basis for all scientific statements; this basis is formulated in what Carnap called the (intersubjective) physicalistic thing language, that is, the ordinary observation language, or the language of data. Only

9. I think this is (among other things) what Richard von Mises had in mind when he suggested "connectibility" as a meaning criterion. It is even more explicit in Schlick's essay "Meaning and Verification" (*Philosophical Review*, 45 [1936]), in which he stipulated that any factually meaningful (descriptive) terms in a language must be connected by a chain of definitional steps with some terms of the language of direct experience.

a non-metrical account of space and time and a qualitative (again topological) description of properties of observable objects are required for this purpose. By an ingenious logical device (the technique of reduction sentences) Carnap attempted to show that concepts of dispositions (capacities or abilities) could be introduced on the basis of terms of the observation language. These latter terms were assumed to be understood directly, and hence not to be in need of definition. (Carnap, at least since 1956, has changed his views on this matter, and now prefers an explication of most concepts of scientific theories by means of postulates and correspondence rules.)

The points just discussed in connection with the first thesis of the unity of science pertain to the logical reconstruction of scientific knowledge-claims, and to the explication of the meaning of scientific concepts. The choice of the intersubjective observation language as a basis for the reconstruction implies a (qualified) adoption of the behavioristic outlook in regard to psychology and the social sciences. I say "qualified" because the data of introspection can well be included to the extent that they themselves are formulated in the language of behavior. The linguistic utterances, that is, the verbal behavior, of human beings quite clearly constitute an important part of the data of psychology, just as the discriminatory responses of animals and humans furnish a basis for the ascription of mental states. According to the early stage of logical positivism, the mentalistic language (as it is used in connection with introspection) was construed as being strictly translatable into the language of behavior. But later analyses showed this view to be grossly oversimplified. (It has the same defects and shortcomings as the phenomenalistic reduction of physical-object statements to statements of immediate experience.) The later view, now adopted by many logical empiricists, is that peripheral behavior is to be taken as a probabilistic indicator of certain central states—the latter to be described (to the extent that the required knowledge is available) in the language of neurophysiology or in the (mentalistic) language of introspection. (The mentalistic language can by metaphorical extension also be made to cover the depth-psychological statements about unconscious states or processes as assumed, e.g., by psychoanalytic theories.)

This leads me, finally, to a brief discussion of the *second* thesis of the unity of science (or of physicalism). This is a much more exciting, but also more problematic, pronouncement. Schlick, Carnap, and Reichenbach, who espoused this thesis, were fully aware of its conjectural and hence precarious character. Essentially it endorses a certain program for the current and future development of science toward a unitary or monistic set of explanatory premises. It is encouraged by the partial but impressive successes in the reductions (in the sense of explanation) of chemistry to physics; of biology to physics and chemistry; and of psychology to neurophysiology. As a distant goal of this program of unitary explanation, some future theoretical physics is fancied, from which all observable phenomena of the entire universe (including organic life and mind) would be derivable. This thesis is, of course, not only problematic but also inevitably vague in that such a theoretical physics may have to be very different from its current stage. All that can be said at the moment is that the "style" of explanation might be somewhat similar to that used in the present stage of the theories of relativity, quantum mechanics, and quantum electrodynamics. If this program is at all successful, it would resolve the much-discussed difficulties of emergent evolution.

It was Schlick, perhaps more distinctly and promisingly than anyone else among the logical positivists, who provided helpful suggestions regarding a coherent conception of the relation of the mental and the physical, or, as the widely used phrase expresses it, "the place of mind in nature." The traditional mind-body problem has indeed remained one of the most recalcitrant difficulties of a scientific empiricism. As many philosophers have seen it, this perplexing problem arises when we ask about the place of the apparently "homeless qualities" of immediate experience in a world conceived of by means of the highly abstract concepts and postulates of physical theories. It was Schlick's contention that the "physical" be conceived of not as a kind or aspect of reality but as a type of conceptual system radically dif-

21

complete list of Carnap's publications is appended to this book);

M. Schlick, *Allgemeine Erkenntnislehre,* forthcoming English translation by A. E. Blumberg (New York, Dover).

Books containing searching criticisms by outstanding philosophers of science include:

Henry Mehlberg, *The Reach of Science* (Toronto: University of Toronto Press, 1958);

K. R. Popper, *The Logic of Scientific Discovery* (New York: Basic Books, 1959);

———, *Conjectures and Refutations* (New York: Basic Books, 1962);

Israel Scheffler, *The Anatomy of Inquiry* (New York: Alfred A. Knopf, 1963).

Some important articles not reprinted in Ayer's collection are included in:

Herbert Feigl and May Brodbeck, eds., *Readings in the Philosophy of Science* (New York: Appleton-Century-Crofts, 1953);

Herbert Feigl and Wilfrid Sellars, eds., *Readings in Philosophical Analysis* (New York: Appleton-Century-Crofts, 1949).

I have tried to expound, defend, as well as comment on the difficulties of a new synthesis (based on both Schlick's and Carnap's ideas) of a monistic solution of the mind-body problem in "Physicalism, Unity of Science and the Foundations of Psychology," contained in Schilpp's *Philosophy of Rudolf Carnap* and in a long essay, "The 'Mental' and the 'Physical,' " in *Minnesota Studies in the Philosophy of Science,* vol. 2, ed. H. Feigl, M. Scriven, and G. Maxwell (Minneapolis: University of Minnesota Press, 1958), pp. 370–497.

My own critique of logical positivism may be gathered from my presidential address, "The Power of Positivistic Thinking," *Proceedings of the American Philosophical Association,* May, 1963.

STEPHEN E. TOULMIN

from logical analysis to conceptual history

I

In the world of fiction, Virginia Woolf and Lawrence Durrell
have accustomed us to a *genre* in which the chosen events are
described through the eyes of each character in turn, and the
reader is left to wonder for himself what more, if anything, could
have been said. In such cases, they have insisted, a prosaic insistence on impersonal narrative, or a Ranke-like demand to be
told "what really happened," reveals a misconception of the
nature of motives, personal relations, and the other categories
of psychological description. The lesson such writers have taught
us is relevant not merely to fiction. For instance, the network
of ideas, influences, and personalities temporarily interwoven
within a philosophical movement, such as logical positivism, itself
has something of the same protean character. Intellectual affilia-
tions, as much as emotional encounters, depend for their appearance on one's standpoint; thus it is inevitable that a dozen separate accounts of the legacy of logical positivism should differ,
perhaps even drastically, in their perspective, proportion, and
emphasis. What are they, after all, but the apperceptions of so
many individual monads, each mirroring a shared totality from
its own particular point of view?

If this is so, there is something to be said for making a virtue of necessity. Instead of feigning an Olympian impartiality, or professing to record the historical fact *wie es eigentlich geschehen,* it may well be better if I here *select* one out of the whole bundle of possible perspectives and tell my tale, quite deliberately, as it appears from the chosen standpoint. The origins, ambitions, and long-term outcome of the logical positivist movement will be most clearly discernible within a self-bounded picture—if the perspective in question is well chosen. So, in what follows, I shall be attempting to depict the relations between logic and philosophy, natural science and language theory, as they developed in the mind of one man: a man who, from the very beginning of the movement, was closely associated with logical positivism and the Vienna Circle, but who was never completely identified with it. And my concluding appraisal of the new intellectual opportunities that philosophers of science owe to the work of Wittgenstein and Schlick, Carnap, von Neumann, and their associates, will take the form of an extrapolation—carrying forward directions that become apparent within logical positivism if one studies it from a single, consistent viewpoint.

My chosen monad is Ludwig Wittgenstein himself. Even before 1914, Wittgenstein's early correspondence with Bertrand Russell had brought him into contact with the originators of philosophical analysis at Cambridge: with Bertrand Russell and Alfred North Whitehead, Maynard Keynes and G. E. Moore, and with their associated circle—Roger Fry, E. M. Forster, G. M. Trevelyan, and the rest. (In his essay "My Early Beliefs," Keynes made a revealing remark, in passing, about Wittgenstein's attitudes toward that original Bloomsbury group.[1]) Returning from

1. Reprinted, for instance, in J. M. Keynes, *Essays and Sketches in Biography* (New York, 1956), pp. 239–55: The allusion to Wittgenstein is on p. 253, where Keynes brackets "Ludwig" with D. H. Lawrence as objecting to the brittleness, superficiality, and—above all—the *irreverence* of the Bloomsbury group. The whole essay is of great importance for anyone who wishes to understand the social and conversational background against which Moore and Russell were developing their philosophical ideas and techniques. Looking back in September, 1938, Keynes acknowledges the defects of the Bloomsbury attitudes and

Cambridge to Vienna, to the Austro-Hungarian Army and in due course to the Italian prisoner-of-war camp where so much of his work on the *Tractatus Logico-Philosophicus* was done, Wittgenstein linked the two prime centers of analytic philosophy; the *Tractatus* was one of the founding documents from which the new positivism of the Vienna Circle took its departure, according to many accounts the crucial one; and it was Wittgenstein who provided the channel by which Russell's work on mathematical logic and philosophy exerted its full influence on Schlick and his other colleagues. So let us follow out here, stage by stage, the changing relations of Wittgenstein's philosophical activities to those of the Vienna Circle philosophers—first serving as a starting point for logical positivism, then for a short time running parallel to it, and finally diverging sharply from it. Such a comparison can help us to appreciate better the course that twentieth-century analytic philosophy has taken and the intellectual debts that philosophers of science today owe to the logical positivists.

II

Let us start in Cambridge at the turn of the century. The alliance between formal logic and philosophical analysis personified by the early Bertrand Russell had, to begin with, nothing specifically "positivistic" about it. In intentions, at any rate, it was philosophically neutral. True: both Russell and his closest ally, G. E. Moore, were in revolt against the British post-Hegelian idealists, notably Bradley. Yet what they objected to in Bradley was not what he said—it was his failure (as they saw it) to say anything significant at all. Absolute idealism was not so much a philosophical doctrine as an intellectual debauch. One could laugh at it, like F. C. S. Schiller in his spoof issue of *Mind;* one could clear it out of the way and start again from scratch; but one could not contradict it, because its arguments were confused beyond the point of rational discussion. So Moore and Russell

---

the truth behind Lawrence's objections with marvelous candor; but in doing so, of course, he exemplifies the respect for intellectual honesty which was the group's greatest virtue.

scorned to debate with their predecessors, and embarked rather on a "new instauration"—a cleansing of the Victorian philosophical stables, to be followed by the reconstruction of philosophy in new and unambiguous terms.

The analytic methods employed in this reconstruction might be either of two alternative kinds: those of a refined lexicography, as in *Principia Ethica,* or those of a purified mathematics, as in *Principia Mathematica.* But in each case the keyword was the *principia.* For theirs was a new and initially uncommitted beginning. Indeed, if you go back to the earliest papers of both Moore and Russell, those written in the late 1890's, you will find that even so characteristic a notion as that of a "sense-datum" is not yet in evidence. Those ideas came later. For the moment, the task was to assemble a disinfected language for philosophy: to insist on clear definitions of those terms which could be defined, to rebut all misleading attempts at defining terms that were essentially indefinable, and to reveal the true logical forms and articulations underlying the sometimes deceptive clothing of grammar and syntax in which everyday language dresses up our thoughts. Were these humdrum ambitions or—as John Locke called them—underlaborers' tasks? They may appear that way to us; but a missionary, reforming zeal will carry one through even the most tedious-sounding enterprises.

Onto this scene came the young Ludwig Wittgenstein. Wittgenstein had been trained not in philosophy but in applied physics, and he first visited England as an engineering apprentice. But his logical interests had already been awakened by Frege, his philosophical curiosity by Schopenhauer, and his enduring puzzlement about the problems of language and representation by one book above all: Heinrich Hertz's treatise *The Principles of Mechanics*—a book whose central task had curious parallels to the one which was shortly to engage Wittgenstein and Russell. For Hertz had faced directly the question that had perplexed Kant before him: how the classical theory of Newtonian dynamics can, at one and the same time, form a mathematical system of axioms and deductions and also describe the *actual* world of nature as contrasted with all *logically conceivable* worlds. (This is a topic to which Wittgenstein subsequently devoted an unusually sustained passage in the *Tractatus,* and this confirms his debt to Hertz.[2] If only—Hertz had argued—one would distinguish with sufficient care between the formal steps by which such a calculus is articulated and the empirical and pragmatic steps by which the resulting axiom system is connected with actual experience, that question would answer itself. Furthermore, one could then circumvent all those fruitless and confused debates about "the essential nature of force" which had disfigured and obstructed the development of nineteenth-century physical science.)

At the outset Wittgenstein found the philosophical program presented in Russell's early writings extremely attractive, but almost at once it landed him in a problem similar to Hertz's. Suppose we did try to reform philosophy, as Russell proposed, by reconstructing language on an explicitly defined mathematical model, and suppose we did in this way arrive at a system of logical articulations within which one could not fail to "reason aright": what guarantee would there be that the resulting formalism had any application to the real world? Christening that axiom system "the propositional calculus" was all very well; but this did not answer the fundamental question, it merely begged it. (To treat the formulas of the system as "propositions" without further ado was merely arbitrary.) What one had to show, and, if possible, to state, were the conditions on which a formally defined calculus could serve a *propositional* function at all. As Hilbert and Hertz had demonstrated, no axiomatic system by itself *said* anything about the world. If such a system was to perform a "propositional," that is, a linguistic, function, some-

---

2. *Tractatus Logico-Philosophicus* (London, 1922), propositions 6.34–6.3611; cf. Heinrich Hertz, *The Principles of Mechanics Presented in a New Form* (originally published in 1894, translated into English in 1899, reprinted in New York in 1956), notably the Introduction, pp. 1–41. The enduring mark left by Hertz on Wittgenstein's mind is shown by his repeated references to one passage in this introduction as the best concise statement he knew of of the differences between genuine scientific uncertainty and mere philosophical confusion: that passage is the paragraph on pp. 7–8 which ends, ". . . when these painful contradictions are removed, the [philosophical] question as to the nature of force will not have been answered; but our minds, no longer vexed, will cease to ask illegitimate questions."

thing more was required: it was necessary to demonstrate that the relations holding between language and the world made such a formalization possible.

At this point a basic difficulty presented itself. As Moore had shown, the procedure of *analysis by verbal definition* could be used only up to a certain point: if applied in ethics, for instance, it soon ran up against an obstacle—the most basic terms (e.g., "good") were seemingly indefinable. The procedure of *analysis by formalization* now encountered a similar obstacle. The use of familiar non-theoretical language to analyze the relations between the language of physical theory and natural phenomena need not have presupposed what it was meant to justify, and so was legitimate enough. But to use the same language for an analysis of language-as-a-whole was open to immediate objection. Russell's program required one to assume that the "true structure" of language was "propositional" (in the required, formalizable sense) *and* that the real world was describable by means of such a language. These assumptions, as Wittgenstein saw, were substantial ones. Yet what more could legitimately be *said* in order to clarify the situation? Once we have questioned the validity of using language to describe the world at all, it does not improve matters if we use that same language in the attempt to describe and validate the relations *between* language and the world. That whole enterprise will be a kind of Indian rope trick—like trying to climb up an unsupported ladder and hold it up, both at the same time.

This dilemma is fundamental for any proper understanding of the *Tractatus,* and so of the origins of logical positivism. At this early stage Wittgenstein evidently accepted Russell's program as being legitimate and worthwhile, not only for mathematics, but also for philosophy. Initially, his questions about the applicability of the propositional calculus reflected no active doubt— on the contrary. Yet his quandary was genuine. Urging people to think of the world as being "composed of facts, not of things," of the unit-elements in a fact as "hanging together like the links in a chain," and so on, was likely merely to prompt the question, "But *why* should we? *Why* must we suppose that language is related to the world in this way?" And, faced with that retort, the Wittgenstein of 1919 could have given, on his own confession, no literal reply. If the propositional calculus was to provide the sole instrument for making literal, meaningful statements, one could then speak *about* its linguistic role only figuratively.

In a manner of speaking, therefore, the whole *Tractatus* had been, as Wittgenstein himself was to acknowledge later, a kind of Platonic myth: not a straightforward theoretical account for which any literal defense could be given (since that was out of the question), but at best a helpful image which might give us some insight into the nature of the language/world relationship —a metaphorical extrapolation of Vaihinger's *Philosophy of As-If* to the point of mere verbal gesturing. And, if we ourselves, with historical hindsight, now try to answer the question, "Why did the young Wittgenstein have to picture the relation of language to the world as he did?," all we can say is, "Because it gave him the guarantee he needed that the propositional calculus, as derived from *Principia Mathematica* by the method of truth tables, would be capable of serving a *linguistic* function."

III

Until 1920, then, Wittgenstein saw no fundamental reason to challenge the philosophical claims Russell had made for the propositional calculus. Yet the very fact that he wrote the *Tractatus* at all proves that his confidence in those claims was not unquestioning. Presumably Russell's analysis of language followed the right lines; but its results were at any rate dubitable, and one must accept them only with the reservations implied by the mythical character of the *Tractatus*. These reservations must not be overlooked, because they distinguish Wittgenstein's own position sharply from that of the Vienna Circle philosophers of the 1920's.

What must be explained is the fact that this contrast was overlooked at the time. For Schlick and his associates thought of themselves as simply carrying Wittgenstein's argument further. Where he hesitated, they trod without fear. Unlike his qualified belief in the philosophical relevance of *Principia Mathematica*, their confidence was unquestioning. For a historian of philosophy, this poses one of the key problems about the origins of logical positivism. True, such a transformation was not unprecedented. Something similar had happened to Descartes 250 years before. In his *Principia Philosophiae* he had put forward an elaborate cosmological parable intended not to contradict the revelations of the scriptural narrative but rather to give an insight into the present structure of the natural world, thereby reconciling (he hoped) a mechanical view of nature with a tolerably orthodox view of mind and the deity. But his more enthusiastic followers dismissed all his qualifications as mere diplomatic eyewash and turned his carefully balanced "mechanic theism" into the Cartesian deism of the Paris salons.[3] Now the logical positivists transformed the spider's web of Wittgenstein's myth into the scaffolding of a "scientific philosophy," reinterpreted the delicately qualified metaphors of the *Tractatus* as bald assertions, and converted a fabric of images woven on a strictly *as-if* basis into a *logische Aufbau*.

How did this happen? Before answering that question, we should take a look at the other main sources of the Vienna Circle doctrines. To begin with, these had been scarcely more doctrinal in intention than Moore's and Russell's early programs. During the years before 1914 scientifically minded intellectuals in Germany and Austria were disgusted with the entire state of official European philosophy. If they had any patience with professional philosophers at all, they reserved it for Schopenhauer; but this could be attributed as much to his polemical attacks on Hegel as to his personal doctrines. Their own preoccupations arose, rather, out of the exact sciences. They followed with sympathy and interest the mathematical innovations of Frege and Hilbert, the theoretical physics of Poincaré, Lorenz, and the meteoric young Albert Einstein, the chemical skepticism of Ostwald, Mach, and other critics of literal-minded atomism. All these arguments relied on a new kind of critical analysis, and it was this critical

3. On Descartes' attempted compromise and its subversion by the Cartesians, see, e.g., Stephen Toulmin and June Goodfield, *The Discovery of Time* (London–New York, 1965), chap. 4, and the Introduction, by Alexandre Koyré, to Rene Descartes, *Philosophical Writings*, ed. G. E. M. Anscombe and P. T. Geach (Edinburgh, 1954).

movement within the exact sciences which now provided the inspiration for the new positivism.

The philosophical aims of the young Viennese positivists were thus the same Augean ones as those of Moore and Russell; but their methods were different. Whereas the young Cambridge radicals had set out to reform philosophy by analysis, the Viennese positivists were determined to reform it by generalizing methods that were already proving their worth in scientific theory. Philosophy must be set on "the sure path of a science"—indeed, integrated with physics and biology into a single "unified science." In practice this involved reconstructing both philosophy and science in the form of axiomatic, mathematical disciplines, as the example of Frege suggested; as empirical, inductive disciplines, in which all generalizations and abstract concepts could be legitimated directly by appeal to observation; or *ideally* (and here they ran into the problems that Wittgenstein encountered) as empirical, inductive sciences whose inner articulations were at the same time formalized on the axiomatic pattern of systems in pure mathematics.

If there *was* a streak of positivism present at this stage, it came in through such men as Mach, Avenarius, and Vaihinger. Above all, Ernst Mach was to be the godfather of logical positivism, if not its chief progenitor. In the early years of the century, Mach held the Professorship in the Philosophy of the Inductive Sciences at the University of Vienna, a chair in which Moritz Schlick was later to follow him. Even now, the formative influence of Mach's rich and complex mind on twentieth-century physics and philosophy deserves more attention than it has yet had. In the 1880's he did pioneer aerodynamic work on supersonic shock waves from explosions; through his critical and historical studies *The Science of Mechanics* and *The Principles of Physical Optics* he revealed a lucid, intellectual self-awareness in exposition; and the insistence on the primacy of experience and observation, characteristic of his work in both physics and the history of science, was associated in his thought with a philosophical commitment to "phenomenalism." All claims to knowledge of the world around us, Mach argued, derived their justification from the evidence of our senses, and this "evidence" must ultimately be interpreted in terms of the direct content of our individual sense fields. Accordingly, the theory of knowledge, if not the whole of science, was reduced for him to *die Analyse der Empfindungen*—the analysis of sensations. Mach's epistemological position, like Hume's, was a "sensationalist" one.

This last idea grew in significance for the Vienna Circle philosophy of the 1920's, for, when the logical positivists set about identifying an epistemological starting point for their theories, they turned in vain to Wittgenstein's *Tractatus*. Although the *Tractatus* provided the basic logical structure for the new positivism, the Vienna Circle philosophy was completed only when the *Tractatus* was run together with Mach's sensationalism. The argument of the *Tractatus* had employed the notion of "atomic facts" to correspond with the "unit propositions" of an idealized formal language and had gone on to show how the significance of more complex propositions might, in theory at any rate, be analyzed by "truth-functional" methods. But Wittgenstein had said nothing to indicate how, in practice, one was to recognize "atomic facts" or "unit propositions": this had not been his purpose. The logical positivists now remedied his omission. Taking a hint from Mach and from Russell's own doctrine of "knowledge-by-acquaintance," they equated Wittgenstein's "atomic facts" with the indubitable and directly known "hard data" of Mach's and Russell's epistemologies. The "unit propositions," which were the ultimate carriers of meaning, thus became *Protokolsätze* and thereby the ultimate carriers of knowledge—each recording one single item of sensory evidence, vouchsafed by one single "sensation" or "sense datum." [4]

4. This account of the origins of the Vienna Circle epistemology needs two qualifications.

First: as it subsequently developed, logical positivism acquired a "physicalist" as well as a "sensationalist" wing. For the physicalists, the *Protokolsätze* were reports of basic observable data about objective situations, involving material objects or physical measuring instruments, rather than about an individual's sensations; but their preoccupation was still epistemological because their basic question remained, "How can our claims to (hypothetical) knowledge of general theoretical truths be validated in terms of our (categorical) knowledge of particular observable truths?"

Second: the Vienna interpretation of the *Tractatus* as implying a "sensa-

Like Mach, therefore, the Viennese positivists for the most part were content to operate with an epistemological unit taken over with little change from David Hume's notion of "impressions." Like Hume again, they identified the realm of the "necessary" and the a priori with that of the "analytic" or "tautologous"; and this at first appeared to be in line with the *Tractatus* account of "logical" truth-or-falsity. Propositions were to be considered meaningful only if they were *either* confessedly logical, and thereby tautologous or inconsistent, *or else* genuinely empirical, in which case their semantic value would be determined by cashing them in for actual or possible observation reports or *Protokolsätze.* The formal truth calculus of the *Tractatus* thus became a method for the "logical construction" of human knowledge, by which higher-level abstractions and propositions of scientific theory were to be built from, or anchored onto, the concept-free, "hard data" of the *Protokolsätze.* The fundamental dichotomy between empirical propositions and logical ones was accepted as absolute and exhaustive: whatever could not be expressed in either form was not truly a meaningful proposition. This ax, it was true, threatened to sever ethical utterances (and much else) from the realm of the meaningful; but a place was soon found for many of the disputed utterances, even though as second-class speech, under the heading of "emotive" rather than "cognitive" expressions.

The resulting philosophy was a clean, functional one worthy of Gropius: geometrical in its lines, with none of that unpositivistic muddleheadedness so common among working scientists. (The logical positivists would cite with admiration Mach's slashing attack on the Newtonian concepts of absolute space and time.) [5] Thus the transformation was under way which proceeded,

---

tionalist" or "observationist" epistemology will be less puzzling if one recalls that the book was circulated with a preface by Russell (later disowned by Wittgenstein) which encouraged this interpretation, and that it was naturally read in conjunction with Russell's own books *Our Knowledge of the External World* and *The Philosophy of Logical Atomism.* Russell's early epistemology was, in fact, very close to Mach's and in certain significant respects anticipated the logical positivist position.

5. E. Mach, *The Science of Mechanics* (Chicago, 1902), originally published as *Die Mechanik in ihrer Entwicklung* (Leipzig, 1883); see especially the

step by step, from the *Tractatus,* through Russell's *Philosophy of Logical Atomism,* to Carnap's *Logische Aufbau der Welt,* and finally to Ayer's *Language, Truth and Logic.* And, despite a dozen subsequent qualifications and changes of name, the same basic dichotomies (between the factual and the logical, the cognitive and the emotive) still preserve a central place in the logical empiricism of the present day.

IV

Meanwhile, Wittgenstein had retired to a distance; first to an elementary school in Wiener Neustadt, later to an Alpine hut in Norway, eventually to a whitewashed eyrie in the tower of Whewell's Court at Trinity College, Cambridge. From the sidelines he watched the development of logical positivism with growing distaste. During the early years of the movement the philosophers and scientists of the Vienna Circle deeply respected his authority, and one or two of them (notably Moritz Schlick and Friedrich Waismann) eventually were able to have extensive personal discussions with him. Yet he remained an onlooker, and an increasingly skeptical one, so that by the mid-1930's he had dissociated himself entirely from ideas and doctrines which others continued to regard as *his* brain children. For his own part he hoped that he had "climbed through, on, over" his earlier doctrines, that he had finally "surmounted" them; and, having kicked away the temporary scaling ladder used in the *Tractatus,* he was distressed to see others picking it up and embedding it permanently in intellectual concrete, for that had never been his intention. The logical positivists were overlooking the very difficulties which the *Tractatus* had been meant to reveal and were turning an argument designed to circumvent *all* philosophical doctrines into a source of *new* doctrines, meanwhile leaving the original difficulties unresolved.

---

preface to the seventh edition (1912), where he labels absolute space and time as *Begriffsungetüme,* or "conceptual monstrosities." The orthodox Machian interpretation of Newton is expounded, e.g., in Max Jammer, *Concepts of Space* (Cambridge, Mass., 1954), pp. 139–42. Its justice is questioned in my paper "Criticism in the History of Science: Newton on Absolute Space, Time and Motion," *Philosophical Review,* 68 (1959): 1–29, 203–27.

What are we to make of this reaction? It would be easy to write it off as a display of temperament on the part of one who was by nature a prima donna. But that would be a mistake. One is at liberty to speculate about ulterior motives, but Wittgenstein also had powerful *reasons* for dissociating himself from the logical positivists; and, if we take the trouble to analyze those reasons, it will help us to define more exactly the scope, strengths, and limits of the Vienna Circle approach.

The fundamental point at issue can be clarified by comparing two approaches to the philosophy of science. In the course of the *Tractatus,* as we said, Wittgenstein cited Newtonian dynamics as providing an extended illustration of his views about the nature of language, and this discussion can usefully be contrasted with the logic of scientific theories subsequently elaborated by such men as Carnap, Hempel, and Nagel. To present my conclusion immediately: For logical empiricists one of the main functions of a "logic of science" has been to provide epistemological guarantees for science, but for Wittgenstein the *Tractatus* was in no sense an exercise in epistemology. On the contrary: As Wittgenstein saw it, epistemological preoccupations were distracting his Vienna Circle colleagues from his real topic, namely, the relations of language to the world, and were leading them to take for granted an impossible theory of language. This distraction, I would add, was attributable above all to the example and influence of Ernst Mach's and Bertrand Russell's sensationalism.

The difference is worth spelling out. According to the *Tractatus,* the function of a formalized theory in science was to provide a possible "method of representing" the relevant kinds of fact about the natural world. As Wittgenstein had learned from Hertz, the applicability of any axiomatic formalism, whether Euclid's, Newton's, or Russell's, is necessarily problematic. It is one thing to lay out such a system in the form of explicit definitions and deductions; it is another to show how the resulting categories and logical articulations can be applied to the world as we know it. Up to that point there was no disagreement between Wittgenstein and the positivists. But now the old epistemological question arose: "Have we any guarantee that a given theory—e.g., Newtonian dynamics—does in fact apply?" And here we reach the parting of the ways, for Mach and the early logical positivists believed that, in principle at any rate, all the abstract terms of a meaningful theory have their "physical meaning" conferred on them through their association with appropriate collections of "sensations" or "observations"; and, interpreted in this way, the statements in our abstract formalism become empirical descriptions of the natural world as we perceive it. Accordingly, in a completely candid science, every general abstract term or proposition is anchored down, logically and epistemologically, to the corresponding set of *Protokolsätze*, while the terms used in the *Protokolsätze* themselves are defined "ostensively," by associating them with the contents of our "observations"—ideally, of our sensory fields.[6]

This was once again a return to Hume, with "sensations," "sense data," and/or *Protokolsätze* standing in for "impressions" and statements that record "impressions." Wittgenstein had no use for any such doctrine. An axiomatic theory, he had argued, defines only a formal *ensemble* of possibilities in "logical space." (It was no accident that he had borrowed his nomenclature from Boltzmann's and Liouville's statistical thermodynamics.) This formal ensemble of possibilities—this "symbolism," "mode of representation," or "language"—could never be anchored *logically* to the world we use it to describe, because logical relations hold only *within* a symbolism. No set of authentic definitions can be contrived which will by itself transform the Newtonian formalism, or any other set of symbolic articulations, into a plain description of the world: if we *do* use the possibilities defined by such a theory as the stock-in-trade of our scientific descriptions and explanations, that fact inevitably remains a fact as much about *us*

6. As will already be apparent, the idea of ostensive definition was to have significant connections with later attempts to construct a methodology for science on the empiricist basis laid by logical positivism: e.g., P. W. Bridgman's "operationalism" in physical science and the psychological methods of Skinner, Hull, and others. The link between logical positivism and physics was John von Neumann, whose "phenomenalist" interpretation of quantum mechanics reflected his "physicalist" epistemology (see note 4 above). The links between logical positivism and contemporary psychology are clearly demonstrated in Charles Taylor's book *The Explanation of Behaviour* (London–New York, 1964), chap. IV, pp. 72–97.

as about the world. "That Newtonian mechanics *can* be used to describe the world," Wittgenstein had declared, "tells us nothing about the world. But this *does* tell us something—that it can be used to describe the world *in the way in which we do in fact use it*." [7] If Mach had played Hume, then Wittgenstein was here playing Kant—repeating Kant's countermove against Hume, but in a linguistic rather than a psychological mode. The crucial idea of "ostensive definitions," by which the logical positivists had hoped to account for the connection between language and the world, was delusory. In the last resort the connections between the linguistic realm and the world—the meanings, uses, or *modes d'emploi* it involves—cannot be made a matter for formal definitions: they are something which we must simply "catch on to."

Using this last phrase, of course, involves running ahead. The idea of "language uses" as something we have to "catch on to" becomes open and explicit only in Wittgenstein's later phase, after his break with the logical positivists was complete. Yet the arguments that led him to this idea were, I believe, implicit even in his earlier views. The work on the *Tractatus* had taught him that the relationship between language and reality was not, and could not be, a "logical" one. One might demonstrate this relationship, but one could not describe it, let alone make it a matter for formal definition: it could be shown but not stated, *gezeigt* but not *gesagt*. Definitions can have a logical force only as between one set of words and another; thus the ambition to establish formal relationships between words and the world, whether by "ostensive definition" or otherwise, was unacceptable. Yet, for Mach, that ambition had been fundamental if epistemology was to give the kinds of guarantees for natural science that he required.

This was the breaking point between Wittgenstein and the logical positivists. They would have to choose between him and Mach; and by and large they chose Mach. Yet they did so without at first consciously renouncing Wittgenstein, for, as they saw it, there was nothing incompatible between the insights of the two *maestri*. In the *Tractatus* the basic symbolism of *Principia Math-*

7. *Tractatus,* proposition 6.342.

ematica, as generalized by the truth-table method, apparently had provided positivism with the logical skeleton it had lacked in, for instance, the writings of Auguste Comte. The idea of "atomic facts" lent itself at once to an epistemological use, if these facts were simply identified with the evidence of Mach's "sensations." And a dozen other gnomic remarks in the *Tractatus* thrown out in passing could be reinterpreted in the same sense. For example, Wittgenstein's insistence that the relationship between language and the world was fundamentally ineffable, that the mode of projection of a map cannot itself be "mapped," any more than we can *see* the light rays we are *seeing with*—this insistence, which he had expressed in the closing proposition of the *Tractatus, "Wovon man nicht sprechen Kann, darüber muss man schweigen,"* was interpreted by his Viennese associates as the positivist slogan "Metaphysicians, shut your traps!" Thus was born the hybrid system of logical positivism which professed to put an end to all metaphysics but succeeded, rather, in rewriting the metaphysics of Hume and Mach in the symbolism of Russell and Whitehead.

v

From this point on, Wittgenstein's philosophical development diverged from that of most of his Viennese colleagues. How soon he recognized the incompatibility of their views, it is hard to say, without more biographical evidence than we yet have. But the seeds of disagreement were there from the start, and it was only a matter of time before they germinated.

The logical positivists, for their part, had satisfied themselves about the applicability of Russell's propositional calculus. They found the process of "ostensive definition" quite unmysterious and embarked with confidence on the formal investigations that were in due course to lead to von Neumann and Morgenstern's theory of games, to von Mises' work on the probability calculus, Carnap's inductive logic, and the rest. To all of this, Wittgenstein had no objection, so long as it was regarded simply as an extension of mathematical methods into new fields—comparable, for instance, to R. A. Fisher's work on the statistical design of scientific experiments. But he himself was not by temperament an applied mathematician, he was a philosopher; and the more he thought about all the things that Moore and the sense-datum theorists, Mach and the logical positivists, were alike taking for granted, the more puzzling he found them. How, for instance, was ostensive definition conceivable? How could "private sensations" be used as an anchor for language? And, if they could not perform this function, how could one then break the hold of the intellectual model that Moore, Mach, and their followers found so seductive?

We are now in a position to locate both the negative and the positive aims that underlay the second phase of Wittgenstein's work, which was represented by *The Blue and Brown Books* and the *Philosophical Investigations*. To put the negative point first: Judging from his experience with both the Vienna Circle and the Cambridge "sense-datum" philosophers, one major obstacle to understanding had been the idea that bare, unconceptualized "sensations" could play a direct part in the building of a language and provide the "hard data" required for epistemology to be 100 per cent secure. Given this central target, the significance of Wittgenstein's later polemic against the idea of a "private language" in which "sensations" are the carriers of "meanings," and the extraordinary amount of space he devoted to demolishing this idea need no further explanation. Like Kant with his motto "Percepts without concepts are blind," Wittgenstein was concerned to emphasize that unconceptualized sensory inputs give no testimony and put us in a position to say nothing, that, as the late John Austin was to put it, *sense data are dumb.*

More positively, however, Wittgenstein soon saw that he must also find some alternative way of indicating how language *does* operate. It was all very well to insist that, literally speaking, the uses of language could not be stated but only shown; but that could no longer be accepted as an argument for silence—*Darüber muss man schweigen.* After all, in the *Tractatus* he had managed incidentally to "show" a good deal about the relation between formalized scientific theories and the world, using as his expository device the model of a "picturing relationship." The problem now was to find comparable ways of "showing" how language operates in spheres of thought, reasoning, and meaning to which the "picture" model of language has no relevance, not even mythical or analogical.

At the corresponding point in Kant's antisensationalist argument, he had launched into what he called his "transcendental deduction," arguing that our existing system of concepts, categories, and forms of intuition alone could yield a *coherent* understanding of experience. Kant was prepared to settle for nothing less than a "deduction" because, in his eyes, it was essential to insulate the fundamental structure of our rational concepts from what he called "mere anthropology": it would never do, for instance, to make the *necessary* truth of Pythagoras' theorem dependent upon the *contingent* truth that, in actual practice, surveyors and other such geometry-users habitually operate with procedures the effect of which is to keep the Euclidean system applicable. Wittgenstein's ambitions were more modest. Certainly the positivistic equation of the "necessary" with the "tautologous" had been too shallow. Tautologies are two-a-penny, and we can construct as many more as required, Humpty-Dumpty-wise, whenever we please: "It's a question of who's to be master, you or the words." But this leaves one central fact unexplained: the fact that some such tautologies are manifestly more indispensable than others, that we "feel" the necessity of some of them (in Keats's phrase) "on our pulses," while we would throw others overboard with equanimity.

This point was not met by turning it, as G. E. Moore did, into a conundrum—"Is the proposition that p is a necessary proposition *itself* a necessary proposition?" To do that would only conceal the fact that we are concerned here with two kinds of "necessity," one of which can plausibly be equated with "tautology," the other of which cannot. We would do better to rephrase Moore's question in the form, "Could we get along without the tautology p?" Nor is it met, I suspect, by replying, with Quine, that the original distinction between "necessary" and "contingent" propositions was never applicable in the first place, except perhaps contingently. For the very questions at issue are: "On what conditions does that distinction remain applicable?" "In what contingencies should we be obliged to admit that the applicability of some fundamental concept, or the relevance of some necessary relationship, was once again in doubt?" Rather, some way must be found of bringing into the open the *human contingencies*— the "anthropological" facts, as Kant would have called them— underlying the adoption of our existing categories and concepts. The central problem with which Wittgenstein had been concerned throughout his career as a philosopher thus drove him away from all questions about syntax and formal semantics into that area of "pragmatics" and "psychologism" which logical positivists and logical empiricists have always dismissed as an intellectual slag heap.

In this second phase, Wittgenstein's style of exposition was as idiosyncratic as before; and those who never attended his lectures can hardly be blamed for missing the point. Whereas in his *Tractatus* he had resorted to myth, he now used parables or fables. To reconstruct two typical samples from memory:

Suppose a young child who has been playing outdoors runs into the house and grasps the kitchen tap, calling out as he does, "Water, water" —this being a word he heard used for the first time only yesterday. And suppose someone now raises the question, "Is the child telling us something, or showing that he has learned the meaning of this word, or asking for a drink?" What are we then to do? Need there be any way of answering that question?

Or again:

Suppose an anthropologist finds the members of a tribe, whose language he does not yet understand, cutting up bolts of longitudinally striped cloth and exchanging them for small cubes of wood, uttering as they hand over the cubes the sounds "eena," "meena," "mina," "mo," and so on, always in the same regular sequence. And suppose he discovers that this exchange proceeds always up to the same point, regardless of whether the cloth is (as we should say) single width or folded double. What should the anthropologist then conclude? Is he to infer that the tribe values cloth only by its length as measured along the stripes; or that the merchants who sell the cloth single width are rogues; or that this tribe's arithmetic has a different structure from ours; or that "eena," "meena," "mina," "mo" are not their words for "1," "2," "3," and "4" after all; or that this is not really a commercial exchange, but some kind of a ritual . . . ? Or might we have no effective way of deciding among these alternatives?

These little stories, with the sting in the final question, all served the same general purpose. They forced the hearer into a corner from which he could escape in only one way. He was thereby compelled to concede that the applicability or inapplicability of our actual categories and concepts depends, in practice, always on previous human decisions, and that these decisions have become "second nature" to us, for one or the other of two reasons, or for both. Either the choices in question were made long ago in the development of our culture, and have been preserved ever since within our conceptual traditions—no occasion having arisen for doubting them; or, alternatively, the practice of using an expression in our way rather than in a conceivable alternative way was drilled into us so early in life that we have ceased to think twice about it unless some unforeseen contingency compels us to reconsider it; or, most commonly, the relationship under discussion reflects choices that were taken at forgotten branch points in conceptual development, both ancient in terms of cultural history and primitive in the development of the individual's speech and thought habits.

By explicitly reconstructing for ourselves the issues that arise at these branch points, we shall normally, though not necessarily, come to see that our actual linguistic practices are understandable, natural—even the most eminently practical—ones to have adopted, given all the circumstances. To that extent we shall do what can be done to satisfy Kant's demand for a "transcendental proof" of the "synthetic a priori." The concepts and categories we actually employ are not the only conceivable basis for a coherent, describable experience of the world; but they do represent a legitimate equilibrium resulting from sequences of interlocking choices, none of which, in the actual context of decision, could have been taken differently except at a certain price. We can ask for more than that only if we misunderstand what is involved in the building of our language.

From this point of view the fables and parables of Wittgenstein's later teaching open a door which connects philosophy to such disciplines as child psychology, anthropology, and cultural history. True, Wittgenstein himself used to insist, quite as much as Kant, that his examples were not intended in any "anthropological" sense. It was not his purpose to offer hypotheses about how children may in fact learn to use language, about how different tribes do in fact use it, or about how our current twentieth-century concepts have in fact developed from earlier ones.[8] Rather, his aim was to bring into sharp focus certain features of our current adult language uses which (like contact lenses) we commonly look *through,* not *at,* and which when misunderstood may lead us to draw conclusions damaging to philosophy. Nevertheless, by the very act of penetrating the logical articulations, necessary truths, and conceptual congruities that define the semantic structure of a living linguistic system to those *empirical counterparts* which underlie them—all the factors determining those forgotten choices and decisions by which the development of our concepts has been guided—by that very act Wittgenstein opened

8. There are many illuminating analogies to be drawn between the philosophy of Wittgenstein and his associates and that other great intellectual product of early-twentieth-century Vienna, the psychoanalytic movement. Wittgenstein himself was aware of this fact: although he protested at the description of his later philosophy as "therapeutic positivism," there was a certain rough justice in the label, and at certain points he used to cite Freud as facing similar problems himself. For instance, Freud had early been compelled to recognize that neuroses may in many cases find their explanation in "fantasy traumas"—unspoken resentments rooted in remembered events that never in fact took place *as the patient recalls them.* In these cases the psychoanalyst will be interested only in the patient's repressed recollection, distortions and all, not in the actual event; for his task is to uncover the concealed motivation of neuroses in the present, not to guess at their historical etiology in the past. In this respect the more recent attempts to build a theory of personality development on Freudian foundations (e.g., those of Erik Erikson) go beyond Freud's own work into an area which he deliberately avoided, and involve hypotheses about time sequences, whereas he was concerned only with interpretations of a patient's present state of mind.

Wittgenstein would similarly insist that his own concern was with the misleading models, misconceived theories of language, incorrect grammatical analogies, etc., underlying fallacious philosophical positions in the present, not with hypotheses about the historical genesis of such fallacious attitudes or about the proper development of our concepts. So the *extension* of Wittgenstein's position advocated in this paper goes beyond his work—quite deliberately—in the same general way that Erikson goes beyond Freud. The most persuasive treatment of Wittgenstein's later philosophy as a kind of intellectual psychoanalysis—concerned (to coin a word) with "cerebroses" rather than with "neuroses"—is that given by John Wisdom in the series of essays collected in *Philosophy and Psychoanalysis* (Oxford, 1953).

to inquiry a whole range of empirical and historical questions more radical and more exciting than anyone immediately recognized.

VI

The logical positivists, having opted for more formalized techniques of language analysis, never faced these issues seriously. In their account of the matter, indicative sentences have a genuinely descriptive use by virtue of the ostensive definitions through which words are ultimately made to "refer to" the world: the resulting statements, or propositions, are logically docile and therefore of potential interest to philosophers. (Where that trail ends, in terms of "extensional ontologies" and the rest, I need not remind you.) Sentences in other moods, or indicative sentences involving non-referential words, were not immediately tractable; but the hope was to domesticate as many of them as possible by restating their essential meanings in formally analyzable terms. As for the remainder, concerning which all such hopes were vain —for instance, aesthetic appraisals or metaphysical declarations— these were regretfully (or cheerfully) written off as merely leading one into a linguistic morass or an intellectual junk pile.

For Wittgenstein, the applicability of Russell's propositional calculus to the world had always been open to question; and in time he abandoned his original belief in the philosophical relevance of that calculus. By the time the Vienna Circle had completed its work the applicability of this formalism was no longer questioned. Quite the reverse: the possibility of giving such a formal analysis was now used as a criterion for distinguishing philosophically acceptable questions, statements, and expressions from those which were intellectually disreputable or incoherent. What was not formalizable could no longer be deemed significant. The triumph of technique was seemingly complete.

Yet, as so often happens with success stories, this one ends with an ironical twist. Let me show how this happened step by step. Our central topic here has been the development of analytic philosophy during the twentieth century, with particular reference to the role of the Vienna Circle philosophers, and we have distinguished three phases in this story. For the first thirty years of the century, *analysis* in philosophy was taken to mean establishing linguistic or logical equivalences and using these equivalences to re-express terms and propositions in philosophically trouble-free forms. For G. E. Moore the task was to extend to philosophically difficult cases the kind of equation represented by, for example, "A brother is a male sibling" or "The word 'brother' means the same as 'male sibling.' " For Russell it meant unpacking hidden logical implications from problematic sentence forms, with the help of the models given by the propositional calculus, so that "The present King of France is bald" was replaced, for philosophical purposes, by "There is now one and only one *x*, such that *x* is a king of France, and *x* is bald." A similar confident eye for equivalences survives even in Gilbert Ryle's "sentence-frame" method, which relies on our ability to recognize at sight that the grammatical form *"He verbed adverbly"* admits of only certain permutations; that, for instance, "Heed adverbs like 'carefully' . . . and 'pertinaciously' cannot be used to qualify such cognitive verbs as 'discover' . . . or 'see,' any more than they can qualify such verbs as 'arrive' . . . or 'conquer.' " [9] And the art of recognizing such equivalences and incongruities reached its high point in J. L. Austin's work on the distinctions between different adverbs of exculpation.[10]

Yet the question was always lurking in the background, *why* all these logical equations and grammatical congruities are as they are, rather than otherwise. Moore's intuitive grasp of syn-

9. Gilbert Ryle, *The Concept of Mind* (London, 1949), p. 151.

10. See, for instance, his famous paper "A Plea for Excuses," in his *Philosophical Papers,* ed. J. O. Urmson and G. J. Warnock (New York, 1961). See also the closely related work of Herbert L. A. Hart and Antony M. Honoré on the legal application of such adverbs in relation to questions of negligence and responsibility in their *Causation in the Law* (Oxford, 1959).

The *incompleteness* of such appeals to "intuited usage" was implicit already in Keynes's description of the way in which Moore would counter disagreement, by using "the accents of infallibility" and "an expression of face as if to hear such a thing said reduced him to a state of wonder verging on imbecility. . . . *Oh!* he would say, goggling at you as if either you or he must be mad; and no reply was possible" (see Keynes, "My Early Beliefs," *Essays and Sketches in Biography,* pp. 243–44). As late as the 1940's Moore remained a master of this method, as those who saw him in philosophical meetings will testify.

onymy, Russell's formal ingenuities, even the "plain man's feel for what you just can't say" which Ryle and Austin both cultivated with such delicacy—in the long run it was inevitable that such claims would be challenged and some more profound way demanded for displaying the ultimate basis of our conceptual equipment. No one had been fully satisfied that Kant's account of "synthetic a priori truths" was the whole story; the claim that all necessary truths were tautologies seemed, if anything, a step backward, yet what alternative was there?

At this point we turn to the second phase of our story. The new styles of analysis introduced by Wittgenstein and Waismann during the thirties met an immediate need. Consider, they said, the choices and decisions implicit in the successive steps by which our current concepts are built; and consider the kinds of changes that would be necessary—in the world we live in, in the ways we live, or in both—for us to be forced to call into question the appropriateness and significance of our existing concepts. By facing directly the very different hypothetical circumstances in which our conceptual arrangements (institutions, forms of life) would have ended up, we shall at the same time come to understand how in our actual circumstance they in fact ended up as they did. In a phrase, the equivalences, congruities, and necessary truths of earlier philosophical analysis represented not eternal, unchangeable verities but *intellectual equilibria;* and the second task for philosophical analysis was to bring to light the conditions on which these equilibria depended.

But, having gone that far, why not go further? If it is a legitimate task for philosophers to go behind our current conceptual relationships and to consider how differently these might conceivably have ended up—supposing the natural world, and/or the structure of our bodies, and/or the development of our cultures, and/or the sequences by which our children learn to talk, had been sufficiently different—why should we stop at mere speculation? Why should we not try to base our understanding of these conceptual relationships on a wider study of how things have in fact happened? Could we not, for instance, look into the procedures by which language uses *are in fact* established and maintained—both in the lifetime of the individual and in the progressive development of a culture—for a more general explanation of what *can* meaningfully be said? And, if the structures of our adult language and understanding are the joint products of our upbringing and of our cultural history (which can hardly be questioned), is it not worthwhile to study them as such and to relate our current adult conceptions of *number* or *good, freedom* or *time,* to the sequence of decisions by which these conceptions came (both ontogenetically and phylogenetically) to their current forms?

There were moments, during the years following 1935, when one or two analytic philosophers came tantalizingly close to following up on these questions explicitly. Consider, for example, Friedrich Waismann's *Introduction to Mathematical Thinking.* This is a fine example of second-period philosophical analysis which unraveled and dissected out the complexities concealed within the simple-looking word "number": it showed how many philosophical difficulties can be circumvented if only we avoid asking, for instance about "irrational" numbers, questions that have been given a meaning only in the case of "integers," or applying unthinkingly to, say, "transfinite" or "complex" numbers all the patterns of argument which were introduced for "real" numbers. As a piece of pure analytic exposition, the book would be hard to improve. Yet its very style may raise expectations it does not satisfy. For suppose Waismann is right—and he clearly is—in arguing that the concept of *number* needs to be analyzed, not in terms of a single array of formal definitions and procedures, but rather by reconstructing an ordered sequence of such arrays, in which the concepts of transfinite, complex, and imaginary numbers are shown trading on the implications of logically prior concepts, such as those of real and rational numbers. How far, we may then ask, does that *logical* sequence of formal definitions reflect, or find a reflection in, temporal sequences, whether psychological or historical?

Does the logical dependence of the concept of transfinite numbers on that of real numbers, for instance, place limitations on the learning sequences by which those number concepts can be *acquired?* That is, should Waismann's analysis be considered as a *prolegomena* to the work of Jean Piaget and Jerome Bruner?

And is the sequence of definitions and dependencies which Wais-mann expounds the only conceivable one, or has it developed in part as the outcome of historical accidents? Do we, for instance, conceive of transfinite numbers as we now do only because Georg Cantor came on the scene just when he did, vis-à-vis Weierstrass, Dedekind, and Hilbert, or might an alternative "mathematical culture" have developed under different circumstances? Wais-mann's *conceptual analysis* would have been even more valuable if only it had been supplemented by something more in the way of *conceptual history*.

This having been said, the irony implicit in our current situa-tion can be made clear, for, within the philosophy of science itself, striking examples of just this kind of *conceptual history* were already being written more than fifty years ago. During the years before 1914, one man above all refined the art of expound-ing the inner complexities of our scientific concepts in such a way as to display their current logical structure as the product of their intellectual history. Who was that man? His name was Ernst Mach. Mach was a man with many strings to his bow: quite apart from the dynamics of supersonic flow and the epistemology of his *Analysis of Sensations,* his books on mechanics and optics were consciously designed to give a "historical and critical" treatment of our fundamental physical concepts.

Accordingly, the limitation of the Vienna Circle philosophy lay not in its debt to Mach; rather, it lay in being indebted to the *wrong books* of Mach. If the logical positivists had studied Mach's conceptual histories more closely, they might have made less dras-tic claims on behalf of mathematical logic and have taken some of the formal starch out of their own philosophies of science. For Mach himself was never a "logical" positivist; and it is the element of conceptual history in his thought which many of us find most refreshing today.

VII

"Every worthwhile philosopher," Gilbert Ryle has said, "must be something of a parricide." Intellectual criticism goes sufficiently deep only if the philosophers of each generation are ready to dis-own the basic axioms of their immediate masters. Yet, even though we slay our intellectual parents, we cannot help but inherit from them—thus, for example, Russell's *Human Knowledge* shows unexpected parallels to F. H. Bradley's *Appearance and Reality,* against which Russell was originally rebelling.[11] While many of us whose philosophical careers began after 1946 reject the positivism of our forebears, it would be presumptuous for us to deny our inheritance entirely. At the very least, we share with our analytic predecessors a common stock of questions and problems about whose answers and solutions we *dis*agree.

What legacy, then, has logical positivism left us? What enduring marks of value has the Vienna Circle made on the philosophy of science? We can give these questions either a pedestrian answer or a more sympathetic one. The pedestrian one would be this: "It has compelled us to face, to sort out, to define, and thus to understand better both (1) the role of formal and linguistic elements in the conduct of our intellectual enterprises, and (2) the relation between these formal and linguistic elements and the historicoecological situation within which they have to be applied. In this way it has compelled us to consider and clarify, more exactly than ever before, the ways in which formal techniques come to serve human purposes as these emerge from the historical interaction between men's minds and their changing ecological situations."

Such an answer would not only be pedestrian, it would also *miss the point* of logical positivism. For the aim of the Vienna Circle was never merely one of clarification. Theirs, as Stuart Hughes has reminded us, was a radical, liberating, apocalyptic movement which thought of itself as a kind of International Liberation Front—*for* scientific enlightenment and *against* the conservative obscurantism of idealist philosophy.[12] All the basic

11. Compare the detailed criticisms of ordinary language advanced by Russell in Part II of *Human Knowledge: Its Scope and Limits* (New York, 1948) ("rough and ready approximations which have at first no beauty and only a very limited degree of truth") with Bradley's arguments, in *Appearance and Reality: A Metaphysical Essay* (New York, 1930), to demonstrate that our familiar human concepts and categories of thought are all concerned with "mere appearance."

12. H. Stuart Hughes, *Consciousness and Society* (New York, 1958), chap. 10, sec. I.

texts of the movement, from Ayer's *Language, Truth and Logic,* back through Carnap's *Logische Aufbau der Welt* to Wittgenstein's *Tractatus,* and even to G. E. Moore's *Principia Ethica,* were intended to put an end to traditional ways of doing philosophy, and sometimes to philosophy itself, considered as an independent discipline. (One must never overlook the missionary element in Moore, as illustrated by the influence of the "flaming advocacy" of *Principia Ethica*—the phrase comes from Roy Harrod's biography of Keynes[13]—on men such as J. M. Keynes.) Just as for Marxists the triumph of "scientific socialism" was to put an end to the confusions and contradictions of earlier class-ridden politics, so for the positivists of the twenties and thirties the triumph of "scientific philosophy" was to put an end to the confusions and contradictions of earlier school-ridden metaphysics. The "diseases" of philosophy were to be "cured" by the "therapy" of philosophical analysis; and so seriously was this view of philosophy taken that, in the 1930's, Wittgenstein quite deliberately drove his best students out of philosophy into other, "humanly more valuable" professions such as medicine or science. He saw it as his own vocation, or doom, to scrub down the Augean stables of philosophy single-handedly.

Yet the victories of Marxism have not led to a "withering-away" of the state; nor has logical positivism led to a "withering-away" of philosophy. Rather, the sterilizer has proved to be a nutrient: after analytic treatment, philosophy has burgeoned more than ever. The logical positivists' critique may have forced us to consider how formal techniques come to serve human purposes, but it has not replaced the understanding of that over-all process by the analysis of formal structures alone; nor has it made a broader understanding of their role less necessary. For the fact is that, in intellectual as in political affairs, apocalyptic ambitions always prove delusory, and revolutionary hopes are bound to be largely disappointed.

Still, it would be deeply unfair to judge logical positivism by the failure of its misconceived aims while shutting our eyes to the

13. R. F. Harrod, *The Life of John Maynard Keynes* (London, 1951), esp. p. 78.

successes of its incidental by-products. For once, the radical sur-gery that was intended to kill philosophy has ended by improving its health. Already, through the work of John von Neumann, the Vienna Circle's preoccupation with formalism and mathematical logic has played a substantial part in the development of com-puter science. Meanwhile, the movement's other principal con-cern, with the analysis of language, is giving birth to a new theoretical linguistics through the work of Chomsky and his asso-ciates. And now, as I have hinted, we find ourselves faced with a further possibility: that of a new science of human understanding, in which the logical structure of our concepts and language uses is seen in its proper relation to conceptual ontogeny (e.g., Piaget and Luria), to conceptual phylogeny (prefigured by Mach), and also to the physiological and anatomical substrates and correlates of concept acquisition and loss as studied, for example, by Lettvin, McCulloch, and Geschwind.

A philosophical movement which has made such contributions to contemporary thought—even if incomplete and as by-products of its main intentions—has no reason for excessive modesty. If this is failure, an onlooker may say, then the failure of logical positivism is as glorious as the success of many philosophical movements.

the
status
of
theories
in
physical
science

NORWOOD R. HANSON

logical positivism and the interpretation of scientific theories

The view from Vienna was always bifocal. Concerning syntax, statements—for the Viennese—were either analytic in their sign design or synthetic; that is, either the negation of P entailed a contradiction or it did not. Concerning its semantics, P was either necessarily true or just contingently true; that is, it was either invulnerable to counterfacts or quite vulnerable, and possibly false. Concerning its epistemological status, P was known either a priori or a posteriori; reflection alone was sufficient to establish P or it was not. Concerning the content conveyed by a statement network, either it was informative about the *facts* of a subject matter or it detailed only the formal arrangement, the structure, the rules of that network; that is, either it discloses what *is* the case or it delineates the grammar, the inferential machinery, linking elements within discourse about the subject matter. Concerning the epistemic content of experiential statements, either they denote sense data or they refer indirectly to material objects. The sense-datum claim was construed in the *Kreis* as being free of all interpretation, speculation, and extrapolation, whereas material-object claims result from such exercises of intelligence.

These bipartite analyses of meaning, truth, and experience typify logical positivism. Such stentorian contrasts generated discussion, criticism, and revision in the late 1920's and early 1930's. But the clarity of dichotomy faded before the realities of discourse, experience, and science—which rarely allowed themselves to be sliced, sundered, and separated. The high spirits of hasty division were halted by the bitter Quinean tablet in the analytic-synthetic case and by a draught of Wittgenstein in the matter of phenomenalism. Bifocals became compound lenses.

However, the earlier division by positivists—between scientific theories and their interpretations—although modified significantly by today's logical empiricists, still depends on distinctions delineated before 1934. Granted, analyses of theories and interpretations have become sophisticated, articulate, and technical in their expositions. But the basic strategy now is just what it was for Schlick and Carnap in the thirties. To wit, a scientific *theory* is (ideally) a deductive structure, an inferential reticulum, an algorithm, a physical *interpretation* of which is explicitly brought about by coupling terms and formal properties of the algorithm to objects and processes within a subject matter. Interpreting a theory is something *done* to formally finished frameworks. It is something clamped onto a theory; or perhaps it is a "hooking" of theory to subject matter somewhat like the hooking of wire mesh over the frame of what will become a modeled statue. Qualifications by contemporary logical empiricists have melted the cutting edges of tools that sliced concepts for the Viennese in 1930. Theories are no longer so sharply demarcated from observation or from interpretation. But the earlier divisions still determine *where* today's thinkers will locate their modifications. Hence we will discuss the logical-positivist view of scientific theories as if this paper were being written in 1934.

The strategy of this paper will be, first, to set out the distinguishing features of a positivistic analysis of theories and their interpretations. Next, we will indicate how spectacular moments in the history of physics support such an analysis—support it in the sense that the analysis is often illuminating as to actual developments in the history of science. Positivists acknowledged Mach and Einstein as philosophical idols. Finally, we shall pursue the rhetorician who asked "What is it to interpret a scientific theory? Are the theory and its interpretations ever apart? *Could* they be apart?" Analysts who hastily construe this as a question of history or psychology or genesis are simply wrong. They are as wrong in this case as they were when construing Wittgenstein's criticisms of phenomenalism to concern only matters of psychology, not analysis. Conceptual inquiry is the name of our game in this third section. It will appear just as strange to regard an interpretation-free calculus as a scientific theory as it is to regard an interpretation-free visual encounter as a scientific observation. Subject-neutral inferences come from the same philosophical basket as subject-neutral experiences. Both are misguided attempts to find the conceptual ground floor of scientific theory and of scientific observation. They are misguided in much the same way. But, before the turkey shoot, we must fatten the turkey!

I

Logical Positivism and Its Interpretation of Theories

Before Euclid, geometrical lore was an unordered collection of carpenter's formulas, surveyor's recipes, minor demonstrations, deductions, displays, and depictions of spatial puzzles and their solutions, as well as some few rudiments of geometrical argumentation. With Euclid all such extant "know-how" became systematized as geometrical *knowledge* within what we call the *Elements*. That work, proceeding from a few primitives and rules, generated first a set of axioms, via which one could move by inference from any single item of geometrical knowledge to any other item—the entire discipline being interconnected with deductive conduitry that has served as our paradigm of systematic knowledge. Consider Copernicus' case against Ptolemy; he claimed that *his* cosmology unfurled "in a Euclidean manner," whereas Ptolemy required *ad hoc* hypotheses to preserve any semblance of system within his *Almagest*. Newton was more explicit: the several and sundry sciences scattered through schools and societies in the seventeenth century were all cemented within one discipline by this heroic axiomatizer. Celestial mechanics, ballistics, tidal theory, dynamics, kinematics, hydrodynamics, hydrostatics, optics, and acoustics—all these tumbled inferentially from the *Principia Mathematica Philosophiae Naturalis,* whose few axioms and rules provide a most powerful intellectual machine.

Hilbert out-Euclided Euclid himself. For, however Euclidean Euclid's ambitions were, his frequent need for diagrams and constructions, as well as his incessant dependence upon intuitive notions, *had* to dissatisfy a super-Euclid like David Hilbert. Within his reconstruction of geometry the primitive terms, the formation rules, and the rules of inference delineate how undefined terms can be combined to form other terms and full statements—whether true or false. Some of the latter are accepted as fundamental—to be called postulates. Given these and the rules of inference, all one needs in a problem are the initial conditions—for example, the numerical values for sides and angles of *this* isosceles triangle—and deducible conclusions tumble forth, all via Hilbert's "rules of the Euclidean game." Indeed, he emptied Euclid's geometry of content. In no way does Hilbert's reconstruction depend upon demonstrations within, or intuitions of, actual spaces. Either the whole of our discursive knowledge of Euclidean geometry is contained completely within David Hilbert's reconstruction, or his axiomatization is deficient—the detection of which, and the remedy, would themselves constitute an exercise within the positivist program of logical reconstruction.

Thus systematic knowledge is always representable, ideally, as an inference game. Such systems will be replete with primitive terms and statements, with construction and transformation rules, with conventions concerning what does and does not constitute demonstration or proof, and with some delineation of what will count as the resolution of any problem set within the framework of that discipline. As the logically distilled essence of geometrical knowledge, the Hilbertian ideal has long served us as a paradigm. Moreover, within a movement such as logical positivism, wherein the pseudoproblems of traditional metaphysics seemed but misuses and misunderstandings of language, such reconstructions as Hilbert's were a magical model for the elimination of chimerical philosophical pursuits. Clearly, to formulate all rules of discourse would, it was mused, identify metaphysics and other speculative enthusiasms as simple errors in the employment of language.

Similar programs have been known before. Lagrange, motivated in much the same way as twentieth-century positivists, construed physical science as analytical mechanics, within which primitives, rules, and postulates might be formulated as strictly as they are within any mathematical inquiry. The only distinction for Lagrange lay in there being more ideas—such as force, mass, and velocity—to be added to the arsenal of algorithmic transformation techniques. Analogously, the Euclid-Hilbert ideal served as a sangraal for the early positivists' conception of a scientific theory —only some additional linking of formalism with subject matter had to be forged. But, where Lagrange sought to achieve this by broadening the set of primitives, Vienna positivists undertook this *and* the introduction of "correspondence rules" and "co-ordinating definitions." Because of the latter, terms constituent of an otherwise uninterpreted theorem get hooked to actual observables (objects and processes) and thereby generate a genuine observation statement, not just a bottom-of-the-page formal conclusion.

Of the positivists' original notions of interpreting theories, then, the following picture is appropriate. The theory is an inferential reticulum. It is a rule-governed, gamelike system of symbols, some tokens within which are propositional (i.e., *true* or *false* in the system). Combinations of these propositions, as well as deductive interrelations between them, are controlled by the explicit transformation rules which make that system what it is. Any element of interpretation, or meaning, which goes beyond these explicit rules is to be exposed—as Hilbert exposed Euclid. Such an element, then, will either be rejected as irrelevant or introduced openly as an assumption which the system cannot do without. Hence everything germane to comprehending such a system will be explicitly stated by the rules or else contained in the primitives and postulates. To that extent the system will be uninterpreted; nothing outside the system will be required for understanding what makes it "go." Such a theory, moreover, would be neutral vis-à-vis any external subject matter. It would be uninterpreted. Hence, linking the theory to a subject matter must be undertaken explicitly, somewhere near the bottom of the page. There the "theorems" are *interpreted* for a subject matter by correlating constituent terms with the names of objects or with descriptions of processes. The result may then be an observation statement, true or false, concerning the subject matter itself.

Take the simplest example: a strictly Euclidean conclusion may be that the smallest 2-space between point A and point B must lie along the straight line which connects those points. But, as Hilbert taught Euclid, this tells us nothing about actual spaces and points *until* we go beyond the formal system itself—outside the "space game." A positivist might then urge that, if "point A" is interpreted as New Haven's East Rock Monument and "point B" is interpreted as Brookhaven's spherical gas reservoir—and, if "straight line" is interpreted as the path in 3-space described by a pencil of light radiation—then an observation statement, informative and factual, will result. It is concluded that the distance between monument and reservoir is 30 miles—the length of the paths described by light rays from sphere to monument. But other definitions of "straight line" suggest different procedures and generate different observation statements. "Straight line" might mean the path covered by a taut wire or the surface of optically flat glass (viewed on edge), etc. Each interpretation generates a different observation statement, the truth or falsity of which must be checked through different procedures. Hence, distinct subject matters might be approached simply by the application of different co-ordinating definitions to one and the same calculus. Thus geometrical optics and physical optics are distinguishable in that the first concerns itself only with straight lines traced by light rays passing through air. The second discipline, however, addresses straight lines construed as light rays passing through media of all kinds—gaseous, liquid, and crystalline. Were "straight line" defined as the paths that light describes through all spaces, across any distances, and even near large masses, the observation statement resulting therefrom would, in certain astronomical applications, turn out to be false. Light rays do not describe Euclidean straight lines as they pass through spaces containing large masses—such as our sun.

What better place is there for the positivist to harness the empiricism of Hume with the logic of Hilbert than in the interpretation of scientific theories? The view from Vienna focuses on a scientific theory as an uninterpreted algorithm designed strictly in terms of criteria appropriate for deductive theories. The interpretation of this algorithm, however, will proceed through co-ordinating definitions that transform uninterpreted symbology into empirically vulnerable observation statements.

Logical positivism, then, must be the great eclectic movement of our age. It took logicians' analyses of mathematical systems as the model for all systematic knowledge. Then it took the empiricists' account of how meaningfully to couple language and three-dimensional subject matters as the model for expressing information. These two models simply were combined, thereby constituting an analysis of the nature and interpretation of scientific theories which was presented at first crudely in Schlick's *Allgemeine Erkenntnislehre,* Carnap's *Über die Aufgabe der Physik,* and Reichenbach's *Axiomatik der Relativistischen Raum-Zeit-Lehre,* and later in the more sophisticated and considerably modified expositions of Hempel, Braithwaite, and the Carnap of today. In all, varying degrees of subtlety are exercised to link the abstractions of theoretical physics to encounters with objects and processes in the laboratory. The early positivist invited us to think of a *theory* as a totally uninterpreted Rosetta stone discovered in a semantical desert arid of meaning, for which, then, an application is sought here, there, in this subject matter, and in those. The primary challenge is always one of linking the "bottom" of the algorithm—its lowest-level deductions—with events in an actual subject matter. From this posture Herbert Feigl speaks of the "upward seepage of the empirical juice that provides a meaning for the otherwise altogether unvisualizable (non-intuitive) concepts of theoretical physics." In the same stance Braithwaite fashioned his "zip-fastener" analogy; correspondence rules permit theory and data to be "zipped" together and thereby transform uninterpreted theorems into observation statements. As more of these observation statements are confirmed in experience, the semantical zipper moves upward, linking theory with subject matter at all algorithmic levels. This will ultimately infuse even the highest postulates with empirical meaning.

Through this bifocal view of theories and interpretations other positivistic doctrines can be perceived. The reliance on logical syntax and empiricist semantics is clear enough. The rejection of anything metaphysical is also obvious; capital letters and purple ink play no role in the design of an algorithm or in the transformation of theorems into observation statements. Moreover, anxieties as to subject matters that resist such reconstruction would indeed constitute pseudo-anxiety. "Unanswerabilia" are equivalent to "nonsense" within this framework of analysis. One also perceives philosophy emerging as a "critique of language." Since *conceptual* mistakes are possible only within the inference framework of a scientific theory, and not while co-ordinating the theory with its subject matter, "idea analysis" will always intertwine with "language appraisal." A view of meaning is also implicit here; it, too, is bipartite. Expressions in the algorithm may be meaningful via one set of criteria; observation statements are meaningful via criteria *in addition* to those operative inside the formalism.

So also the further commitments of logical positivism are linked with this influential analysis of scientific theories and their interpretations—the doctrines of *tautology* (to which classical necessity was reduced), of *verification* (which as "testability" dominated semantical discussions in the thirties and forties), the role of the *protocols* (themselves possessed of material content to be diffused throughout the uninterpreted theory language), the distinction between the *material and formal* modes of speech (so apparent in the division between an algorithm and its interpretation), and finally the pervasive thesis of *physicalism* (wherein observational hypotheses of the "less exact" sciences are revealed to be subsumable in principle under the design principles of an ideal *physical* theory).

II

When Ernst Mach characterizes Newton's conception of *mass* as "unfortunate" he gives reasons that gladden logical positivists. Newton defines "mass" as the "quantity of matter in a body." This quantity, however, is measured as the product of the body's *volume* and *density*. Mach notes that "as we can only define

'density' as the mass of unit of volume, the circle is manifest." [1]
There is no way of determining the mass of a body other than via
its interaction with other bodies. To be meaningful in physics, a
concept like mass must be "cashed" in terms of the observable
effects *differences* in mass have on the differentiable behavior of
interacting bodies, and these differences must be quantitatively
describable. Thus we have Mach's own definition: ". . . bodies of
equal mass . . . , mutually acting on each other, produce in each
other equal and opposite accelerations." This definition differs
from Newton's inasmuch as it makes a difference in what we
actually observe bodies doing. However attractive psychologically,
Newton's words provide no conceptual leverage for observing differences in mass. Within the *Principia,* then, *mass* is co-ordinated
with no observables whatsoever. Mach linked this important
parameter with quantitatively differentiable features of the subject matter of physics. He "hooked" mechanical theory to the
world much more firmly than did his illustrious predecessor.

Within Newton's theory one also finds a notorious reference to
absolute space, which

. . . In its own nature, without relation to anything external, remains
always similar and immovable. . . .

. . . But since it is impossible to know, from the positions of bodies
. . . whether any of these do keep the same position to that remote
body [at absolute rest] it follows that absolute rest cannot be determined from the positions of bodies in our regions.

Newton further postulated an "absolute, true, and mathematical
time, which of itself, and from its own nature, flows equably
without relation to anything external." Newton conceded that "It
may be that there is no such thing as an equable motion whereby
absolute time can be accurately measured." In short, Sir Isaac
seeks to set our minds on concepts that lie beyond the discrimina-
tions of observation: these ideas were supposed to make a difference to observational science, yet they make no difference in
observation.

Despite Newton's vague assertions about absolute space and

1. Ernst Mach, *The Science of Mechanics* (La Salle, Ill., 1960), p. 237.

absolute time—and despite their systematic untestability—the hope of making relevant observations was an inspiration for several physicists. Since mechanical experiments were ruled out ex hypothesi as being beyond practical fulfillment, *optical* exploration seized the imagination of many. Since light was an undulatory disturbance within some subtle medium—traditionally called the ether—why then the earth's very motion as it sweeps through this all-pervading ether ought to generate something detectable like an "ether wind." The refined researches of Michelson and Morley constituted the experimental attempt to locate some observable effect of our motion through this ether; such an effect should appear as differences in signal return when light impulses are shot across very long distances in directions simultaneously parallel and normal to our own orbital path through the ethereal envelope. The fact that Michelson and Morley detected no such effect has been called "the greatest negative result in the history of science." How does one explain this negative result, granting that the ether is *that which undulates* when light is transmitted, even *in vacuo,* and granting also that an undulating medium with the properties required of an ether *should* have generated some differentiable results under the conditions of Michelson-Morley experimentation?

In 1892 Fitzgerald urged that any body moving at high speed relative to the ether *shrinks* ever so slightly. How much? The amount of contraction was supposed to be just enough so that the travel time for light signals in an interferometer arm *parallel* to the earth's motion would just equal the travel time in the perpendicular arm. The contracted interferometer-arm length could not be detected by direct measurement, because the measuring meter stick would contract also. Indeed, Fitzgerald argued that, inasmuch as the ether *must* exist, the negative result obtained by Michelson and Morley must be *explained away* by a hypothesis which places both the ether and the arm contraction beyond any possibility of empirical disconfirmation—a disturbing dodge for anyone with positivistic sensibilities.

H. A. Lorentz then fashioned an electromagnetic theory which, although compatible with the Fitzgerald contraction, is not as objectionably *ad hoc.* The postulates of Lorentz' theory are:

1. There *is* a stationary ether.
2. Electrons in motion *do* contract according to the Fitzgerald contraction relation.
3. Atoms, and hence all matter, deform in the same manner as electrons.
4. Moving matter has a "local time."
5. All mass is fundamentally electromagnetic.

Lorentz' theory explained away all experimental failures to detect a motion relative to the ether—a motion resulting from our earth's orbital motion. Moreover, Maxwell's equations (which required a stationary ether) would now have the same mathematical structure for bodies *or* for light sources in constant motion relative to a stationary ether—provided only that the contracted-length and local-time transformations were made. Lorentz' theory thus effected *apparentias salvare* in the best traditions of Claudius Ptolemy. But, against this *"ad hoc-*ery" and these "untestabilia," Einstein's theory of special relativity was more satisfying; it was more responsible, from a positivistic point of view. There is nothing of the *ad hoc* within his hypotheses. Einstein's concepts are semantically and operationally respectable; his observational suppositions are eminently testable, sooner or later. Resistance to further observation is never considered a virtue within the Einsteinian framework of inquiry.

Newtonian mechanics unfolds with the three axioms of motion and with the law of gravitation as postulates. These generate an algorithm which deals with diverse interactions such as Kepler's laws, projectile behavior, pendulums, ballistics, planetary perturbations, etc., all of which have been confirmed in countless experiments. Newton construed *mass* as a body's property that does not vary with speed and dealt similarly with *gravitation*. Acceleration is thus invariant with respect to Galilean transformations. Therefore, Newton's first and second laws, the law of gravitation, and all relations inferrible from these are *invariant;* they have the same form relative to any inertial reference frame. This is the principle of relativity. Consider travelers on a ship moving at constant velocity in a calm harbor: no mechanical experiment can reveal to them whether the ship is moving or lying at anchor. One must look to shore to detect changes in position, if any. Table tennis can be played on deck without adjustment for the ship's uniform motion. Newton recognized this when he conceded that there was no way to learn whether or not a body was at absolute rest.

The validity of Newtonian dynamics in all inertial frames was taken for granted. However, when it was noted that Maxwell's equations were *not* invariant, but seemed rather to require an absolute frame of reference, new attention was drawn to the problem. Since Newton's mechanics satisfied the principle of relativity it seemed thereby to supply a more universal description of nature than did Maxwell's theory. Yet the latter was so comprehensive, its prediction of radio waves so completely verified by Hertz, that it demanded profound respect. Parallel to this invariance limitation of electrodynamics was the negative result of the Michelson-Morley experiment.[2] This conflicts with the Galilean transformation of velocities. The speed of light is 3.0×10^8 m/sec. According to Galilean transformation theory, an astronaut moving toward Polaris at one-third the speed of light should receive the star's light at 4.0×10^8 m/sec. If he were receding from Polaris, however, the starlight would catch him while moving at 2.0×10^8 m/sec. Thus we have Galileo, Newton, and light. But the ether-wind experiments indicate that the astronaut would measure the starlight's speed as 3.0×10^8 m/sec under *all* values of relative motion, whether "head-on" or "going away." The Fitzgerald and Lorentz "explanations" of this unexpected event have been cited. How did Einstein attack the same problem? He proposed two postulates:

1. The principle of relativity applies to *all* the laws of physics, not just to mechanics. That is, it applies to Maxwell's equations too.

2. The speed of light in empty space is an experimental constant in *all* inertial frames, regardless of their relative velocities. With the light source head-on, or going away from it, c always has the same value.

Thus: "We must grant classical mechanics a measure of 'truth';

2. The 1887 result demonstrated no ether wind to about 1/20 of the orbital speed of the earth. Many other tests have been made. The latest (1958) used short radio waves and found no ether wind to 1/1000 of the earth's orbital speed, i.e., to 30 m/sec. In other words, the speed of light can be considered to be an experimental constant to one part in 10 million.

it supplies the actual motions of the heavenly bodies with a delicacy of detail little short of wonderful. The principle of relativity must therefore apply with great accuracy in the domain of *mechanics*. But that a principle of such broad generality should hold with such exactness in one domain of phenomena, and yet should be invalid for another, is *a priori* not very probable."

Starting from these postulates, Einstein then deduced a set of co-ordinate transformations between two inertial frames—transformations different from the Galilean ones. These are called "Lorentz transformations," and they are essentially of the same form as Galilean transformations with the experimentally observed constancy of c "plugged in." Lorentz transformations reduce to Galilean ones when velocities are small compared to c. Departures from Galilean transformations become observationally detectable only at speeds approaching c. These occur in subatomic processes, such as those encountered in accelerators, and also in certain astronomical events.

How would this velocity transformation be applied to the rocket ship approaching Polaris at $c/3$? (Let the reference frame of the ship be RF' and that of Polaris be RF. Light from the star has a speed $u = -c$ while $v = c/3$.) What would the astronaut measure for u', the speed of the received light in his frame, RF'?

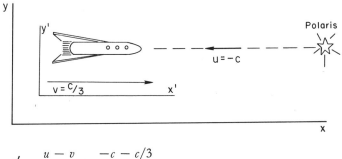

$$u' = \frac{u - v}{1 - \dfrac{uv}{c^2}} = \frac{-c - c/3}{1 + \dfrac{c^2/3}{c^2}}$$

$$= -c \ (not \ -4c/3 \text{ as in the Galilean transformation}).$$

If the rocket were *receding* from Polaris at $c/3$, then $v = -c/3$.

$$u' = \frac{-c + c/3}{1 - \frac{c^2/3}{c^2}}$$

$= -c$ (*not* $- 2c/3$ as in the Galilean transformation).

These results are consistent with Einstein's second postulate.

It is in cases like this that some philosophers balked at special relativity. They knew by experience that if one walks at 3 mi/hr into a 9 mi/hr wind it feels like a 12 mi/hr wind; if one walks at this speed *with* the wind, it feels like but a 6 mi/hr wind. Why would the same relations not hold for a rocket approaching or receding from a source of light?

Einstein's reasoning—so dear to the Viennese positivists—was as follows: relations between velocities in moving systems, as expressed by Galilean transformations, are *completely consistent with our everyday experience;* they have been established by direct and indirect measurements. There is no operational reason to reject them: what navigator or billiards player would? But, when we make the same relations hold at speeds approaching c, we undertake extrapolation based on intuition only. Such an extrapolation may or may not agree with whatever predictions, tests, or measurements can be contrived, *provided* the extrapolation remains a genuinely testable hypothesis! (Exit Fitzgerald and Lorentz.) In fact, the consistent failure of all ether-wind experiments to detect *any* change in c indicates clearly that some *different* relation must hold at such speeds. Algorithmic reconstruction, operational interpretation of terms, testability, falsifiability of predictions—indeed, all the medals on the positivists' tunic—are brilliantly displayed in the case for special relativity.

Einstein's view was that progress in understanding nature will result from studying phenomena *we can detect* and measure, building our conceptual schemes strictly around these. Spurious concepts such as Newton's mass, absolute space, and absolute time, which everyone admits to elude empirical identification, are nebulous ideas that cannot constitute any sound scientific theory. Rather, when we approach new areas of inquiry, like the electrodynamics of moving bodies, we must attend to established principles such as the principle of relativity in mechanics. And, when we become suspect of transexperiential extrapolations of algebraic relations (like the Galilean transformations), we must look to the best observational study available (e.g., the ether-wind experiments) to guide us in formulating new relations. This concentration on the detectable, the measurable—and the implicit rejection of the undetectable-in-principle and the constitutionally unmeasurable—came to dominate early logical positivism. The untestable came to be construed as the illegitimate offspring of poor grammar, sloppy logic, slushy semantics, and unstructured and undisciplined observational techniques. The theory of special relativity, being a repository of testability criteria, became also the gold mine for positivistic explorations in methodology, meaning, and measurement—all matters of moment for the physical interpretation of algorithms.

Suppose that our rocket ship is 50 feet long, at rest in frame RF', and moving in the $+x$-direction at $c/2$. What length would this rocket have in RF? This would be a difficult measurement to make, but not conceptually impossible. Station a string of fast cameras along the x-axis. These would be synchronized to run at the same rate. Moreover, some means of identifying which frames are being exposed simultaneously for observers in RF would have to be designed. After the films are developed there would be a camera station, x_1, where the rocket's tail shows in the center of one film frame. A search would then be made of all other film frames exposed *at that same instant* in RF to locate which one "caught" the rocket's head. This is station x_2. The distance, $x_2 - x_1$, would then be the observed length (in RF) of the moving rocket. How would this compare with the rocket length, L', as measured in RF'? This requires the Lorentz transformation,

$$x' = \frac{x - vt}{\sqrt{1 - \beta^2}},$$

and the expressions

$$L' = x_2' - x_1' = \frac{x_2 - x_1 - v(t_2 - t_1)}{\sqrt{1 - \beta^2}} = \frac{x_2 - x_1}{\sqrt{1 - \beta^2}} = \frac{L}{\sqrt{1 - \beta^2}}$$

because $t_2 = t_1$ when *simultaneously* taken pictures are selected. So now

$$L = \sqrt{1 - \beta^2}L'$$
$$L = \sqrt{1 - 1/4}L'$$
$$L = 0.87L'.$$

Thus the 50-foot rocket would appear in RF to have shrunk by 13 per cent to a length of 43.5 feet.

What, then, would observers in RF' find for the length of an identical rocket at rest in RF? Would it appear 13 per cent *longer* to them? Why? Which frame is at rest and which one is moving? There is no operationally sound way of identifying any *preferred* inertial frame. Yet how could observer RF and observer RF' each find the other's "moving" rocket to be shorter than his own, without there being some kind of a contradiction? [3] As a model of uncomfortable conclusions embraced because of their logical connections with the data of experience, this served as a beacon for all positivistic explorations in epistemology, ethics, metaphysics, and meaning.

Imagine now a sequence of rockets in RF', all 50 feet long and 500 feet apart. As this rocket train passes, observers in RF, using this same procedure, would measure these spaceships to be 43.5 feet long and 435 feet apart. This contraction of moving objects thus is not just a property of *matter* at high speed; it is a property of the moving spatial frame itself and hence of all the objects in it. Such a "contraction of space" is different from the specific and unique contraction of one of the arms in a Michelson

---

3. [For observers in RF' properly to measure the length of an identical 50-foot rocket, they would have to proceed just as described above. They would note positions x_1' and x_2' at the *same* instants in *their* reference frame. That is, they make $t_1' = t_2'$. Then, using

$$x = \frac{x' + vt'}{\sqrt{1 - \beta^2}},$$

$$L = x_2 - x_1 = \frac{x_2' - x_1' + v(t_2' - t_1')}{\sqrt{1 - \beta^2}}$$

$$= \frac{L'}{\sqrt{1 - \beta^2}}.$$

Therefore, $L' = \sqrt{1 - \beta^2}L$; $L' = 0.87L$; $L' = 43.5$ feet! Logical inference thus forces us to a consequence contrary to our Galilean intuitions. Objects which pass an observer at substantial fractions of C thus appear to contract in the direction of travel by the factor $\sqrt{1 - \beta^2}$.]

interferometer, a contraction which Fitzgerald first proposed, and Lorentz later developed, to explain away the negative results of the ether-wind experiments. Einstein's spatial contractions as laid down in special relativity have an affinity with more comprehensive spatial deformations in the general relativity of 1916.

This epoch-making work of Einstein constituted a textbook of logical positivist philosophy of science. What begins as a semantical uneasiness about designations like absolute space and absolute time leads to a philosophical reappraisal of the empirical foundations of entire networks of concepts; this in turn leads to the construction of a formalism which is then hooked, via correspondence rules, to observable processes within the world. It is thus no historical accident that the distinguished microphysicist Werner Heisenberg proclaimed himself a positivist, insisting that he concerned himself only with "observables"—as against wave mechanicians in the Schrödinger–De Broglie tradition. The conceptual division between theoretical structures and their interpretations, plus the further rule that the interpretations themselves met "operational" criteria, were widely regarded as simply characterizing the structure of the actual theories and *de facto* procedures that made contemporary physics the powerful set of conceptual innovations it has been. Indeed, from these pronouncements of great physicists, and these illustrations from scientific breakthroughs, it almost appears that the Viennese analysis of theories and of their interpretations is not only conceptually sharp but *historically* illuminating as well. The inescapable conclusion is that the rational structure of modern science and the logical positivist's analyses of scientific theory are one and the same. A refusal to accept the philosophy from Vienna might appear to make an understanding of what has made contemporary science great quite impossible. With so formidable a conviction to oppose, one's pulse quickens with anxiety as one challenges both the philosophical analysis and the historical suggestion. To this we now turn.

III

Return again to the rhetorical question with which we first served notice of our intentions. Are theories and their interpretations ever separable? What would an interpretation-free physical theory really be like?

The initial move from this question must be to stress that it does not concern psychology, history, or genesis. The slogan contrast between "the context of justification" and "the context of discovery" is often advanced to stifle queries that are fundamentally *conceptual* in character. Too many explorations into the *concept* of discovery have been dismissed by contemporary analysts as turning on issues of psychology and history, when it is our very *ideas* of discovery, of creativity, and of innovation which are at issue in such inquiries. Similarly, any philosopher who remarks that, in fact, one *never* encounters uninterpreted scientific theories must be prepared to be told that he is confusing matters of fact with matters of analysis. But this charge is simply mistaken.

When the older Wittgenstein undertook his searching epistemological investigations—to the dismay of classical sense-datum theorists—he was often accused of concerning himself overmuch with matters of psychology. Apparently he had not the wit to distinguish an *analysis* of the perceptual act from *descriptions* of the observer's responses when he confronts Gestalt puzzles like the duck-rabbit, the wife-mother-in-law, the Necker cube, and the reversing staircase. But most philosophers now realize that Wittgenstein carried the day. It was his *analysis* of complex concepts such as *seeing, seeing as,* and *seeing that* which exposed the crude, bipartite philosophy of sense datum versus interpretation as being the technical legislation it really is. By means of *philosophy* he destroyed the dogma of the immaculate perception. Philosophers telling the world how it *must* use discourse precisely to describe what the philosophers are presently interested in—this never is an elevating spectacle, even when undertaken by distinguished phenomenalists like Russell, Broad, Price, and Ayer, or by their Viennese counterparts Schlick, Carnap, Feigl, and Neurath. Aside from internal difficulties, phenomenalism failed to give satisfactory answers to the rhetorical questions "Could an observation lack an interpretation? What would an interpretation-free observation be like?" Of course, the atypical signal registrations of inebriates, idiots, and infants may constitute *de facto* interpretation-free sense encounters with phenomena. But these certainly are not observations—not in any sense that the last five hundred years of scientific inquiry would recognize as an "observation." The sharp, bipartite decomposition of *observation* into sense-data awareness as against interpretation does *not* constitute a valid analysis of the *concept* of observation in science, past or present. It is, rather, the substitution of a technical, prescriptive recipe— useful for certain varieties of philosophical cookery—for the concept of observation as it sustains scientific discourse, thought, and theory.

An analogous objection must be raised against the positivists' tandem account of theories (i.e., their syntax) versus their interpretation (i.e., their semantics). Such an account does *not* constitute an analysis of the concept of theory in modern science. It is, rather, philosophical legislation which has its roots in the same soil that nurtured the phenomenalism of the early Carnap, Schlick, and Reichenbach. Dichotomy was the rule for analysis then; its bipedal tracks are still evident within much philosophy of science today, especially in studies of scientific theories.

If we were to empty geometrical optics of its content—extract every morsel of physical interpretation concerning the paths of light rays, the edges of shadows, the properties of umbra and penumbra—the result would not be the *theory* of geometrical optics, but pure geometry *simpliciter*. To take the interpretation out of geometrical optics is to take the optics out of optics. The *theory* of geometrical optics (in the positivists' sense) is simply geometry, not optics at all. To put my position more generally, if you extract the physical interpretation from a physical theory, the result will not be physics, but algebra, pure and simple. What then *is* the interpretation-free theory within, for example, contemporary microphysics? It is little more than a motley combination of classical matrix algebra, non-commutative operator calculus, and sundry mathematical inelegancies that never would have been introduced into the algorithm of quantum electrodynamics had they been in any way avoidable.

Well, why were they unavoidable? Anyone concerned with physical theories only as elegant syntactical structures could easily undertake—independently of interpretation—to fashion his algorithm within the best tradition of mathematical systematization.

Redundancies, inconsistencies, divergencies, and ambiguities might then be stripped away from the formal calculus without awkward questions of hooking the calculus to some subject matter. Now, if this is always possible, why is it historically the case that it is never done? Is it just logical ineptitude and mathematical laziness which made meson theory and quantum electrodynamics into the formally inelegant systems they surely are? Was it simply a lack of positivistic sensibilities which loaded Laplace's *Mécanique céleste* with bundles of tiresome trigonometric functions? Was it just Newton's lack of concern for logical niceties which made his hydrodynamics a jumbled toolbox of computational recipes?

Now, the hydrodynamics of Euler and Bernoulli had a beautiful formal design (it is a mathematician's delight) which to achieve they had to give up trying to apply their "theory" to any actual subject matter. It is a symbolic toy, of little use to students of hydraulics, fluid flow, or even plumbing! And Lagrange's *Mécanique analytique* was also a favorite of the formalists. But, again, this achievement resulted from defining the desperately difficult subject matters of mechanics as virtually out of bounds for Lagrangean premises. Indeed, there may be an inverse relationship between the degree of formal elegance built into a physical theory and the possibility of applying it to really intricate phenomena at the frontiers of research. If the investigator's eye is fixed upon perplexities within the subject matter, his theory is sure to be syntactically inelegant. But, if his concern is with formal elegance, attention will not long remain on the intricacies within the data themselves. A history of physical theory could be written as variations on this one theme.

When concern with the formal structure of scientific theory is pressed so far that the scholar divorces syntactical matters from any concern with applications or with subject matter, the result must be the account fashionable among the logical positivists, for whom the idea of a *scientific theory* contracts into a concentration on matters of syntax only. This is to *change* the normal senses within which "scientific theories" are referred to. After all, a physical theory is primarily a theory *about* some physical phenomena—processes and events in nature. To restrict one's philosophical attention, focusing now only on syntactical structure, and later on the host of semantic issues involving interpretation and meaning—this is to have failed to recognize that "physical theory" is an *indissolubly* complex concept to begin with. Complexity never constitutes a good argument for reluctance to undertake analysis. We can all grant that. But complexity is not confusion. When analysis results in destroying complexity in the name of clearing up confusions, to that extent it destroys the concept in question. It slices it out of existence. To talk of the formalism *within* a physical theory is *not* to be talking about the *physical* theory itself. To discuss only the "interpretation" of the theory also is not to be discussing the theory itself—as our earlier example from special relativity should make clear. If the early positivists had addressed themselves to the more realistic and more complex problem "Theories: Their Constituent Formalisms and Interpretations," their concern would have been more in line with the conceptual realities of modern science. For, much as sensation and interpretation constitute indissoluble aspects of *observation,* and much as warp and woof constitute indissoluble aspects of *textiles*—so also formalism and interpretation constitute indissoluble aspects of *scientific theories.* To chop theories apart into *formalism* and *interpretation*—and then to identify only the formalism with the "theory"—is the simple mistake of misplaced discreteness.

All this becomes pointed when one considers some facts of scientific life—to wit, at the frontiers of research into the unknown not only are the observations "theory-laden," but even the most provisional theories *already* have their interpretations, their applications, their observations, built firmly into the system itself. To argue this persuasively one must caricature the orthodox positivist position. As if *describing* great moments in the historical development of science, early positivistic analyses of physical theory seemed to suggest that the scientist *first* designed his algorithm, *then* set up correspondence rules and co-ordinating definitions, and *finally* clamped his theory to a subject matter within which he determined to what degree observation statements tumbling out of the pure-theory-plus-interpretation were confirmed by the phenomena themselves. If the subject matter allowed itself to be construed à la "theory," then further observation statements were generated to serve as *predictions* which, if also confirmed in the data, raised the probability of the theory's being "true" vis-à-vis that set of phenomena. The examples elicited to support this account are familiar; Riemann's elliptical geometry lay available as an algorithm (= a physical theory?) for a century before Einstein clamped his interpretation onto it, ultimately to construct the theory of general relativity. The leading co-ordinating development was the rendering of the term "straight line" as "that geodesic path described by a ray of light through any volume of space." The conclusion from this adaptation of algorithm to subject matter was that the very structure of local spaces was itself a function of the large masses, or lack thereof, located within given spatial envelopes. Mass-free spatial volumes *are* Euclidean; therein light traverses Euclidean geodesics, that is, the line of intersection along two Euclidean planes. But, in vicinities dominated by large masses, for example, by our sun, the geodesic line traversed by light may not be a Euclidean straight line at all, but rather the "shortest" line in a Riemannian space, or even in a Lobachevskian space, or in any one of several other possible spaces.

These positivistic rewritings of the history of physics too often stand unchallenged because of the clarion call that they constitute *analysis* and have nothing to do with the "context of discovery." But philosophy of science may differ in this respect from "pure philosophy"; it *does* have a subject matter. If a proffered analysis fitted no science whatsoever—neither its history nor its present state—if it illuminated nothing problematic within research and resolved no perplexities found therein, then philosophy of science would be an arid, worthless, logic-chopping discipline indeed. What actually happens in science, however, *is* relevant to conceptual analysis—even if only questions concerning what philosophers are right *about* are raised. And, for every case history that can be contorted to fall within the concept mold of early positivism, there are just as many that do not conform at all.

Consider the business of data-gathering—a remarkably prominent undertaking at the frontiers of inquiry, where theories are thin and problems fat. When setting out data points on a graph, the objective is to map ways in which variations in the intensity of one parameter can be construed as a function of variations along some other parameter. Thus, in ideal gases, variations in pressure relate inversely to variations in volume. In ideal fluids, variations in pressure are inversely related to variations in flow velocity; the viscosity of a lubricant is directly related to its temperature, etc. As one records such data points on a graph it is instructive to reflect on what obtains with maps themselves. A map of Baltimore shares few features with the city itself; the tints of urban areas, the contour lines of elevation, the representation of bridges, airports, and monuments—on an aerial map these differ from what one encounters in an aerial photograph. One thing the map must share with its subject matter, however, in order to *be* a map of Baltimore, is the geometrical structure, the shape, accorded to the city's boundaries, the street layout, the configuration of lakes and hills, etc. Lacking that verisimilitude, the map would not be useful for travelers or geographers.

Data charts are useful also because they indicate, by the structure of lines connecting the data points—that is, the slopes and intersections of those lines—certain corresponding structures in the fluid, dynamical, or mechanical phenomena being represented. Because cold oil flows slowly, one expects a chart to locate high viscosities at low temperatures; as the temperature is increased, data points again slope according to expectation—viscosity decreases smoothly and regularly. It is the *de facto* physical relationship between an actual lubricant's viscosity and temperature which makes chart representations of such a substance directly useful to builders of engines, oil coolers, and hydraulic systems. Further data enable one to *correct* what may have been a *mis*representation of the structure as set out in the chart. Therefore, a chart which is informative as to the properties of substances (like oils and viscosities) will be informative *because* it possesses structural features found also in the lubricant itself. In a way, the data chart and the oil have the *same* structure—which is why engine designers can wear white shirts even when solving difficult problems about connecting-rod lubrication.

This situation is unchanged when one represents the parametric structure of a subject matter *not* by a chart, nor by a geometrical display of intersecting data curves—but instead by algebraic expressions which give the slopes and contours of those same intersecting lines within a suitable Cartesian space. The myriad algebraic descriptions found in aerodynamics and in fluid mechanics generally, in celestial mechanics and in experimental microphysics—all these function in the same way. They are primarily expressions which *describe* structural relationships within and between observable parameters constituting phenomena. This is particularly true at the frontiers where observations and measurement data constitute the primary data; there, algebraic expressions are introduced as a convenient shorthand for encapsulating a bewildering chaos of laboratory phenomena. Data charts, with their display geometry, do the same things, but not so tersely or economically. Algebraic descriptions of phenomena are ready-made for inferences; data charts are not. But the charts and the algebra have exactly the same relationship to the phenomena.

Hence the *algebraic* accouterments of a theory may *not* signal that a *pure* algorithim is being applied to a subject matter via correspondence rules. On the contrary, the algebra may be structurally related to physical processes in the most intimate way imaginable. Algebraic representations of flow parameters, pressure parameters, friction parameters, and vorticity parameters do not have to be "co-ordinated with," "correlated with," or "interpreted for" processes adjacent to a high speed airfoil. Rather, the algebraic expression of such parameters *is* the structure of the processes themselves. Just as when Wittgenstein remarked that "the cat is on the mat" and "a R b" do not have the *same* structure, but that "a R b" *is* the structure of "The cat is on the mat," so also our algebraically expressed parameters do not *have* the same structures as aerodynamic processes around an airfoil; rather, those expressions *are* the structures of those processes. It is not true that the algebra must be *interpreted* to fit the phenomena, or "hook" into it, or be clamped onto it. Rather, the algebra was introduced initially just to give us knowledge of such processes and their structures—in the same way that maps were introduced initially to give us knowledge of land masses and their structures.

There *are* conventional aspects of maps and charts; special symbols, terminology, and graphic devices focus our attention on features in the terrain. [An aerial photograph of Baltimore is just as bewildering to a lost aviator as would be an unobstructed aerial view of this city. But an informative aerial chart of Baltimore will focus attention on prominent landmarks via familiar cartographic conventions so as to orient the aviator within the map's structure and, *eo ipso,* to locate him within the city's structure as well.] There are innumerable conventional devices within physical theories also. They punctuate what is fundamentally an algebraic formalism. But from all this prescription and convention it should not be concluded that the algebraically expressed theory is therefore just pure mathematics, an axiomatized formalism. Indeed, the structural representations provided by a theory's algebra at the observational level is a most significant feature of scientific research. This is what dominated the explorations of Galileo and Kepler. $S = \frac{1}{2} at^2$; $T^2 = r^3$—these are structural representations of the observed phenomena themselves, ballistical in the one case, astronomical in the other.

Of course, these restricted expressions of structure are eventually subsumed under higher algebraic generalities via the powerful and flexible techniques afforded by the general theory of functions. The occasion for such subsumptions, however, the reason for clustering low-order structural representations under higher-order ones, is always to represent *phenomenal structures* (as encountered in observation) in the most general and universal form. This is never achieved by striving first for an abstract, elegant, general, and universal formalism, only later trying to apply it to subject matters so that deduced conclusions might (perchance) have the same structure as some three-dimensional process. That entirely reverses the order—not just the historical and psychological order, but the epistemological and conceptual order as well. Even in a "context of justification," of concept analysis, the story of abstract-formalism-plus-operational-interpretation is just wrong. It does violence to the working concept of scientific theory, the whole of which not only is different from the sum of its parts as identified by logical positivism—it even has *different* parts.

Algebra as the structure of observed processes does not need additional semantic interpretations, as abstract algebraic expressions generated in a calculus may.

This is the signal feature of scientific theories misrepresented by the bifocal analyses of philosophers whose comprehension of modern science grew out of restricted exposures to logic, mathematics, and the associated problems of axiomatics. For earlier positivists the criteria that revealed an algorithm to be "well-made" were familiar and clear. What better motivation was there for excursions into the philosophy of science than the hope of injecting into natural science the familiar clarity of mathematics itself? And what of the procedure? Dwell first on the well-formed algorithm and *then* turn to its interpretation, or the "fitting" of that algorithm to a subject matter. This procedure, however comfortable to analysts of positivistic posture, does more violence to the concepts of *physical theory* and of *observation* than do the zoologist's scalpel and stains to the life of a jellyfish.

IV

Perhaps the only way a zoologist *can* learn about a jellyfish *in vivo* is to section it and stain it; otherwise it would remain unexposed, transparent, and featureless—a living turmoil of tissue. But conclusions drawn about animals from sectioning and staining should be cautiously clamped onto the living organism. So, too, the analyses of positivists concerning physical theories have given us much to be thankful for. Their examinations of meaning, of formal design, of semantics and syntax, are among the sharpest and clearest the history of thought has ever known. Many problems that would have been discussed only *sotto voce,* if at all, are now at the forefront of our attention. All hail to logical positivism! Nonetheless, when analytic techniques carry such conviction as to distort our understanding of the subject of analysis —scientific theory—it is time to reconstitute our comprehension of the objects and the objectives of the inquiry.

There are algebraic expressions that serve at the level where we set out our observations and their structures. And there are also algebraic expressions that formally embrace unvisualizable *designata* within ever more abstract reaches of scientific theory.

Intratheoretical relationships between these two different kinds of algebraic expression are intricate and difficult to construe. But one way *not* to construe them is to conclude without argument that algebraic expressions operative at the observation level simply *spill* deductively from higher-level algebraic claims within an uninterpreted algorithm—only *then* to be co-ordinated with objects and processes in the three-dimensional subject matter itself. For perhaps this very co-ordination is *initially* operative in our coming to grasp the significance of the observations themselves, in understanding the structures of processes and what makes them "go." Were there only one case wherein the conceptual development of a scientific theory proceeded from algebraic *expressions of structure* at the "theorem" level on up through sophisticated symbolic subsumptions, ultimately to issue in algebraic expressions of the highest generality and the sparsest semantic content, this one example would require an analysis wholly different from that urged by positivists. The Viennese account given would not serve us well in such a case. It does not even begin to help us when theories such as aerodynamics and quantum electrodynamics hold the floor. For such cases the early logical positivists, and their contemporary devotees, advance a Procrustean analysis into which they jam the writhing and squirming disciplines of modern physical theory, thus cutting away the living parts that do not fit the logical analysis. Either that, or they ignore such aspects of the sciences altogether. Perhaps they proceed even to the ultimate rejection, dubbing what they find to be analytically uncomfortable fit only for discussion under the heading "Context of Discovery."

To all this, a contemporary enthusiast of logical empiricism might riposte:

No living member of the original *Wiener Kreis* would now divide "theory" (i.e., algebraic formalism) from "interpretation" (i.e., correspondence rules, co-ordinating definitions, physical semantics) as sharply and inflexibly as has been done in this paper. The position vis-à-vis theories and interpretations here construed as typical logical positivism is, indeed, now explicitly argued against by Carnap and by Hempel. The former now makes the correspondence rules an integral and inseparable part of the theory itself. He now intertwines semantic issues with syntactical ones, granting that no full understanding of either, as constitutive of physical theories, is possible in the absence of the other. And Hempel now concedes all observation in science to be "theory-laden." He challenges all attempts to divide observation languages from theoretical languages. Hempel even denies the conceptual possibility of there being an interpretation-free physical theory.

Good; so be it! There are, then, no logical positivists around today. Carnap and Hempel have changed. Their criticisms of the early, youthful, and iconoclastic Viennese philosophy are therefore further support for section III of this paper. But the spectacular intellectual shock effect of logical positivism derives not from the guarded and sophisticated expositions of the 1960's but from the strident, stentorian, and sinewy sallies of the twenties and early thirties. The historically significant movement known to the world as logical positivism dates from that era. Everything since, including this paper, expresses concern for the Procrustean simplicities of the initial doctrine and to that extent must be demarcated from it as we have done, the 1967 Rudolph Carnap, Herbert Feigl, and Carl Hempel notwithstanding. These men are no longer positivists.

The major philosophical flaw in the early analysis of physical theory offered by the Vienna positivists can be couched in the form of an epigrammatic postscript:

It is not a question of *meaning* being pumped up (or "seeped up" [Feigl] or "zipped up" [Braithwaite]) through an already designed algebraic formalism. Rather, the facts of scientific life require us to attend to *formalisms* being pumped up (via the general theory of functions) from algebraic expressions *already* rich with meanings, charged with structural representations of phenomena, and informative as to what matters most within our observational encounters in physical science. No correspondence rules or co-ordinating definitions are required semantically to inform algebra of this kind, for it "corresponds with" and is "co-ordinated with" its physical subject matter in the most intimate way imaginable *ab initio*—a pointed fact which deflates most of the positivistic apparatus inventoried in this paper.

MARY B. HESSE

positivism and the logic of scientific theories

I. INTRODUCTION

There is a certain periodicity in the history of the philosophy of science: between positivism, empiricism, inductivism, and skepticism at one pole, and rationalism, deductivism, and dogmatic metaphysics at the other. In this, philosophy of science is often responding to the progress of science itself. Many historical examples can be given of developments in science leading to a swing toward positivism. The nominalism of Ockham is a reaction against the use of substantial forms as "theoretical entities" in fourteenth-century physics; Newton's inductivism and positivism are a response to the unintelligible character of gravitational action at a distance if this is understood metaphysically; the pervasive positivism of later eighteenth- and early nineteenth-century physics—seen in Black, Coulomb, Lavoisier, Fourier, Ampère—is an attempt to eliminate the multitude of elastic fluids, ethers, and distance forces of Cartesian and Newtonian physics; twentieth-century constructivism, reductionism, and operationism are consequences both of nineteenth-century metaphysical mechanism and of the bizarre characteristics of modern theoretical physics. Also, scientific developments have led to swings toward rationalism, and a parallel catalogue could be enumerated of the rationalist and metaphysical systems constructed from, and in attempted justification of, theoretical science. As examples, Aristotle, Descartes, Leibniz, Kant, and Whitehead come immediately to mind.

Meditation on the past four or five decades of philosophy of science reveals some interesting variations on this theme. In spite of much lip service to science, it must be said that the early Russell, Mach, Bridgman, and the Vienna positivists were ultimately skeptical regarding the significance of scientific theories as genuine discoveries. To deny that these could be understood as discoveries of the hidden mechanism of nature was clearly one method of handling the paradoxes of nineteenth-century mechanism and the disturbingly unfamiliar world that twentieth-century physics appeared to reveal, if indeed its theories were to be taken realistically. Yet there is another sense in which those who were thus skeptical about the power of theories to reveal the unobservable were robustly rational about the power of science to make well-grounded inferences concerning the observable but not yet observed. Once the "given" was firmly identified, they thought, it must be possible to give rational grounds for the inferences that science in fact makes about the not yet given, as long as the not yet given is expressed in empirically testable predictions that can, if successful, themselves take on the status of the given. Indeed, this conviction was one of the grounds for skepticism about distant inferences to theories; it was also an incentive for capturing as much of the theoretical superstructure as possible in observational terms by means of definition and reduction.

Since the days of the early logical positivists, the pendulum has swung away from inductivism toward deductivism, but it certainly has not approached rationalism, much less systematic metaphysics. It is now fashionable to hold that in the currently orthodox deductivist accounts of science we have outgrown the strait jacket of positivism and have allowed theories to range abroad in the guise of freely adopted postulate systems, only some of whose consequences require observational interpretation. But there is another sense in which theories are now taken less seriously than they were by the positivists. For the positivists, theories were at least a problem: if theories were to be regarded as an essential element in scientific thinking, then *some* account was obligatory regarding both their *meaning* and their *inductive justification.* Nowadays these problems have for the most part been abandoned as insoluble or as pseudoproblems. And, although many implications of positivism in relation to theories have been repudiated, some of the very assumptions which led to these problems remain fundamentally the same in the deductivist account and still lead to paradoxical consequences. The legacy of these assumptions requires critical scrutiny, but at the same time we need to recover some of the healthy conviction of the early positivists that science is ultimately intelligible and rational and that we need not abandon the search for meaning and justification, even in the face of modern physics.

What I shall do here is sketch the basic tenets of positivism concerning scientific theories; show how criticisms of some of them led to the subsequent deductivist account of theories; examine the inadequacies of the deductivist account, especially in regard to the problems of meaning and justification; and tentatively suggest a road forward. This road will not lead us back to positivism, but it shares some of the concerns of positivism, notably that of exhibiting a unity of theory and observation which is closer than that permitted in deductive accounts.

II. THREE PROBLEMS ABOUT THEORIES IN LOGICAL POSITIVISM

I am going to summarize the logical-positivist account of theories in four points. Without detailing all the refinements that various writers have added, these points do, I think, capture the essentials of a position common not only to those associated with the Vienna Circle but also to the early Russell and Bridgman, as well as to many philosophically minded scientists from the 1920's to the present, including the so-called Copenhagen school of quantum physicists. The four points are as follows:

1. There are *observation predicates,* which have direct empirical reference. These are variously identified in terms of sense

data or the "thing language" of ordinary descriptive discourse.

2. There are *observation statements,* containing observation predicates, whose empirical truth or falsity is directly determinable (they are directly verifiable or falsifiable) when the relevant empirical situation is presented.

3. Science also employs *theoretical predicates,* which do not have direct empirical reference. These must be given meaning in some fashion through observables.

4. Finally, science employs *theoretical statements,* which are not directly confirmable or falsifiable, and which must be shown to be indirectly confirmable or falsifiable through their logical relations with observation statements.

All this clearly presupposes a radical distinction between observation and theoretical predicates, and, although this distinction was often admitted, even by positivists, to be largely pragmatic and relative to a given language community, consequences were built upon it which often seemed too substantial for such a pragmatic foundation to bear. Later on we shall consider this distinction in more detail and suggest that its significance does not reside in the four points just mentioned. But meanwhile, because it is now fashionable to emphasize the pragmatic nature of the distinction and to disregard its consequences, it is important to notice that the distinction was first introduced as a response to real philosophical problems about theories which remain unsolved.

Carnap begins his classic paper "Testability and Meaning" (1936) with the sentence "Two chief problems of the theory of knowledge are the question of meaning and the question of verification." [1] Other philosophers have recognized a chief problem of scientific ontology in the question of real reference. Let us see what it is about theoretical science that raises these three questions and how the four points of positivism were intended to provide answers.

Perhaps we should begin with the problem of real reference, because it was this that set the stage for the other two questions.

1. Partly reprinted in *Readings in the Philosophy of Science,* ed. H. Feigl and M. Brodbeck (New York, 1953), p. 47.

If we go back in the empiricist tradition, as far back as Bacon and Locke, and ask "What are theories about?" we shall receive the answer "They are about hidden entities whose existence and functions become known to us by means of aids to the senses (telescopes, microscopes, barometers) and by the inference of hidden causes from their observable effects." That this was the aim of science no one doubted, although even Bacon, and to a greater extent Locke, doubted the possibility of gaining *knowledge* about entities that lay too deeply hidden beneath appearances. There was no problem about reference or about meaning with regard to unobservables. Ordinary descriptive language, it was thought, suffices to describe small unobservable mechanisms, and there is no problem about what it is to be such a hidden entity or about why it is hidden. In the age of the Copernican revolution it would indeed have been reactionary to hold that everything that exists must be obviously present to the senses of one particular species inhabiting one minor planet. Rather, the problem was how can we get to know about hidden causes?

The history of science does not always put things in the same order of importance as does philosophy. In science itself the question of *how* we know was set aside, and more and more elaborate accounts were given of *what* we know, purporting to describe entities of increasing hiddenness and more and more unfamiliar characteristics. Nineteenth-century ether theories are usually said to be prime examples of such uncritical realism and of the absurdities to which it led. In fact this does less than justice to most nineteenth-century physicists, who were only too well aware that new accounts of theory construction were required for the new theories to be properly understood. The question then became not how we get to know the truth about hidden entities but how we can justify the use of familiar language to describe things so distantly inferred, and what it is we are referring to when we so use it. The positivists met this question by retreating to the firm base of the observable, where there was thought to be no doubt as to what we are talking about, what our language means, or how we know our assertions to be true. When we raise these three questions with regard to theories, we can take it for granted that there are no such problems with respect to observation.

1. According to the positivists, then, what are theories about? They are essentially about observables. Only observables can enter the evidence for theories, and only predictions about observables can be of any interest in the application of theories to the world. Hence, although there may be hidden causes of observables, these cannot be known, are not the real referents of theories, and are not relevant to the logic of science.

2. What do theories mean? Here various answers have been given. There were attempts to define theoretical predicates explicitly in terms of observation predicates. Sometimes, as in Russell's early logical constructionism, observation predicates were held to be names of sense data: "Physics cannot be regarded as validly based upon empirical data until the [light] waves have been expressed as functions of the colours and other sense-data." [2] Later, observation language was held to be the "thing" language of ordinary descriptive discourse, as in Eddington's "A physical quantity is defined by the series of operations and calculations of which it is the result," [3] and Bridgman's development of this idea in his demand for operational definitions of physical quantities.[4] But the view that there could be explicit definition and hence complete equivalence between every theoretical predicate and some set of observation predicates was soon abandoned, for two main reasons. First, it was shown that in many existing theories, including Maxwell's electrodynamics, quantum theory, and even Newtonian mechanics, such exhaustive translations cannot be carried out; yet no theorist would wish to abandon otherwise satisfactory theories on this ground alone. Second, and more important, it was pointed out that explicit definitions of each theoretical predicate in terms of observation predicates would cripple the theory in its proper role of expanding to correlate other observation statements. Observation predicates alone do not ensure the performance of this role; hence theoretical predicates, if equivalent to sets of observables, cannot perform it either.

2. B. Russell, "The Relation of Sense-data to Physics," *Mysticism and Logic* (London, 1918), p. 146.

3. A. S. Eddington, *The Mathematical Theory of Relativity* (Cambridge, 1923), p. 3.

4. See P. W. Bridgman, *The Logic of Modern Physics* (New York, 1927).

A weaker suggestion was to give conditional or reduction definitions of all theoretical predicates in observable terms. For example, we might conditionally define the magnetic-field strength at a space-time point (s,t) as follows: "The magnetic field strength is H if and only if a very small magnetic pole M placed at (s,t) is subject to a mechanical force MH." This is clearly an incomplete definition, in that it says nothing about the field strength in the absence of the small pole M, although the theory contains statements about H when no pole is present. Moreover, it presupposes a particular theory about non-disturbance of the original field when an indefinitely small pole is introduced, but use of the concept "magnetic-field strength" is not necessarily dependent upon the correctness of this theory. Because of these and other more ingenious objections to more ingenious formulations of the reducibility thesis, Carnap admitted in his "Methodological Character of Theoretical Concepts" (1956) that "in agreement with most empiricists" he considered that theoretical concepts have a weaker relation to observables than is required for reduction definitions, and that therefore they must be accounted for in a different way. What that way was we shall consider in connection with the deductivist account of theories.

3. How do we know that theories are true? Generally speaking, the logical positivists' answer was that we do not *know* that theories are true, because their truth or falsity cannot be decided directly by observation. *Verifiability* was therefore agreed to be too strong a requirement. But theories may be *confirmable* by observation. In "Testability and Meaning" Carnap defines confirmability of theoretical predicates as reducibility to observation predicates by reduction definitions, and confirmability of theoretical sentences as confirmability of all their descriptive predicates. This definition, of course, shares the fate of the reducibility thesis, and, apart from that difficulty, it was already an abandonment of the attempt to *justify* theoretical statements in general, because a statement in which all the predicates have been reduced to observation *predicates* may still be about unobservable *entities* —e.g., "small charged particles"—and therefore not directly verifiable or falsifiable.

The criterion of confirmability was close to the center of the platform of logical positivism, but it was never intended as a basis for answering the questions of meaning or justification. It was rather a criterion for deciding whether a theory is empirical—an answer to the question of *demarcation* of the empirically significant from the metaphysical. The general requirement of empiricism was put in the form of "making some difference" to predictions about observables. For a statement to be a significant part of a scientific theory, therefore, the statement had to be necessary for the derivation of some observation statements; hence, it had to be falsifiable in principle, although it need not be verifiable. Many problems arose in the attempt to formulate this criterion of empirical significance precisely, and they have been adequately summarized by Hempel, Scheffler, and others.[5] What I particularly want to emphasize here is that the position of those who emphasized the problems of empirical significance, or meaning, was already a retreat from the question "*What* do theories mean?" From their position, the answer to this question could only be "Their meaning is exhausted by their empirical content, that is, by the observation statements which are their potential falsifiers." In other words, the theory as such does not have meaning; the observables have meaning, and this meaning is comparatively unproblematic. Nor was the criterion of empirical significance intended as an answer to the question "When is a theory justified?" For, although it began as a criterion of verifiability or confirmability, and became a criterion of falsifiability, both of which seem to be relevant to the question of the truth of the theory, it could tell us only that a theory with false observational consequences is false. It did not pretend to tell us whether any parts of a theory were more highly confirmed by observables than others, what the criteria for a good theory would be, supposing its observed consequences to be true, nor how to choose between theories with the same observed consequences, all of which are true. In other words, with respect to theories, the various criteria of empirical meaning failed to pro-

5. C. G. Hempel, "Problems and Changes in the Empiricist Criterion of Meaning," *Revue Internationale de Philosophie,* 9 (1950), partly reprinted in C. G. Hempel, *Aspects of Scientific Explanation* (New York–London, 1965), p. 101; I. Scheffler, *The Anatomy of Inquiry* (New York, 1963).

vide either an account of meaning or an account of justification. The criteria did, however, focus attention on the deductive character of theories, seen essentially as postulate systems from which observation statements were derivable. And writers on deductivism were forced to admit that their legacy from logical positivism included the problems of meaning and justification of theories.

III. MEANING AND JUSTIFICATION IN THE DEDUCTIVIST ACCOUNT

Meaning

In the deductivist account, theoretical predicates are not given explicit definition or even reduction definitions in terms of observables. The question of meaning arises in a form borrowed from the logic of formal postulate systems: If the postulates of the theory give the syntax and basic logic of the system, what gives its extralogical *semantics* or *interpretation*? A minority view, first stated explicitly by N. R. Campbell in 1920,[6] was that this interpretation is given by a *physical model* which is intelligible, ultimately in observation terms, independently of the theory and its explanandum, and which therefore contributes to the theoretical predicates an interpretation not derived from any direct connection with its explanandum. Campbell's well-known example is the dynamic theory of gases, for which a system of Newtonian particles is an observational model. We shall return to this view later.

More commonly, however, deductivists regarded such physical models as nonessential heuristic devices and argued that no *direct* interpretation of the theoretical predicates is required, only a *partial* interpretation resulting from the deductive relation between theoretical statements and observation statements. According to this view, the "meaning of theoretical predicates" is sometimes said to be *implicit* or *contextual,* in contrast with the explicit empirical meaning of observation predicates. Just as we do not explicitly define the terms "point" and "line" in a formalized geometry, but allow their meaning or rules of use to be implicitly conveyed by the postulate set, so it is held that a

6. In *Physics: The Elements* (Cambridge), later reprinted as *Foundations of Science* (New York, 1957).

theoretical term such as "electron" means just that entity related to other entities of atomic physics in ways specified by the postulate system of physics. Physics differs from formalized geometry, however, in that some consequences of its formal postulates are translatable by means of the so-called *correspondence rules* into observation statements. This guarantees physics its empirical content, which a fully formalized geometry lacks. But in this view physics also differs from a *physically* interpreted geometry in that some of its predicates are not directly interpretable, whereas all the terms of a physical geometry—"point," "line," "plane," "curvature"—are so interpretable (at least by a process of idealization). If this distinction between theoretical and observation predicates is accepted, therefore, the parallel between physics and geometry is imperfect and does not suffice to explain the notion of implicit definition of theoretical predicates.

A more serious objection can be brought against implicit definition and partial interpretation. Interpretation of a formal system in the logician's sense cannot in fact be "partial"—either it is interpreted or it is not, and to interpret such a system is to give a *model* for it, where *model* is now used in the logician's sense. To give a logical model is to specify a set of entities with their predicates such that, when the postulate system is interpreted in the domain of these entities, the postulates are true in that domain. If no such model is specified for the postulates of a scientific theory (and the contextualist certainly does not require that one should be specified), the best that can be said is that the postulate system "implicitly defines" a *set* of possible models, that is, all those that would realize the postulates, and that the deductive relation of the postulates to observables further limits these possible models to those that include the observable entities and their observable relations. Thus the "implicit definition" is not an interpretation of the theoretical predicates but a definition of a set of possible models that partially intersect in the observable consequences of the theory. In any interesting case there is likely to be an indefinite number of such models. It is not at all clear that the notion of their "set" is well defined, and in any nontrivial case some of them are likely to be inconsistent with others. The notion of a set of models therefore cannot add anything to

the cognitive content of the theory over and above its already interpreted observation consequences, and in the absence of further
clarification of the sense in which theoretical predicates are "implicitly defined" we must conclude that deductivist accounts, like
positivist accounts, do not provide a solution to the problem of
meaning of theoretical predicates in its original form.

Of course, it is possible to hold, as most deductivists do, that
no such solution is required, because there is no such problem;
that in fact theorists have been mistaken in thinking that the aim
of theoretical science is explanation in terms of hidden entities
described in intelligible language. If there were indeed a special
class of "observables," and if science were about only these, then
the deductivist account of meaning might be adequate. But even
then it would not be easy to rest content with the deductivist
account of justification. I shall now try to show that the failure
of deductivism here is basically also a failure of its theory of
meaning.

Justification

There is no doubt that deductivism has given a sophisticated
account of theoretical predicates and postulates which is certainly
more adequate for scientific theories than were the attempts of
early positivism. But it is unfortunate that while this has been
happening the discussion of justification has been left far behind,
still wrestling with highly simplified versions of inductive inference. This is partly because of the intrinsic difficulty of the subject of confirmation, but mainly, I think, because of a loss of
nerve induced by powerful attacks on the notion of a rationally
grounded inductive logic. These attacks came first from Wittgenstein's *Tractatus*[7] and later from the work of Karl Popper.[8] Popper's premise is that there is no logic except deductive logic.
Therefore, there is no *inference* in connection with theoretical
systems except the deduction from them of observable implications and the consequent possibility of falsifying these systems by

7. L. Wittgenstein, *Tractatus Logico-Philosophicus* (London, 1922).

8. See especially *The Logic of Scientific Discovery* (London, 1959) and
"Truth, Rationality and the Growth of Scientific Knowledge," in *Conjectures
and Refutations* (London, 1963).

modus tollens. It is true that from time to time Popper has spoken as if his account gives at least a criterion of choice between competing theories, and he even speaks of a progressive approach to truth as one theory supersedes another. But, if one scrutinizes these claims carefully, one finds that they contain no element of *justification* of any theory, even in the weak sense of a procedure for choosing between competing unfalsified theories the one that is most likely to be true.

Popper's criterion of choosing the more *falsifiable* of two competing theories is not adequate to this task. In the first place, it applies only when one of the theories *includes* (entails) the other, for in Popper's view there is no plausible method of comparing the falsifiability of theories not related in this way. The definition of degrees of falsifiability in terms of atomistic potential falsifiers which he once proposed would have made any pair of theories comparable in falsifiability, but I think that even Popper no longer takes this suggestion seriously. Second, the criterion grossly misdescribes the procedures of scientists in deciding which theories to adopt. The notion of the theory that is the most falsifiable and that accords with all the known facts in practice is not even a well-defined notion. If such a theory could be identified, it would also be the most risky and least reliable one. Popper's arguments notwithstanding, theorists, even in moods of greatest abandon when nothing material is at stake, do not put to the test highly bizarre and therefore highly falsifiable theories just for the joy of seeing them tumble. On the contrary, they *know,* even without testing, that some bizarre theories would be falsified, and we must therefore say that they have an implicit theory of inductive inference. Popper's later accounts in terms of a concept of the "approach to truth" fare no better. This turns out to be an approach along a road which leaves more and more actually *falsified* theories behind, but for which "truth" is and remains infinitely far away. All that can be said about the leading theories still on the road is that they have not yet been falsified, not that they are ordered in any way with respect to nearness to the truth.

Much more significant than Popper's theory of falsifiability and rejection of inductivism seems to be his insistence on the *universal* character of all scientific statements, including observation statements, and his account of all predicates, including observation predicates, as being essentially *dispositional*. In this, Popper's theory of language is a fundamental rejection of the most deeply embedded assumptions of positivism. It is my conviction also that these assumptions have to be rejected if we are to progress beyond the limitations of positivism. But Popper's account is vitiated by his refusal to recognize that there are rules of inductive inference which can be rationally discussed. I shall take it from now on that there are indeed such rules, which are intrinsic to all scientific inference and manifest in the procedure of scientists. The task of the logician of science is to systematize or explicate these rules and to provide such kinds of justification for them as are appropriate and possible.

The best discussions of confirmation are found in the writings of Carnap and Hempel, but the difficulties in this area are such that neither of these philosophers has been able to carry his account much beyond the explication of simple inductive generalizations of the "All ravens are black" type and their statistical counterparts. Almost no progress has been made with the problem of devising a confirmation theory for theories. Let us examine some of the reasons for this.

Hempel's classic paper "Studies in the Logic of Confirmation" (1945) [9] is best remembered for his discovery of the so-called paradoxes of confirmation, which have given rise to an enormous literature. Yet this problem is nothing but an irritating technicality compared with Hempel's real aim in the paper, which was to formulate criteria of adequacy for the confirmation of statements related to evidence in deductive systems. This was in fact the first attempt to develop a confirmation theory for science understood in the deductivist sense, and its limitations have much to teach us about the adequacy of the deductivist account itself.

Hempel inquires what general conditions ought to be satisfied by a confirmation theory which explicates accepted forms of theoretical inference. Of the conditions he discusses, the following are specially relevant to the confirmation of theories.

9. Partly reprinted in Hempel, *Aspects of Scientific Explanation,* p. 3.

1. *Special consequence condition*: If E confirms H, E confirms every logical consequence of H.

2. *Converse consequence condition*: If H entails E, then E confirms H.

At first sight the special consequence condition does seem intuitively desirable in order to explicate the following familiar type of theoretical inference. A theory is proposed on the basis of a set of experimental laws that are entailed by the theory, as for example, Galileo's law and Kepler's laws and descriptions of the orbits of the comets are entailed by Newton's theory. Further as yet untested consequences are then drawn from the theory, for example, the laws of the tides, which are predicted with confidence on the basis of the confirmation of the theory by its observed consequences. Indeed, sometimes confidence in the consequences of the theory is so strong that it enables *corrections* to be made even to laws already accepted; for example, Newton's theory corrected Kepler's third law. Condition (1) allows such inferences to have high confirmation. But this condition runs into serious difficulties, as we shall see, especially if it is combined with condition (2).

Condition (2) seems to be required to allow evidence which is entailed by a theory to confirm that theory. But if it is taken together with (1) we get the following counterintuitive case. Suppose H entails E_1 & E_2; then E_1 confirms H by (2), hence E_1 confirms E_2 by (1). But suppose further that H is equivalent to E_1 & E_2; then certainly H entails E_1 & E_2. But it is unreasonable to expect E_1 to confirm any arbitrary E_2 which may be conjoined with E_1 to form H; indeed, usually it will not do so. This example shows that, if conditions (1) and (2) are both accepted, any evidence will confirm any statement whatever by the mere construction of a suitable H by conjunction.

For this reason Hempel originally rejected (2) and retained (1), thus demanding a stronger relation between hypothesis and evidence than mere entailment, if the evidence is to confirm the hypothesis. But accepting (1) and rejecting (2) means that the confirmation relation cannot be a relative probability, for in a probabilistic confirmation theory (2) is always satisfied for empirical E. Furthermore, (1) is then not in general satisfied, for, if E_1

is to confirm E_2 probabilistically, there must be a stronger relation between E_1 and E_2 than their joint deducibility from some hypothesis H.[10] These difficulties in Hempel's criteria were first demonstrated by Carnap, and Hempel has now agreed that condition (1) rather than (2) should be abandoned and that a probabilistic confirmation function provides a better explication of confirmation than does a function satisfying his original criteria.[11] There are in fact several cogent arguments in favor of probabilistic *c*-functions, and in Carnap's work this type of confirmation theory has received detailed development. But, whether or not a probabilistic theory is adopted, the consequences of this discussion for the deductive view of theories are serious. As the extensive literature on Hempel and Oppenheim's paper has shown,[12] it has proved difficult to formulate deductive criteria for explanatory theories in such a way as to eliminate trivial cases while including those which seem to conform to intuitive concepts of explanation. But the criteria suggested in this debate have not touched the problem of explicating the kind of predictive inference just discussed. Yet the example of Newton's theory and the laws it explains shows that such predictions are frequently made with great confidence.

The situation is even less satisfactory if the deductive account of theories as *uninterpreted* postulate systems is considered from the point of view of justification of predictions. Consider an un-

---

10. These results are easily proved as follows:

Let $c_0(p)$ be the prior probability of a proposition p, and $c(p/q)$ be the conditional probability of p given q. (i) Suppose H entails E. Then $c(H/E) = c_0(H)c(E/H)/c_0(E)$. But $c(E/H) = 1$, and, if E is empirical evidence (not logically true), $c_0(E) < 1$. Hence $c(H/E) > c_0(H)$, and (2) is satisfied. (ii) $c(E_2/E_1) = c_0(E_1 \& E_2)/c_0(E_1) \geq c_0(E_2)$ according as $c_0(E_1 \& E_2) \geq c_0(E_1)c_0(E_2)$, that is, according as E_1 and E_2 are probabilistically positively dependent or independent. Thus (1) is satisfied only if there is a positive dependence between E_1 and E_2 as determined by the distribution of prior probabilities. The fact that E_1 and E_2 are both deducible from some H is not sufficient for such dependence, for this deducibility is always trivially true for any pair of propositions.

11. R. Carnap, *Logical Foundations of Probability* (Chicago–London, 1950), p. 471; Hempel, *Aspects of Scientific Explanation*, p. 50.

12. See C. G. Hempel and P. Oppenheim, "Studies in the Logic of Explanation" (1948), partly reprinted in Hempel, *Aspects of Scientific Explanation*, p. 245, and Hempel's discussion there of subsequent objections raised against this paper.

interpreted system T to which is attached a set of correspondence rules C, such that the conjunction of T and C enables some observation statements to be derived. Every observation predicate in the derivable observation statements must be connected by means of some correspondence rule with some uninterpreted terms of the system. But, because system T in this view contains no observation predicates, there cannot be any reason *derivable from the statements of T* why one observation predicate should occur in a given correspondence rule rather than in another. If the task of *T&C* is merely to *explain* given observations in the deductivists' sense, then there is no problem about the form of the correspondence rules, because both T and C have been set up in such a way that the observation statements are derivable from their conjunction. But suppose T is to be used predictively, that is to say, new observation statements are to be asserted with confidence on the basis of *T&C* *before* the new statements have been tested directly. This may well involve asserting observation statements containing new observation predicates that do not occur in C. In this case new correspondence rules are required, but ex hypothesi these cannot be derived from *T&C*. So *T&C* cannot entail any predictions involving new observation predicates, and in the deductivist account there is no other way in which such predictions can be made confidently on the basis of the theory.[13]

The deductivist may reply that to assert a "theory" is to assert an uninterpreted postulate system *plus* all the correspondence rules required for application of that theory in all relevant experimental domains. But it is doubtful whether this can be maintained. In the first place it is not likely that "all relevant experimental domains" are known, and the predictive power of a theory consists precisely in its capacity for extension into domains not initially seen to be relevant. Even if these domains could be

13. Compare Campbell's account (*Physics: The Elements*, p. 134) of the prediction of laws of gas viscosity (a new observation predicate) from the kinetic theory and correspondence rules involving only the observation predicates (pressure, volume, temperature) found in Boyle's and Charles's laws. If the kinetic theory were interpreted only in these observation predicates, it would be impossible to know what function of its theoretical predicates should be identified with viscosity, and hence what law of viscosity should be predicted.

known, the correspondence rules containing observation predicates not in *C* would be redundant to the explanation situation in which the theory was first set up, and the deductivist still would be faced with the question "What reason can be given in terms of the *known* laws and the uninterpreted theory based on them for inclusion of these extra correspondence rules?" Following Campbell, I shall suggest below that reasons have to be given by referring to analogical arguments from observables, including observational models; but this solution implies that the theory *T* is not merely an uninterpreted postulate system and so is not open to a deductivist who holds that it is.

It is interesting to notice that both Hempel and Carnap early admitted that in the context of justification deductivism is not enough. In "Studies in the Logic of Confirmation" Hempel says: "Unquestionably scientific hypotheses do have a predictive function; but the way in which they perform this function, the manner in which they establish logical connections between observation reports, is logically more complex than a deductive inference." [14] Generally speaking, however, arguments such as we have discussed have not been attended to by deductivists, and, where they have been noticed, they have been taken merely to reinforce the generally accepted conclusion that no account of the inductive inferences involved in theories is possible. With regard to both meaning and justification, the deductivist account of theories has shown itself to be grossly inadequate.

IV. A REVISED MODEL OF THE OBSERVATION LANGUAGE

It is time to recover the confidence of the early positivists that the meaning and truth of science is not opaque to the rational understanding. But it is also time to scrutinize their legacy of assumptions about the nature of the observation language, for it is these which have led to the present stalemate. I have characterized these assumptions in terms of the alleged direct empirical

14. *Ibid.*, p. 28. Cf. Carnap, *Logical Foundations of Probability*, p. 471: "The logical connection which a scientific hypothesis establishes between observation reports is in general not merely of a deductive kind; it is rather a combination of deductive and nondeductive steps. The latter are inductive in one wide sense of this word."

reference of observation predicates and the direct decidability of observation statements. These assumptions are generally taken for granted by positivists and there are few detailed arguments concerning them in the literature. One of the most explicit statements of later positivism is to be found in Carnap's "Testability and Meaning," where he makes two relevant points. First, he holds that an *observable* must be a primitive of the metalogic of theory structure, in terms of which other concepts such as "confirmation" and "testability" are defined; this is because the question of what it is to be "observable" is a question of psychology and physiology, not philosophy. Even if these sciences could provide a clear answer to the question, the immediate difficulty about this suggestion is that it generates a vicious regress. What is it to be an observable for psychology or physiology, and hence to be an empirical basis for their theories of "observability"? Next, in approximate replacement of a definition, Carnap "explains" the concept of observability as follows: A predicate P is observable for a person N if, for some object b, N can under suitable circumstances come to a decision to accept or reject $P(b)$ with the help of a few observations. He continues: "There is no sharp line between observable and non-observable predicates because a person will be more or less able to decide a certain sentence quickly. . . . For the sake of simplicity we will here draw a sharp distinction between observable and non-observable predicates. . . . Nevertheless the general philosophical, i.e. methodological question about the nature of meaning and testability will . . . not be distorted by our over-simplification." [15]

Now, it is first of all not clear in this explanation that any predicate is in principle *non-observable,* for surely there are some people for whom in some circumstances there could be quick decidability about any predicate, however apparently "theoretical." Even in the case of theoretical predicates in physics, such as "ionized," "attracting," "particle emission," there *are* circumstances under which appropriately educated persons can come to quick decisions. What is overlooked in this pragmatic account of

15. Carnap, "Testability and Meaning," in *Readings in the Philosophy of Science*, p. 64.

observability is that the pragmatic conditions themselves *include* those theories which are currently acceptable or under consideration, and that therefore it cannot be true that making an initial distinction between observables and non-observables on pragmatic grounds leads to *no* distortion in the subsequent discussion of the relation of theory to observation, however oversimplified the distinction is admitted to be.

If one asks why it has for so long been considered necessary to accept the comparatively unproblematic character of the observation predicates and statements in contrast to those of theories, there seem to be two replies, neither of which has been made very explicit. First, the pragmatic account of observability is only a cover for a much more deeply rooted belief, stemming from phenomenalism and the British empiricist tradition, that there are entities (and their properties) which are directly given in perception and that more or less well-defined areas of language directly describe these. In later versions of this belief the direct descriptions are not usually held to be incorrigible or even transparently clear and distinct, but it is still held that there is a vast difference between the minimal doubt and obscurity which attach to them and the highly dubitable and not altogether intelligible assertions of complex scientific theory. That psychology and physiology are appealed to by latter-day proponents of this view is itself an indication that the difference between the observable and the merely inferred is taken to be an *ontological* difference, that is, a difference in the relation of the sensory equipment to the observed and the theoretical, respectively. Second, a half-conscious fear of vicious circularity has inhibited investigation of alternative accounts of the observation language. If we have no firm observational basis on which to stand, how can we begin to analyze the meaning and justification of theories that are erected upon observables? Worse, if observation itself is said to share the uncertainties of theories in any important degree, how can we avoid being sucked into a logical vortex in which we lose all contact with empirical evidence?

Any viable alternative account of the observation language must show not only that we can keep afloat in such a vortex but that we can even make progress through it. I shall now attempt briefly to outline a new model for the observation language which gives just these assurances.

A Self-Correcting Confirmation Theory

For the sake of brevity and ease of comprehension it is necessary to consider a highly oversimplified world, whose conditions for an adequate observation language we shall investigate. It will, I hope, be clear that the various simplifications can be relaxed without changing the principles of this model language, although probably not without raising some severe technical difficulties.

Consider a world consisting of N individuals (which may be situations, events, objects, processes). These are to be described by means of a set of K primitive monadic predicates, each of which may or may not apply to each individual. We shall suppose that application of a given predicate to a given individual is the result of a learned association between certain aspects of the individual and the predicate token. It matters little what this particular learning process is; it need only be such as to allow the discrimination of individuals who elicit this predicate and the ability to reapply the predicate to further individuals in agreement with the usage of the language community. The essential point in this model, however, is that application of a predicate to an individual is always subject to what we shall call *error*, and that a definite, small prior probability can be assigned to the occurrence of this error. For simplicity we may suppose that the prior probability of reporting a predicate P of an individual to which P applies is a constant $1\text{-}\epsilon_1$, and of reporting P of an individual to which P does not apply is a constant ϵ_2, ϵ_1 and ϵ_2 small, for all predicates and all individuals.

If it is possible for the application of predicates to be in error and to come to be known to be so, it is necessary that in the relation of the language to the world there should be some place for the notion of *correction* of errors. This is provided by the fact that the application of predicates (assumed to be for the most part correct, because the ϵ's are small) reveals certain regularities in the relations between predicates. That is to say, for example, it may be found that when a predicate P has been applied to some individuals, Q has always or usually been applied to those individuals as well. We shall visualize each predicate as being like a knot in a network of relationships with other predicates, where we may take the strengths of the strings between knots to be some increasing function of the proportions among individuals in which the predicates have been reported as co-occurrent or co-absent.

We shall suppose that we have a probabilistic confirmation theory which is adequate as an explication of the more elementary kinds of inductive inference. This is not so utopian a presupposition as it may sound, because we are dealing in this model with a highly simplified, finite world in which it would not be too difficult to assign prior probabilities to all possible distributions of predicates among individuals so that intuitively acceptable consequences of inductive and analogical arguments are given high confirmation on appropriate evidence. It can be shown that some postulate like Keynes's Principle of Limited Independent Variety is necessary to determine such a prior distribution, which we shall call the c_0-distribution. Keynes's Principle ensures that, when predicates are reported to have often occurred together in observed individuals, there is a greater than prior probability that they will occur together in future observations.[16] Let us call postulates having this characteristic *clustering postulates*. The justification for assuming a clustering postulate is to be found in the kinds of theoretical inference which are describable and confirmable in terms of it, not in any a priori considerations, for these are, as has often been pointed out, excessively weak. But we are not seeking here to solve the problem of induction in any traditional sense; we are trying only to systematize kinds of inductive argument, including theoretical argument. A clustering postulate is a comparatively small price to pay for such an outcome, for any confirmation theory must contain an explication of the following kind of simple analogical inference: Given that individuals a and b share a high proportion of their observed predicates, though differing in a few others, infer that they will share further predicates as yet unobserved. In the absence of a postulate that ensures confirmation of this inference, it is difficult to see how any

16. For a full discussion of this principle, see J. M. Keynes, *A Treatise on Probability* (London, 1921).

inductive argument can be explicated, for even the substitution instances of a general law are never in practice similar in *all* respects, and inference from "All observed *P*'s have been *Q*'s" to "The next observed *P* will be *Q*" is itself an analogical argument of this kind. Clustering postulates can be formulated so as to provide necessary and sufficient conditions for this and similar types of analogical inference.[17]

Given the c_0-distribution determined in this way, it is possible to calculate by use of Bayes's theorem the probabilistic *c*-value of any as yet unobserved application of a predicate to a given individual on the basis of existing evidence. But here we must make an important distinction. All our evidence is necessarily in terms of *reports* that *P* applies to *b,* and we have assumed that there is a finite probability that such a report may be in error. We must therefore make a distinction between a report and "what really is the case." But we have no access to "what really is the case" unless we can find it in other reports of predicates applying to various individuals, and these reports themselves may be in error. What must be done in this situation is to try to identify errors on the basis of other reports, some of which may make the correctness of a given application extremely improbable. There is no circularity here, however, any more than there is in any proper use of a method of successive approximation. To see why not, we shall introduce the notion of a *theory.*

A theory in this model language is a specific assignment of predicates to individuals, which may be a *complete assignment* (in that it specifies for each individual whether it does or does not

17. Consider a language consisting of two individuals, *a* and *b,* and four two-valued monadic predicates, P_1, P_2, P_3, P_4. Denoting the two values by P_r, $\overline{P}_r$, $(r = 1, \ldots, 4)$, and assuming $c_0(P_r x) = c_0(\overline{P}_r x)$, for all x, the confirmation conditions for three inferences of the type mentioned can be formulated as follows:

$$c(P_4 b / P_1 P_2 P_3 P_4 a \cdot P_1 P_2 P_3 b) > c(\overline{P}_4 b / P_1 P_2 P_3 P_4 a \cdot P_1 P_2 P_3 b)$$
$$c(P_4 b / P_1 P_2 P_3 P_4 a \cdot P_1 P_2 \overline{P}_3 b) > c(\overline{P}_4 b / P_1 P_2 P_3 P_4 a \cdot P_1 P_2 \overline{P}_3 b)$$
$$c(P_4 b / P_1 P_2 P_3 P_4 a \cdot P_1 P_2 P_3 b) > c(P_4 b / P_1 P_2 P_3 P_4 a \cdot P_1 P_2 \overline{P}_3 b) .$$

Denoting by S^n the relation of being alike in just n of the *P*'s or $\overline{P}$'s, the necessary and sufficient conditions on the c_0-distribution are:

$$\frac{c_0(S^4 ab)}{c_0(S^3 ab)} > \frac{c_0(S^3 ab)}{c_0(S^2 ab)} > 1 .$$

possess each of the K predicates) or only a *partial* assignment. Given the c_0-distribution, every theory has a certain prior confirmation. Each report of the application of a predicate to an individual is evidence for the partial theory that that predicate does belong to that individual, and the posterior c-value of this partial theory on this evidence is easily calculated:

Let p be the statement $P(b)$, that is, "P really applies to b," and j be the report $P(b)$, that is, "It has been reported that P applies to b." Then we have

$$c(p/j) = \frac{(1 - \epsilon_1)c_0(p)}{(1 - \epsilon_1)c_0(p) + \epsilon_2 c_0(\sim p)} .$$

In this way it is possible to calculate for every theory its posterior c-value on the basis of any evidence consisting of reports. A theory may "contradict" certain of the reports, in the sense that it ascribes "not-P" to an individual already reported to be P. But a theory which contradicts too many reports will of course have a low c-value, because the ϵ's are small. It is now clear that what has to be contrasted with the *report* that something or other is the case, is not what *really* is the case, to which we have no access, but rather what *in a given theory* would be the case, which may in a small proportion of cases contradict what has been reported. It does not follow from this that the theory which contradicts the fewest reports is the theory with the highest c-value, for the amount of "correct" evidence according to this theory may be counteracted by the higher c_0-value of some other theories. For example, if a clustering postulate is built into the c_0-distribution, preference will be given to theories which cluster individuals, that is to say, those which allow individuals to be classified in more or less well-defined classes with high similarity between members of a class and comparatively low similarity between any member of a class and a non-member of that class. In this case, evidence that reports some individuals as belonging to no such class may be contradicted by a clustering theory which has higher c-value on the basis of all the evidence than does a non-clustering theory which contradicts none of the evidence.

At this point further refinements can be introduced. We may straightforwardly accept that theory which has the highest c-value as a result of this calculation, or we may decide to reject those parts of the evidence which are contradicted by given theories and recalculate their c-values on the basis of the remaining evidence. Without going into these detailed possibilities, however, we can see already how this simplified model offers an alternative to the positivist observation language.

First, it is no longer the case that descriptive predicates are given "meaning" only by direct empirical reference. It is almost universally accepted that, even when there appears to be direct reference, the application of such a predicate may be in error, but this is usually taken to mean an error relative to "what is really the case." In our model, on the other hand, we must speak of error *relative to a theory*. This allows the possibility that the error may occur not only as a result of lack of attention to what is observed but also in a sincere and careful report, when ascription of a predicate *does not fit in well with the general outlines of an otherwise highly confirmed theory*, where "not fitting in" is determined by the c_0-distribution. This is to say that correct application of a predicate depends on both a careful response to a stimulus situation *and* the relations of this predicate to other predicates in this and other individuals. A particular set of such relations is what constitutes a theory. It is therefore possible for the application of a predicate to an individual to be correct in one theory and incorrect in another equally well-confirmed theory, and this is true for *all* predicates, not just for those previously labeled "theoretical" as opposed to "observational." It follows that observation statements are not directly confirmable or falsifiable in a single empirical situation, for the correctness of application of the predicates contained in them will differ in different theories, and confirmation or falsification will depend on all the reported evidence in other situations, together with the verdicts of different theories on the correctness of these reports, and on what theory is taken as best confirmed.

Thus two of the characteristics of observation predicates and statements which in positivism have seemed to distinguish them from theoretical predicates and statements are seen to be illusory, namely, the directness of empirical reference and the immediacy of confirmation or falsification. But this does not lead to circularity of justification, although both meaning and justification become questions that are more complex and more interrelated than positivists imagined. Is there, then, any distinction to be made between observation predicates and theoretical predicates in this model? Before discussing this it is useful to consider the status of the so-called theoretical or unobservable *entities*.

Theoretical Entities and Predicates

The concept of a theoretical entity has been no clearer in the literature than that of a theoretical predicate. If an entity is completely unobservable in the sense of never appearing as the subject of observation reports and being wholly unrelated to entities which do appear in such reports, it is difficult to see that it has any place in science. This, then, cannot be what is meant by a theoretical entity. The usual application of this term seems to be to entities, such as atomic particles, to which *monadic* predicates are not ascribed in observation reports, but which certainly have *relations* with observable entities. Suppose the planet Neptune had turned out to be wholly transparent to all electromagnetic radiation, and therefore invisible. It might still have entered planetary theory as a theoretical entity by virtue of the force relations between it and other planets. Furthermore, the monadic predicate "mass" could have been inferred of it, although mass was never applied to it in an observation report. Similarly, photons, protons, and mesons have relations with observable entities, although they themselves may be "unobservable" in the sense of not being subjects of monadic predicates in observation reports, at least not in prescientific language. In attempting to show that problems which arose for positivist accounts of theories are solvable in this new model, it is necessary to reformulate the problems in terms of the new account. My suggestion that theoretical entities be taken as those to which monadic predicates are not ascribed in observation reports is therefore intended as an *explication* of this notion in the new account rather than as an analysis of what positivists themselves have meant by "theoretical entity." Whatever they may have meant, and this is far from clear, their typical problems about the existence of and reference to theoretical entities do seem to arise only insofar as these entities are not subjects of monadic predicates in observation statements. If a monadic predicate *were* ascribed to an entity in an observation statement, it is difficult to understand what would be meant by calling such an entity "unobservable" or by questioning its "existence."

Another ambiguity about theoretical entities lies in the question of what kinds of monadic predicates can be applied to them. They are not necessarily predicated only by "theoretical" predicates (indeed I shall suggest below that there may not even be any such predicates in the usual sense); they may be entities, all of whose predicates are unobservable *in the domain of that and similar entities* although observable in the domain of different entities. Examples of the second possibility are the *mass* of an electron and the *force* between two hydrogen atoms. There is, however, no place for either kind of unobservable entity in our simplified model, because by definition no monadic predicate can be reported of such an entity, and, inasmuch as there are no relational predicates in the model, no inferences can be made to it either.

The notion of a theoretical *predicate,* on the other hand, can be represented in the model if a somewhat weaker interpretation than usual is given to what it is to be a theoretical predicate. It is usually assumed that a theoretical predicate is one which is unobservable in the domain of *any* entity. However, it is not at all clear that any predicates unobservable in this sense are used in science unless they are explicitly defined in terms of predicates observable in *some* domain. For example, "ionized" might be said to be a purely theoretical predicate, but it is explicitly defined in terms of *charged particles* having certain *masses,* exerting *forces,* and so on, where the italicized predicates all have some application to observed entities. It may be objected that in such explicit definitions even "charge," "particle," etc., have meanings different from those they have in observation statements; in other words, that all predicates are used "in a different sense" when they refer to theoretical and observable entities respectively. There is some truth in this observation, but it is not clear as it stands. If it means that "charge" predicated of a theoretical entity has a sense *unrelated* to that of "charge" predicated of an observable entity, we are back with the uninterpreted theoretical terms of the deductivist account, for if there is *nothing* in common between the two uses, why use the word "charge" of a theoretical entity at all? If, however, the claim that the meanings are different implies only that charged elementary particles are different kinds of entities from charged pith balls, this is true, and can be expressed by saying that the predicate co-occurs and is co-absent with different predicates in the two cases. This fact is represented in the present model better than in most accounts. It has already been noticed that in this model the conditions of correct application of a predicate depend partly on the other predicates with which it is reported to occur. Thus the conditions of correct application of "charge" are different in the cases of elementary particles and pith balls. This seems to capture sufficiently what is in mind when it is asserted that charge "means" something different in the two cases. It does not, of course, make the statements in which "charge" occurs true *by definition* in either case, because their truth value will depend on observation reports in which this and other predicates are asserted of these and other entities, and these reports are empirical, although their truth values are not decidable independently of one another.

I conclude that a given predicate retains its identity—whether used of observable or theoretical entities—though not necessarily its conditions of correct application. Predicates like "ionized," which appear to be purely theoretical, are in fact explicitly definable in terms of other predicates observable of some entities, and I shall assume, at least for purposes of this simplified model, that there are no primitive theoretical predicates which are unobservable of all entities. What are usually called theoretical predicates are those which have *few* applications to observed entities, perhaps because in most entities they are "hidden." Examples would be "charged," which is not directly observed of many kinds of entities, although in physical theory there are ascriptions of "charged" to most primitive entities; or "frequency" of so many cycles, which is more commonly ascribed to air molecules, spectral lines, etc., in theories than it is directly observed of vibrating strings.

In the model, then, theoretical predicates are those which have fewer occasions of reported application and therefore a proportionately greater reliance on co-occurrences and co-absences with other predicates in the inferences into which they enter. Because they are reported less frequently, the posterior c-values of theories containing them will, in general, be comparatively low. It is difficult to give a realistic account of how these predicates might work in our simplified model, but something along the following lines may be suggestive. Suppose a "good" theory is one which not only agrees with most of the evidential reports but also correlates them "economically" by clustering individuals in fairly well-defined classes. Then significant theoretical predicates might be those which are reported rather seldom, but which have particularly important distributions in the theory with highest c-value. They may, for example, provide between them an economical set of necessary and sufficient conditions for class membership, as do the characters of plants exploited in a botanical flora, even though these may not be the characters in terms of which the species were originally identified and may not be the most evident to the naked eye. In other words, it may be that the more "observable" predicates are in a sense redundant, although it would not have been possible without them to have identified which actually was the set of sufficient reports for identifying an object as a member of a given class.

Conclusion: Meaning and Justification Again

What, then, in this model of the observation language is the answer to the two questions regarding meaning and justification which we have traced through half a century of philosophy of science? The clue seems to lie in two characteristics of the new model which were absent in earlier accounts.

1. The meaning of the observation predicates, as well as of the theoretical predicates (in our weakened sense), has elements both of empirical association in situations of easy empirical reference and of contextual relation with other predicates which co-occur or are co-absent. To show that observation predicates have the second element as well as the first, and that theoretical predicates have the first as well as the second, is to show that the problem of the "meaning of theoretical predicates" as conceived in the

deductivist account does not exist. The meaning of predicates in general is to be construed in terms of this twofold process of application, of which the model gives oversimplified examples.

But, inasmuch as both observation and theoretical predicates sometimes appear in theoretical statements that are not directly decidable because they are statements about unobservable *entities*, this solution to the problem of meaning cannot provide a solution to the problem of justification unless another condition is met.

2. The model exemplifies the general condition that inference about unobservable, and observable but not yet observed, entities takes place by *analogy*. The idea that the confirmation theory should give high c-values to analogical argument was built into its c_0-distribution. If we consider the difficulties into which the deductivist account runs when it attempts a justification of theoretical inference, or of prediction of observables from given observables via theories, it is clear why analogical argument is required here. Take first the problem bequeathed by Hempel, which can be put essentially as follows: What is the relation between two consequences, E_1 and E_2, of a theory H such that we are justified in predicting E_2 with confidence, given E_1? Or in terms of probabilistic confirmation, if H entails E_1 & E_2, what additional conditions are required of H in order to satisfy $c(E_2/E_1) > c_0(E_2)$? The answer, I suggest, is that there has to be a relation of analogy between E_1 and E_2.[18] In our model, this is easy to see, although in such a simple world the "theory" appears to be somewhat trivial. In this model, evidence reporting certain predicates of a given individual a is good evidence for the occurrence of certain of those predicates as yet unobserved in another individual b if and only if a and b are already known to have a high proportion of predicates in common, although they may also be known to be different in other respects. What is the "theory" from which both evidence and prediction follow? Simply that a and b share all the predicates which it is reported and predicted

18. For a development of this idea see my "Concilience of Inductions," in *The Problem of Inductive Logic*, ed. I. Lakatos and A. Musgrave (Amsterdam, 1968), p. 232.

that they share. But, if our model could deal with relational as well as monadic predicates, and even predicates of the second and higher types, it would be clear that our requirement of analogy is capable of more general application. In fact it is just a reformulation of the condition insisted upon by Campbell and his successors, that a theory should be interpreted in terms of a physical model or "analogy" for which the physical laws are already known. Thus the system of Newtonian particles bears to gas theory essentially the same relation that one individual bears to another in our model when there is a strong analogy between them, an analogy which allows highly confirmed predictions of further similarities.

We have in a sense come full circle to the early positivists' insistence on "observability" and inductive inference to experimental laws, rather than to deductive theories in a "theoretical" language. We have been able to make this circle without gross misrepresentation of the theoretical development of science because our analysis of the observation language is more complex than that of the positivists and reveals the distinction between the theoretical and the observational to be one of degree rather than kind. Whether this analysis is adequate for all types of theory and theoretical inference, particularly in modern physics, is a question too extensive for us to prejudge here. Its discussion would involve a confirmation theory based on a language containing the real-number continuum, for which many as yet unsolved mathematical problems arise. But perhaps enough has been said to indicate that both the problems and the techniques of the positivists can be pushed further than their deductivist successors thought possible. There is no reason to despair of a logic of scientific theories nor to fall back into a kind of historical relativism in which theoretical inference is regarded as being fundamentally irrational.

DUDLEY SHAPERE

notes toward a post-positivistic interpretation of science

I. POSITIVISM AND ITS OPPONENTS: A DIAGNOSIS

1. *Philosophical Functions of the "Theoretical-Observational" Distinction*

The distinction between "impressions" and "ideas," formulated during the development of British empiricism in the seventeenth and eighteenth centuries, was introduced primarily to fulfill two fundamental purposes. For, in maintaining that all ideas are based on impressions, the distinction embodied the views that (1) all meaningful concepts (terms) obtain their meanings from experience and (2) all meaningful propositions (statements) are to be judged true or false, acceptable or unacceptable, by reference to experience. Thus the distinction proposed—or, more accurately, promised—to make possible the solution of two crucially important philosophical problems: the problem of the *meaning*

I am indebted for discussions leading to many of the ideas in this paper to the students in my graduate seminar at the University of Chicago. I also wish to thank Professors Kenneth Schaffner and Sylvain Bromberger for valuable help on many points.

115

of terms (concepts) and the problem of the *acceptability of statements* (propositions).[1] Corresponding to these two positive aims of the distinction were the negative or critical ones of the elimination of meaningless or metaphysical terms and statements, and of false or unacceptable meaningful statements: for the precise way in which "ideas" were supposed to be based on "impressions" was held to provide, at the same time, criteria for the rejection of all those ideas or alleged ideas which are not so grounded.

As a lineal descendant of this empiricist distinction, formulated specifically with reference to the interpretation of scientific meaning and knowledge, the positivistic distinction between "observation" and "theory" has, with appropriate alterations, inherited the functions of its predecessor. True, the tendency in this century has been for the newer distinction to be stated (as above) as being concerned with terms and statements, thus avoiding, hopefully, the misleading psychological overtones of the word "ideas" (or even "concepts" and "propositions"). And, correlatively with this non-psychological approach, the newer distinction has been stated in terms of the definability or reducibility of theoretical terms, and of the justification for accepting or rejecting a theoretical statement, rather than, with Hume, in terms of the origin of such terms and statements. In addition, views of the exact manner in which theoretical terms and statements are supposed to be "based on" observation have also deviated in radical ways from what the classical empiricists probably would have wanted to say, even had they formulated their theses non-psychologically. Nevertheless, the newer, scientifically oriented distinction continues to serve the purposes of characterizing relationships be-

---

1. In the empiricist-positivist tradition, discussion has also centered on the meaning (or meaningfulness) of statements as well as—and sometimes instead of—concepts. But, despite the fact that the history of science contains a multitude of cases in which the introduction of new concepts, or the abandonment of old ones, played a crucial role in developments, little attention has been devoted to the problem of the acceptability of concepts. Presumably the reason for this was a belief, often tacit, that that problem would be solved automatically with the solution of the problem of the acceptability of statements. This belief, however, is highly questionable, and a close examination of reasons for introducing new concepts and abandoning old ones is needed in science.

tween meaningful (or scientific) terms and true or acceptable statements on the one hand, and experience on the other, while at the same time providing criteria for the elimination of those terms and statements which do not satisfy such relationships.

But, in twentieth-century philosophy of science, the distinction between theory and observation has been utilized to serve a further purpose which was not served by the more general classical distinction between ideas and impressions. For, in its concern with theories rather than with ideas, the modern distinction has had to deal with *rival sets* of terms and statements in a way that Hume, for instance, did not. Hume did not explicitly discuss competing sets of ideas organized into the kinds of systems which in science are called theories. And it is here that philosophy of science in the twentieth century has added a new dimension to the traditional discussions (although, as we shall see, the newness and importance of this dimension have only recently become apparent and pressing).

For twentieth-century philosophy of science, and particularly the positivistic tradition, has utilized the theoretical-observational distinction not only for the purpose of analyzing the meaning and acceptability of *single* theories. It has also applied the distinction to the analysis of the basis on which *different* theories may be said to be in competition, one being chosen as more adequate than its competitors. The fact that two different theories "deal with (at least some of) the same observations" ("overlap in their observational vocabularies") provides a basis for comparing the *meanings* of the terms and statements of the two theories as well as the *relative acceptability* of the two theories.

Nevertheless, the problem of the comparability of theories has tended to play a subsidiary role in twentieth-century philosophy of science—that is, as will soon become clear, until quite recently. For it has usually been tacitly assumed (until recently) that, because the meanings of the theoretical terms of any one theory are at least partially determined by the observation terms with which they are correlated, and because there is a common pool of observation (observation terms) from which different theories can draw (i.e., with which their theoretical terms can be correlated), it follows as a matter of course that two theories may be compared with regard to their meanings insofar as they contain or are correlated with the same observational vocabulary. And one theory would be judged more acceptable than another if, for example, its degree of confirmation were higher than that of the other. In the case of meanings and of acceptability, then, the observational vocabulary provided an objective ("theory-independent") basis for interpreting and judging single theories; and the solution of any problems concerning the comparison of different theories would follow as a matter of course once the exact details of the basis for interpreting and judging single theories were laid out.

But in the last several years the problem of comparability (with respect to both meaning and acceptability) has increased in seriousness until it would not be an exaggeration to say that it is now one of the central problems in the philosophy of science, around which the treatment of a large number of other problems revolves. This shift of emphasis has been due primarily to two factors: (1) the failure of successive efforts to clarify the theoretical-observational distinction and to make it serve the purposes for which it was introduced; and (2) problems raised by the presentation of radical alternatives to that distinction in its positivistic forms. I will discuss these two factors briefly in turn.

2. Difficulties of the Theoretical-Observational Distinction

Attempts to solve the problems of meaning and acceptability by use of the distinction between theoretical and observational terms and statements have encountered severe difficulties. The distinction itself has proved resistant to clear and ultimately helpful formulation. Interpretations of the notions of "observation" and "theory" have proved highly suspect, and unobjectionable analyses of the meaning relations that are supposed to hold between observation terms and theoretical terms, and of the relations that are supposed to hold between evidence statements (observation statements) and theoretical ones, have not been forthcoming. Efforts to modify the basic approach—for instance, by considering the distinction to be a matter of *degree* rather than a sharp difference of *kind*, or by considering it to be a difference between kinds of *uses of terms* rather than a difference between kinds of *terms,* although such approaches have perhaps not yet had full opportunity for development and critical scrutiny—do not seem promising, for these types of approaches still require the very criteria for distinguishing observation and theory that they have sought to avoid.

The literature on these topics is well known, and the objections are familiar; and in any case the present essay will be concerned in general with very different kinds of objections and with an attitude toward the distinction which is different from that embodied in the usual objections. However, there is one by now familiar objection that must be reviewed briefly here, inasmuch as it marks out a transition to a view of science which stands in radical opposition to that of the empiricist-positivist tradition and has, both by its own freshness and its own failures, helped to bring about the shift of emphasis (noted above) in the problems of the philosophy of science.

The objection in question holds that, with regard to their meanings, the "observation terms" that serve as the basis for the scientist's work are *not*—as the empiricist-positivist tradition generally has tended to view them—completely free from "theory." What the scientist considers to be language appropriate for the presentation of empirical evidence seems not to be anything like the neutral "observational vocabulary" of the philosophers —not like the "red patch-here-now" of the sense datum or phenomenalistic analysis of observation, nor like the pointer readings of the operationalists, or even like the ordinary tables and chairs referred to by an everyday thing language. Far from it: according to this criticism, not only is the *relevance* of observations at least partly dependent on theory; even *what counts* as an observation, and the *interpretation* or *meaning* of observation terms, is at least partly so dependent. All "observation terms" in science are, in this view, at least to some extent "theory dependent" or "theory laden" in a sense which is passed over by the usual ways of making the distinction. Data are not "raw"; there are no "brute facts."

3. *The Approach of Feyerabend and Kuhn*
On the basis of this point, as well as of the other difficulties,

mentioned earlier, in formulating the distinction between "observation" and "theory" so that it will do the jobs set for it, a number of writers have concluded that the meanings of observation terms are not dependent merely in part on their theoretical contexts but are *wholly* so dependent. "The meaning of every term we use," Paul Feyerabend declares, "depends upon the theoretical context in which it occurs. Words do not 'mean' something in isolation; they obtain their meanings by being part of a theoretical system." [2] In particular, according to Feyerabend, this holds for so-called observation terms.

The philosophies we have been discussing so far [i.e., versions of empiricism] assumed that observation sentences are meaningful *per se*, that theories which have been separated from observations are not meaningful, and that such theories obtain their interpretation by being connected with some observation language that possesses a stable interpretation. According to the point of view I am advocating, the meaning of observation sentences is determined by the theories with which they are connected. Theories are meaningful independent of observations; observational statements are not meaningful unless they have been connected with theories. . . . It is therefore the *observation sentence* that is in need of interpretation and *not* the theory.[3]

Advocates of this view do not stop with the claim that observation terms are theory dependent; the background point of view (theory, "paradigm" [4]) also is, according to Thomas Kuhn, "the source of the methods, problem-field, and standards of solution accepted by any mature scientific community at any given time. . . . And as the problems change [with change of fundamental point of view or "paradigm"], so, often, does the standard that distinguishes a real scientific solution from a mere metaphysical speculation, word game, or mathematical play." [5] Such basic shifts of viewpoint entail "changes in the standards governing permissible problems, concepts, and explanations";[6] and

---

2. P. Feyerabend, "Problems of Empiricism," in R. Colodny, ed., *Beyond the Edge of Certainty* (Englewood Cliffs, N.J.: Prentice-Hall, 1965), p. 180.

3. *Ibid.*, p. 213.

4. T. S. Kuhn, *The Structure of Scientific Revolutions* (Chicago: University of Chicago Press, 1962).

5. *Ibid.*, p. 102.

6. *Ibid.*, p. 105.

after such a change, "the whole network of fact and theory . . . has shifted." [7] What counts as a "fact"—the meanings of observation terms—is different, "incommensurable," from one theory (or at least one fundamental theory or paradigm) to another, and so is what counts as a real problem, a correct method, a possible explanation, an acceptable explanation, and nonsense or metaphysics.

Indicating ways in which the meanings of "observation terms" depend on a background of theory, the position advanced by these writers has certainly brought out forcefully the inadequacies of usual formulations of the distinction between theory and observation. Their view has also suggested that the analysis of many other supposedly "metascientific" concepts, such as "explanation," cannot be divorced completely from consideration of substantive developments in science. But in their extreme view that all such concepts are completely theory dependent they have made different fundamental theories "incommensurable," incomparable, and have failed to account for the fact that different theories—or different usages of the same terms or symbols—do in many cases exhibit a continuity in the development of science. Again, it is not necessary to repeat in detail the multitude of criticisms that have been leveled against the Feyerabend-Kuhn approach; for our purposes here, it is enough to note that, for all the value and suggestiveness of those writers, their views have not been formulated in a way which resolves the major problems of contemporary philosophy of science but only makes them more glaring.

4. *The Problem of Comparability*

In arguing for the successively stronger theses (*a*) that there is no observational vocabulary which serves as the common basis for comparison of theories, (*b*) that there is no separable component of the scientist's evidence talk which is common to all theories or even to more than one (fundamental) theory ("each theory will have its own experience," [8] according to Feyerabend),

---

7. *Ibid.*, p. 140.
8. Feyerabend, "Problems of Empiricism," p. 214.

and (c) that what counts as an "observation term" and the meanings of such terms are wholly dependent on theory rather than vice versa, the Feyerabend-Kuhn approach has moved the problem of the comparability of theories from the periphery to the foreground of contemporary philosophy of science. The traditional empiricist-positivist approach, it will be remembered, accounted for the comparability of theories by maintaining that two rival theories, despite their differences, can be compared because they both talk about (deal with, try to take account of, explain, organize, systematize) at least some of the same observations. That view, which had long suffered from grave objections anyway, now faces the most serious challenge. But a satisfactory answer is not necessarily to go to the other extreme and hold, with Feyerabend and Kuhn, that science is not "objective," that it does not make real progress, that it is always relative to a background framework which itself is purely arbitrary and immune to rational criticism.

Thus the problem of comparability assumes far greater importance than before. Other problems, hitherto largely ignored, are also brought into prominence by this refocusing of the philosophy of science. For example, the positivistic tradition has made a sharp distinction between "scientific" terms—terms occurring within science, like "space," "time," "mass," "electron"—and "metascientific" expressions—terms or expressions used in talking about science, like "is a theory," "is a law," "is evidence for," "is an explanation." And, for that tradition, the "metascientific" expressions could and should be given an analysis which is independent of any particular scientific theories, laws, evidence, explanations. For positivism, to give such analyses was, indeed, one of the main duties of the philosopher of science. However, the Feyerabend-Kuhn approach has argued, as we have seen, that fundamental scientific revolutions (changes of "paradigm" or "high-level background theories") alter something (everything?) not only about the admittedly substantive content of science but even about what counts as, for example, an explanation (the meaning of "explanation"). The question is thus raised as to whether even allegedly "metascientific" concepts like "explanation" are not to at least some extent "theory dependent" and, therefore, whether, or to what extent, they can be used to talk about different theories. Indeed, the very possibility or significance of the general distinction between "metascientific" and "scientific" concepts becomes suspect, and, with it, a large part of the positivistic conception of the program and method of the philosophy of science.

The problem of comparability now appears in a new and deeper guise: for, with regard to both concepts allegedly occurring "within science" and concepts used in "talking about science," it becomes necessary to inquire whether there are any such concepts, or separable components of such concepts, which are common to more than one theory (or perhaps even *necessarily* common to *all* theories, at least to all those of certain types). And, if there are (as seems *prima facie* to be the case, despite Kuhn and Feyerabend) any common concepts or components of concepts, what gain if any is there, for the understanding of science, in analyzing them? Must we, in order to point out concepts that are (or perhaps must be) common to several or perhaps all scientific theories, or to point out metascientific concepts applicable to any scientific theory, point to something so abstract as to be rather empty and unilluminating? And, having found such concepts, must we face the possibility that future developments in science will force us, in order to maintain them as "common" or "applicable," to make them still more general—and empty? The whole problem of "comparability" thus becomes not simply *whether* or not there are similarities between different "theories" (regarding either the terms occurring in them or the terms used in talking about them) but rather, even granting the existence of such similarities, the extent to which pointing out those similarities and analyzing them is significant or illuminating for the attempt to understand science.

5. *Further Comments on the Relations between the Positivistic and Feyerabend-Kuhn Approaches*

The problem of comparability of theories, as it is exposed in the debate between the positivistic and the Feyerabend-Kuhn camps, may be expressed in the following way: How are we to give an account of the scientific enterprise according to which

123

observations (experience, data, evidence) will be both *independent* of theory (any theory?) and *relevant* thereto? The difficulty is that, *prima facie,* a tension exists between these two requirements, for independence seems to demand that the meanings of observation terms be totally pure of any theoretical infusion, whereas relevance seems to demand that they be permeated, at least to some extent, by theory. And, when the problem is put in this way, it appears that, whereas the empiricist-positivist tradition in its concern with the objectivity of science has overemphasized independence, writers like Kuhn and Feyerabend have dwelt on relevance to the exclusion of independence. But an adequate interpretation of science must do justice to both features, and the problem is to steer a safe course between these two demands.

Nevertheless, this way of putting the comparability problem still relies on the notions of theory and observation for its formulation. And, in view of the difficulties which have plagued these notions, we must consider whether an attack on the comparability problem from this point of view is advisable. We should note particularly that the notion of theory is today in a worse state than ever. Consider first the view of (high-level background) theories advanced by Feyerabend, which is paralleled in many respects in Kuhn's notion of paradigms. Elsewhere I have argued that their approach, although it takes as the fundamental determinant of scientific meaning and acceptability the notion of a theory ("high-level background theory" or "paradigm"), fails to give an adequate analysis of that concept.[9] For it is unclear what is to be included in and excluded from Kuhn's "paradigms" and Feyerabend's "high-level background theories." In order to give his background theories sufficient pervasiveness and scope, Feyerabend declares that "in what follows, the term 'theory' will be used in a wide sense, including ordinary beliefs (*e.g.,* the belief in the existence of material objects), myths (*e.g.,* the myth of

9. D. Shapere, "The Structure of Scientific Revolutions," *Philosophical Review,* 73 (1964): 383–94, and *idem,* "Meaning and Scientific Change," in R. Colodny, ed., *Mind and Cosmos* (Pittsburgh: University of Pittsburgh Press, 1966), pp. 41–85.

eternal recurrence), religious beliefs, *etc.* In short, any sufficiently general point of view concerning matter of fact will be termed a 'theory.' " [10] Similarly, Kuhn's "paradigm" consists of a "strong network of commitments—conceptual, theoretical, instrumental, and methodological," [11] including "quasi-metaphysical" [12] ones.

But the problem of what is supposed to be a "part of a theory" is not confined to such questions as whether Kepler's mysticism was an integral part of some underlying "theory" he held, or whether absolute space was an integral part of Newton's science. In the second part of this paper we will several times encounter cases where it is not clear whether *admittedly scientific* propositions should be judged "part" of a certain theory or not. The positivistic analysis of scientific theories as interpreted axiomatic systems is of no help whatever in such cases. For considering a theory in this way presupposes that we already know *which* propositions *are* part of the theory, in order to axiomatize them; but the problem is to decide which propositions *are* to be considered members of the set to be axiomatized. Here again, philosophers of science are indebted to the Kuhn-Feyerabend view, even for its deficiencies, because the exposure of the difficulties in its notion of theories has brought out the essential triviality (with respect to the present problem) of the positivistic view. There is today no completely—one is almost tempted to say remotely—satisfactory analysis of the notion of a scientific theory.

It should be emphasized that the inadequacies of attempted analyses of the concepts of theory and observation do not imply that those terms ought to be eliminated from legitimate scientific discourse, or that they will not have a place in a full interpretation of science. They are, after all, terms which have perfectly good and common scientific uses. What has failed, so far, are not those uses but rather the *technical* distinction, which, while supposedly doing justice to those actual uses, was really introduced to perform certain philosophical functions.

10. Feyerabend, "Problems of Empiricism," p. 219, n. 3.
11. Kuhn, *Scientific Revolutions,* p. 42.
12. *Ibid.,* p. 41.

6. *The Generation of Artificial Problems by the Theoretical-Observational Distinction*

The distinction between "theoretical" and "observational," and the relations between them, have proved extraordinarily difficult to formulate, particularly in a way which would deal successfully with the specific problems for the sake of which the distinction was introduced—namely, as we have seen, the problems of meaning, acceptability, and comparability. But from the point of view of the present paper there are yet further deficiencies of the distinction which are even more important to recognize, inasmuch as they will be found to suggest fresh and constructive steps to be taken in the attempt to understand science. First of all, it seems reasonable to ask whether some problems that have arisen within the context of discussions relying on the theoretical-observational distinction are *created, at least in part, by the limitations of that technical distinction and the roles for which it was introduced. If so, then the problematic character of those created "problems" must be reconsidered in the light of the failures of the background against which they arose.* That this is in fact true in at least one case may be argued as follows.

One of the most notorious problems arising within the context of discussions employing the notions of theory and observation as analytical tools is the so-called problem of the ontological status of theoretical entities, or the question of whether a "realistic" interpretation of scientific theories can be upheld. Can such terms as "electron"—often taken as a paradigm case of a theoretical term—be said to designate entities, or must reference to electrons be looked upon as only, for example, the employment of a convenient fiction, instrument, or calculating device? Now, there are, no doubt, real difficulties in the way of understanding precisely what is involved in such assertions as "Electrons exist"; but the perplexity about the ontological status of theoretical entities must be attributed at least in part to this problem's being formulated against the background of the theoretical-observational distinction, rather than entirely to some intrinsic opaqueness of the concept of existence. For, once we make a sharp distinction between "theoretical" and "observational" terms, and lay it down that the former are to be interpreted via the latter, we are easily led to be puzzled, not only about the interpretation of the former, but also about whether they have to do, literally and explicitly, with anything that exists. Observation terms are clearly meaningful and clearly they refer to entities that exist (this is particularly obvious if we "adopt a thing language" to provide our "observational vocabulary") or properties that are real. The problem, with regard to the ontological status, as well as the interpretation, of a class of terms distinct from these is apparently merely in the sharpness of the distinction. (The problem of interpreting theoretical terms was understood to involve, as one aspect, the question of what if anything such terms were "about.") It was all too easy to view the distinction between observational and theoretical as paralleling a distinction between existent and non-existent.

The evolution of the theoretical-observational distinction only made matters successively worse with regard to the problem of ontological status. If theoretical terms could, as early positivism maintained, be exhaustively defined via observational ones, then it was unnecessary to assume the existence of theoretical entities: theoretical terms could be treated as a convenient shorthand, and theoretical entities as convenient fictions. With the view that theoretical terms could be only partially so defined, the puzzle arose again: did the "extra meaning" necessitate reference to entities, even unobservable ones? To avoid this inference (an unpleasant one for positivists) it was proposed that the "extra meaning" was contributed by the place of the term in the "system." Thus again, if theoretical entities can be said to exist in any sense at all, they do not exist in the same sense that tables and chairs exist. There were many who could not but feel uncomfortable at this evident taking away with the left hand what had been given with the right. Finally, the abandonment of the sharp distinction by many, and its replacement by, for example, the "continuum" view—a view whose major purpose is to deal not with the problem of ontological status but with the difficulties of the theoretical-observational distinction itself—seem to leave the problem high and dry. As Grover Maxwell, wrestling with the problem, expresses his discomfort, "Although there certainly *is* a continuous transition from observability to unobservability, any talk of such a continuity from full-blown existence to non-existence is, clearly, nonsense." [13] Where on the alleged continuum is one to draw the line? Similar uneasiness is engendered by the view that certain terms are used "theoretically" in some contexts and "observationally" in others.

Further prominent doctrines of one phase or another of the positivistic tradition co-operated to generate the problem of ontological status—although those further doctrines, also relied to some extent for their precise formulation on the theoretical-observational distinction. Among these other doctrines was the verifiability theory of meaning. According to this view—expressed here in simplified form, of course—a statement is meaningful if and only if there exists a method of verifying it. Theoretical terms, in contrast to observation terms, were alleged to refer to what is unobservable; hence, if methods of verification of existence statements are restricted to observation, statements such as "Electrons exist" are unverifiable if taken literally and thus are meaningless unless interpreted non-literally. The failure of the verifiability theory, and serious problems regarding the sense in which theoretical entities are "unobservable," did not remove the deep suspicions that, being unobservable, theoretical entities cannot be talked about meaningfully, at least not in any literal sense. And it followed that theoretical terms must be given some interpretation which does not involve reference to such entities.

A second positivistic doctrine which aided in making the problem of ontological status appear unduly serious was the view that scientific theories are "interpreted axiomatic systems." Modeling so much of their approach to the philosophy of science, as they did, on mathematical logic, the positivists talked about the linkages correlating theoretical with observational terms ("co-ordinating definitions," "rules of interpretation," "correspondence rules," etc.) as being analogous to the interpretation of a formal system in mathematics and logic. Such linkages in logic are clearly unlike the kinds of connections which can be asserted to hold between existent things (e.g., causal interaction); and so, the use

13. G. Maxwell, "The Ontological Status of Theoretical Entities," in H. Feigl and G. Maxwell, eds., *Minnesota Studies in the Philosophy of Science,* vol. 3: *Scientific Explanation, Space, and Time* (Minneapolis: University of Minnesota Press, 1962), p. 9.

of this analogy automatically leads one to suppose that, inasmuch as observables exist, theoretical terms also are linked to observational ones in ways different from the ways in which existent entities can be related to one another. Once again we seem compelled *by the very approach employed*—in this case, by the employment of the logical model (although even here the theoretical-observational distinction is relied upon)—to say at the very least that we are puzzled by statements about the "existence" of theoretical entities. It appears that a great deal—not necessarily all—of the gravity of the problem of the ontological status of theoretical entities is the result of adopting a certain approach or set of approaches to the philosophy of science. The problem—or at least part of the problem—arises simply *because* we employ a certain technical distinction (theoretical-observational) as well as certain other doctrines (verifiability theory of meaning) and analogies (logical models of scientific theories and their interpretations) which in turn rely heavily on that distinction. None of these views has proved successful; and so one must suspect that a problem which arises at least in good measure against the background of those views may, to that extent at least, not be the problem it has been made out to be. On the contrary: to some extent, at least, it may well be a pseudoproblem.

7. Need for Reconsideration of the "Ontological Status" Problem

Thus, many of the puzzling features of such statements as "Electrons exist" can be attributed merely to demanding an analysis of those statements within the context of the theoretical-observational distinction and associated doctrines, to utilizing that distinction as an analytical tool for the framing of problems and solutions in the philosophy of science. But it is by no means necessary that we approach such statements in this way; and in view of the protracted failure of the technical distinction between theory and observation and because of the way in which it (together with associated doctrines) led to the creation, or at least the exaggeration, of the problem of ontological status it may not even be the best way. Indeed, the multitude of weaknesses that have been exposed in the positivistic *grounds* for worrying about the legitimacy of existence-claims for "theoretical entities" may even encourage us to take a new look at that problem. Such a fresh examination would have to be far more radical than the approach of Feyerabend and Kuhn. Because, for all the divergence of their position from the positivistic view that theories are comparable by virtue of their dealing with a common core of "observation terms," they nevertheless approach their problems with that distinction in mind. The "revolution" of Feyerabend and Kuhn does not consist in denying the utility, the centrality, of the notions of theory and observation in stating and dealing with the problems of the philosophy of science, but rather, simply in reversing their respective roles: it is now theory ("high-level background theory" or "paradigm") that determines the meaning and acceptability of observation, rather than vice versa.

In the course of such a radical re-examination of the problem of ontological status further limitations of the theoretical-observational approach may well emerge. After all, designed as it was to deal primarily with the specific problems of meaning, acceptability, and comparability, it is only natural that that distinction might not do other jobs equally well. Indeed, we might expect that, while some problems—like that of the ontological status of electrons, waves, space-time, or fields—might be exaggerated or distorted by formulating them in terms of that distinction, still other problems, and other interesting and important features of science, may well have been pushed into the background and ignored because of the central place accorded to the theoretical-observational distinction and the problems it was introduced to handle. And it may be that those other problems and features have not just *failed* to be noticed because philosophers were too busy with theoretical-observational work; it may be that that distinction actually *obscured* the existence of those problems and features, that the limitations of that distinction and the complex of problems it was designed to deal with actually drew attention away from those other problems and features.

But it is not only the difficulties and limitations of the theoretical-observational approach that make a re-examination of existence-claims in science an attractive venture; there are more positive grounds for the undertaking. For there are a great many clear cases of scientific terms usually classed as "theoretical" which we are strongly inclined (or, as some would have us believe, tempted) to use in statements predicating existence or non-existence of them. The number of such clear cases is surely comparable to the number of clear cases of terms that we feel strongly inclined to classify as either "theoretical" or "observational." We need not fear, therefore, that we will be worse off initially in reopening the problem of ontological status than those who began to approach the interpretation of science by examining clear cases of "observational" and "theoretical" terms and statements. But more: the very multitude of cases in which existence assertions seem so natural in science is itself a fact that cries out for explanation. It suggests that we try to determine what underlies this inclination, this feeling of naturalness, and to see whether what underlies it may not be sounder reasons than have been noticed by the positivistic tradition. Certainly we should at least look into this subject very carefully before agreeing to dismiss this inclination as illegitimate—as a philosophical or metaphysical overlay, imposed on a science which is indifferent to questions of existence, or to which such questions are irrelevant.

Indeed, we will find that there is a sound basis in science for existence-claims of the kinds mentioned above. But the approach that brings this out will also, even if only in a preliminary way in the present paper, enable us to see a number of other classical problems of interest to the philosopher of science in a new light (including problems discussed earlier in this paper); and a number of further problems, hitherto ignored or at least treated lightly by philosophers of science, will be exposed and brought into prominence by the approach used.

II. EXISTENCE AND THE INTERPRETATION OF PHYSICS

8. *The Logic of Idealization in Physics*

Our discussion will begin with a consideration of three examples. These cases are meant to bring out the fact that, in at least some actual physical reasoning, a distinction is made between the way or ways in which entities can or cannot exist and the way or ways in which, for the sake of dealing with certain problems, it is possible and convenient to treat those entities,

131

even though, on purely physical grounds, we know that they could not really be that way. For the sake of convenience (and not to introduce a pair of technical terms) we shall refer to the concepts so distinguished as, respectively, "existence concepts" (or "existence terms") and "idealization concepts" (or "idealization terms"). The precise characteristics of these concepts will be brought out in the examples to be discussed. It must be remembered that for some purposes it might be necessary to point out differences between the cases classified together here, and, furthermore, that not all concepts employed in physics fit appropriately into *either* of the two classes distinguished here. The present section will focus primarily on idealization concepts, discussion of existence concepts being postponed until the next section.

1. A "rigid body" is defined classically as one in which the distances between any two of its constituent parts (particles) remains invariant. (Call this Definition R1.) If a force is applied to the body at any point, then, in order for the body to remain rigid in this sense—i.e., in order for the distances between any two points to remain the same—that force must be transmitted instantaneously to all other parts of the body. In other words, the force must be transmitted with infinite velocity. But according to the special theory of relativity, energy and momentum (and hence forces) cannot be transmitted with a velocity greater than that of light. Therefore, with the application of a force at one of its points, all the parts of a body cannot begin moving simultaneously; the body must be deformed. It is thus impossible, according to the special theory of relativity, that there should exist any such things as rigid bodies in the classical sense.

Nevertheless, the concept of a "rigid body" is employed by writers on special relativity, including, in a way that is central to his exposition, Einstein in his original 1905 paper on the subject.[14] How is such usage to be reconciled with the contradiction

14. A. Einstein, "On the Electrodynamics of Moving Bodies," *Annalen der Physik*, 1905; reprinted in translation in *The Principle of Relativity* (New York, Dover), pp. 35–65. Einstein declares that "the theory to be developed is based—like all electrodynamics—on the kinematics of the rigid body, since the assertions of any such theory have to do with the relationships between rigid bodies (systems of co-ordinates), clocks, and electromagnetic processes. Insufficient consideration of this circumstance lies at the root of the difficulties

described above? There appear to be three general types of attitudes taken toward the role of the concept of rigid bodies with respect to the special theory of relativity.[15]

a. One may argue that for certain purposes the only sense of

---

which the electrodynamics of moving bodies at present encounters" (p. 38). Some thinkers (e.g., E. A. Milne) maintain that the concept of a rigid body need not be taken as playing a fundamental role in special relativity. I will not consider their arguments here, for I am presently concerned only with whatever rationale there might be for employing the concept, in any sense, in discussions of relativity. Einstein himself appears to have vacillated somewhat in his opinion of the centrality of the concept of rigid bodies to his theory; but in general he seems to have held that the concept is central and fundamental. This attitude is revealed in the following comment:

> One is struck [by the fact] that the theory (except for the four-dimensional space) introduces two kinds of physical things, i.e., (1) measuring rods and clocks, (2) all other things, e.g., the electro-magnetic field, the material point, etc. This, in a certain sense, is inconsistent; strictly speaking measuring rods and clocks would have to be represented as solutions of the basic equations (objects consisting of moving atomic configurations), not, as it were, as theoretically self-sufficient entities. However, the procedure justifies itself because it was clear from the very beginning that the postulates of the theory are not strong enough to deduce from them sufficiently complete equations to base upon such a foundation a theory of measuring rods and clocks.

(Einstein, "Autobiographical Notes," in P. A. Schilpp, ed., *Albert Einstein: Philosopher-Scientist* [Evanston, Ill.: Library of Living Philosophers, 1949], p. 59.)

The *kinematic* use to which Einstein puts the notion of a rigid rod in his 1905 paper raises the question of the relevance of the *dynamic* difficulty noted in this paper; indeed, one writer, discussing these points, declares that "the concept of an infinitesimal rigid rod is *kinematically admissible* in the relativistic scheme, but there is a *dynamical* difficulty" (J. L. Synge, *Relativity: The Special Theory* [Amsterdam: North-Holland, 1965], p. 32, italics his). For our purposes, we need not be concerned with Synge's use of the word "infinitesimal" here. However, full conceptual clarity would certainly seem to demand an explanation of how a concept can be used in one context (kinematic) when the introduction of dynamical considerations (simply exerting a force on the object) leads immediately to a drastic contradiction of a fundamental principle of the theory concerned. In any case, reference to rigid reference frames (systems of co-ordinates) cannot evade the difficulty, because the bodies whose behavior is being referred to such reference frames will exert forces on them. Thus, the distinction between the kinematics and dynamics of rigid bodies does not obviate the need for an understanding of the sense in which a concept which contradicts a fundamental principle of a theory can nevertheless be usefully employed in expositions of that theory.

15. Apart from the view held by Milne and others (see note 14) that "rigid body" is to be considered a derivative and not a fundamental concept in the theory of relativity.

"rigid body" needed is the notion of a body which does not change its shape or size when *free* of external forces:

R2. A rigid body is one in which, if the body is free of all external forces and in equilibrium with respect to internal forces, the distance between any two constituent parts will remain invariant.

This is apparently the, or one, sense in which Reichenbach and Grünbaum employ the expression "rigid body" in their attempt to analyze the logical status of the concepts of space and time in science, and particularly in special relativity.[16] It must be noted, however, that this is *not* the sense in which the expression is ordinarily used in physics, where, according to R1, a rigid body is one in which, even if the body is *not* free of external forces, the distance between any two constituent parts will remain the same. In the sense of R2 *all* bodies are rigid,[17] whereas, according to the physical usage R1 (e.g., in the classical theories of rigid and elastic bodies), under the action of external forces some bodies are spoken of as rigid and others as not (and this is the interesting case for those branches of physics). It is the status of *this* notion of rigid body—R1—that is in question in the argument of the second paragraph of this section, not the notion expressed in R2.

b. One can maintain that the classical notion, R1, is adequate as an approximation, for practical purposes: that in many cases bodies can be constructed or visualized in which, under the con-

---

16. "Definition: *Rigid bodies are solid bodies which are not affected by differential forces, or concerning which the influence of differential forces has been eliminated by corrections; universal forces are disregarded*" (H. Reichenbach, *The Philosophy of Space and Time* [New York: Dover, 1958], p. 22, italics his). The reference to "bodies which are not affected by differential forces" corresponds to our R1; the remainder of the definition corresponds to our R2. Grünbaum's primary use of the expression "rigid rod" is stipulated implicitly in one of the opening questions of his book: "What is the warrant for the claim that a solid rod remains rigid or self-congruent under transport in a spatial region free from inhomogeneous thermal, elastic, electromagnetic and other 'deforming' or 'perturbational' influences?" (A. Grünbaum, *Philosophical Problems of Space and Time* [New York: Knopf, 1963], p. 3).

17. Or, in Grünbaum's terms, all bodies are either equally rigid or equally non-rigid.

ditions of some problem, the deformations produced by the prevailing external forces are so small that they can be ignored for
the purposes of the problem. In this sense some rods are rigid
enough (in the *classical* sense) to permit us to speak of, for instance, rigid measuring rods or rigid reference frames. Thus, for
example, the bodies whose behavior is being referred to our system of "rigid" co-ordinates may be so far away, or so small in
mass compared to the masses of the rods constituting our reference frame, that the distortions produced on the reference frame
by those bodies can be neglected for the purposes of the problem
under consideration (and therefore for more general purposes of
theoretical analysis and exposition, where these requisite conditions may be assumed to hold). Fock gives a somewhat different
practical justification of the employment of the classical concept
of rigid body, although his justification is still in the spirit of the
present approach.

[For the reasons discussed earlier] the notion of an absolutely rigid
body may not be used in Relativity Theory.

However, this does not preclude the use of the notion of a rigid
measuring rod in discussions of relativity. For this notion merely presupposes the existence of rigid bodies whose shape and size remain unchanged under certain particular external conditions such as the absence of accelerations or impulses, constancy of temperature, *etc*. Such
rigid bodies can be realized with sufficient accuracy by solid bodies
existing in nature and they can serve as standards of length.[18]

c. However, many writers have considered such a situation
unsatisfactory. Treating the notion of rigid body in the classical
sense as an approximation has seemed to such writers insuffi-
ciently rigorous for employment in a theory in which the notions
of rigid reference frames and rigid measuring rods are claimed to
play so fundamental a role. In all strictness such a notion of rigid
body should be applied only under special circumstances (e.g., for
rigid reference frames, where the reference frame is overwhelmingly—relative to the problem under consideration—more massive
than the bodies considered in reference to it, or else sufficiently

18. V. Fock, *The Theory of Space, Time, and Gravitation* (New York: Pergamon, 1964), p. 106.

distant therefrom). Furthermore, it has seemed desirable to develop the theory of elasticity within the framework of special relativity. In connection with such considerations attempts have been made to develop a relativistic analogue of the classical concept of a rigid body. The first such effort was made by Born in 1909; however, his proposed definition was shown to fail by the successive criticisms of Ehrenfest, Herglotz and Noether, and Von Laue.[19] Other efforts have been made, including the following by McCrea:

R3. We shall . . . define a *rigid rod as one along which impulses are transmitted with speed c.* . . . Since the theory [of special relativity] permits the existence of no 'more rigid' body of this sort, there is no objection to adopting the term *rigid* in this sense.[20]

If there exist no rigid bodies in McCrea's sense, it is not because the theory prohibits their existence, but rather because there are no bodies with a dielectric constant equal to 1 (in which case, impulse signals would be transmitted through such bodies with the velocity of light c; otherwise, the velocity of transmission in them would be less than c). As a matter of fact, no such bodies are known.

In both cases (*b*) and (*c*)—the cases that are relevant to the contradiction pointed out at the beginning of this section—we see that rigid bodies do not exist. The concept of a rigid body (in either the classical or the McCrea sense) is therefore often referred to as an "abstraction" or "approximation" (Fock) or as an "idealization" (Synge—see the quotation at the end of this paragraph). Such references must not obscure the radical difference in the status of the classical and McCrea concepts. As far as the special theory of relativity is concerned, we might discover a body with a dielectric constant equal to 1—in which case a McCrea rigid body

19. For a discussion of Born's definition and the criticisms thereof, see W. Pauli, *Theory of Relativity* (New York: Pergamon, 1958), pp. 130–32; see also Synge, *Relativity: The Special Theory*, p. 36, and *idem, Relativity: The General Theory* (Amsterdam: North-Holland, 1964), pp. 114ff.

20. W. H. McCrea, *Sci. Proc. R. Dublin Soc.*, 26 (1952): 27, italics his; quoted in W. G. V. Rosser, *An Introduction to the Theory of Relativity* (London: Butterworths, 1964), p. 239.

would have been found, and the point of calling that concept an "idealization" would be lost. But, if the special theory of relativity is correct, there *cannot be* a rigid body in the classical sense at all. The classical concept of a rigid body, insofar as it is employed in the context of relativistic physics, *must* be considered an "idealization": bodies simply *cannot* be of that sort. And the reason why that concept must be so considered is not some general philosophical thesis to the effect that *all* scientific concepts are "idealizations"; on the contrary, the reasons are purely scientific ones laid down by the special theory of relativity. It is thus clear that, if we look for reasons for calling the classical concept of rigid body an "idealization," the existence of these purely scientific reasons makes the following philosophical argument—advanced by Synge—superfluous: "In such measurements the infinitesimal rigid rod plays a fundamental part. Do such rods exist in nature? In one sense, we can say at once: Certainly not! None of the sharpened idealizations of theoretical physics is to be thought of as actually existing—they are like the point of Euclidean geometry." [21]

Nevertheless, despite the fact that there could be no such things as classical rigid bodies according to the theory of relativity, it proved useful, in the context of discussions of that theory, to talk in terms of such bodies. Furthermore, as we have also seen, it is possible to do so, at least in the context of certain kinds of problems. As the above quotation from Synge continues: "But in the world of these sharpened concepts, the idea of a rigid rod is useful and kinematically admissible." [22]

Nowhere in classical physics does one find any allegation (on scientific grounds analogous to those supplied by the special theory of relativity) that the existence of absolutely rigid bodies is an impossibility. If one wanted, then, to call the concept of a rigid body an "idealization," one had to appeal either to an assertion that there are in fact no bodies satisfying the definition or to extrascientific considerations such as a Synge-type argument to the

---

21. Synge, *Relativity: The Special Theory*, p. 32.
22. *Ibid.* For discussion of Synge's expression "kinematically admissible," see note 14 above.

effect that no scientific concept could be other than "idealized." However, just as there could, as far as the special theory of relativity is concerned, be rigid bodies in McCrea's sense, so also there might have been, as far as classical physics was concerned, absolutely rigid bodies in the classical sense. In particular, there was no reason (of a physical kind) why elementary particles could not be rigid bodies. We shall return to this point later.[23]

2. We now pass to our second example. According to the Lorentz theory of the electron[24] (and difficulties in this regard have remained in all post-Lorentzian theories of the electron[25]), that particle cannot be a geometrical point, having zero radius. This results fundamentally from the fact that the electrostatic energy of a charged sphere of radius r and charge e is (except for a numerical factor) equal to e^2/r; this formula implies that a charged sphere of zero radius would have infinite energy, or, if

23. The case of the shift from the classical to the McCrea definition is relevant to the problem of the comparability of scientific theories. For, although we have here two different "definitions," the concepts concerned are not, as Kuhn and Feyerabend would have them be, "incommensurable." On the contrary, we see here physical reasons why an old definition proved inadequate, and how it was possible to continue to use that concept in discussion of the new theory even though the old concept contradicted a fundamental principle of the newer theory. We also see that the two concepts, although they appear on the surface to be very different, are nevertheless quite comparable, the common element being expressible in the statement "A rigid body is one through which signals are transmitted at the maximum possible velocity." The disagreement concerns what that maximum possible velocity is. The classical definition has an *implication*—that signals must be transmitted instantaneously through a rigid body—which is contradicted by special relativity. McCrea's definition concentrates on this implication (rather than directly on the old definition—hence the appearance of radical dissimilarity) and modifies it to meet the relativistic requirement.

24. H. A. Lorentz, *The Theory of Electrons* (New York: Dover, 1952), esp. pp. 213–14.

25. Technical reviews of the more modern form of the problem are found in J. Schwinger, ed., *Quantum Electrodynamics* (New York: Dover, 1958); R. Stoops, ed., *The Quantum Theory of Fields* (New York: Interscience, 1961), esp. the papers by W. Heitler, "Physical Aspects of Quantum-Field Theory," and R. P. Feynman, "The Present Status of Quantum Electrodynamics"; see also the excellent survey of the problem in H. M. Schwartz, *Introduction to Special Relativity* (New York: McGraw-Hill, 1968), sec. 7–5, pp. 271ff. A nontechnical discussion is given in L. de Broglie, *New Perspectives in Physics* (New York: Basic Books, 1962), pp. 41–50.

we apply the Einstein relation $E = mc^2$ between energy E and mass m, infinite (rest) mass.[26] However, the electron does not have infinite energy or mass.[27] Nevertheless, for certain purposes —for the solution of certain problems—and under certain circumstances, it is convenient and possible to treat the electron *as if* it were a point particle.

We have written the solution of the potential problem as a sum of boundary contributions and a volume integral extending over the source charges. These volume integrals will not lead to singular values of the potentials (or of the fields) if the charge density is finite. If, on the other hand, the charges are considered to be surface, line, or point charges, then singularities will result. . . . Although these singularities do not actually exist in nature, the fields that do occur are often indistinguishable, over much of the region concerned, from those of simple geometrical configurations. The idealizations of real charges as points, lines, and surfaces not only permit great mathematical simplicity, they also give rise to convenient physical concepts for the description and representation of actual fields.[28]

---

26. Application of the Einstein formula is admissible only if we allow "the Lorentz theory" to have two "versions": Lorentz' and the relativistic reformulation of his "theory." The ambiguity here, of course, arises from the lack of precision, in usual discussions, as to what is to count as "(part of) a theory." There is, however, no difficulty in the present discussion so long as we are clear as to the issues involved.

Note that when the word "theory" has been used in discussions in this section, no technical meaning has been presupposed; on the contrary, we have referred to specific theories whose contents are specifiable in any particular context. Thus, in the context of the first example of section 8, the expression "special theory of relativity" refers to two propositions (the principle of relativity and the principle of the independence of the velocity of light from its source) and their consequences.

27. There seems to be some disagreement as to whether this conclusion is based on experimental fact alone or on some stronger ("theoretical"? "logical"?) consideration. De Broglie, for example, remarks that, "if the charge is assumed to be a point charge, . . . the interaction between the particle and the electromagnetic field results in the energy of the particle at rest, and hence its mass (according to the principle of the inertia of energy), having an infinite value, *which is inadmissible*" (*New Perspectives in Physics*, p. 45, italics mine). Landau and Lifshitz refer to the "physical absurdity of this result" (L. Landau and Lifshitz, *The Classical Theory of Fields* [Reading, Mass.: Addison-Wesley, 1962], p. 102).

28. W. K. H. Panofsky and M. Phillips, *Classical Electricity and Magnetism* (Reading, Mass.: Addison-Wesley, 1962), p. 13. Panofsky and Phillips later

As in the case of classical rigid bodies, we see from the present case again that it is on *scientific* grounds that treatment of the charged particle as a dimensionless point is considered an "idealization." The conclusion that the electron *cannot really be* a dimensionless point is not, in this case either, a logical or epistemological overlay superadded to the science concerned— a conclusion drawn solely from a more general and sweeping philosophical thesis to the effect, for example, that *all* scientific concepts are idealizations, or that all bodies are (or must be) extended, or that our ordinary concept (usage) of the expression "material object" and related terms implies that talk of dimensionless material objects is absurd.

Furthermore, not only is the *impossibility* of considering electrons really to be dimensionless points based on purely scientific considerations; the *rationale* for considering them *as if they were* —the possibility of so treating them, and the reasons why it is convenient to do so—is also scientific in character. As Panofsky and Phillips note, the fields that occur when we consider the source charges to be localized in a point are "often indistinguishable, over much of the region concerned, from those of simple geometrical configurations." It is thus *possible* to treat the source charges (at least in many problems) as if they were concentrated at a point, *even though we know, on purely scientific* (i.e., not metaphysical or linguistic) *grounds, that electrons cannot really*

---

declare that ". . . in classical electrodynamics the only thing known about the electron is that it has a certain total charge, and any calculation of its radiation field cannot involve details of how this charge may be distributed geometrically within the electron. On the other hand, it is impossible to assume that the charge has zero physical extent without introducing various mathematical divergences. But *certain features of the radiation field are actually independent of the radius of the electron, provided only that it is small compared with the other dimensions of the radiation field*" (*ibid.*, p. 341, italics mine). This, of course, constitutes a (physical) reason for being able to *ignore* the question of the radius rather than specifically for *idealizing* it as being of zero extent; but it can serve as a supplementary rationale (in addition to the kinds of reasons adduced in the passage quoted in the body of the present paper) for one's being able to consider the electron as having some specific radius, including zero. Indeed, Panofsky and Phillips continue, "In our discussion of the electron and its behavior we shall assume that it has a finite radius, but we shall ascribe physical significance only to those properties which are independent of the magnitude of the radius" (*ibid.*).

be that kind of thing. Furthermore, it is *convenient* to treat them in that way, for "The idealizations of real charges as points, lines, and surfaces not only permit great mathematical simplicity, they also give rise to convenient physical concepts for the description and representation of actual fields."

The electron as it really is cannot, therefore, have the zero-radius characteristic which is attributed to it for the sake of dealing with certain problems; and this distinction—between the electron as it really is and the electron as idealized because it is possible and convenient to treat it in a certain way—is one which, in this case at least, is made on purely scientific grounds.

This point is not vitiated by the fact that there are also difficulties in the Lorentz theory in considering the electron to have a *non-zero* radius. However the negative charge was held to be distributed over the extended Lorentz electron (and there were, consistent with the basic theory, a number of alternatives which could be held regarding this distribution[29]), the question naturally arose why the constituent parts of this negative charge did not repel one another, causing the explosive disruption of the electron. In order to ensure the stability of the electron it is necessary, as Poincaré showed,[30] to introduce cohesive forces that counterbalance the Coulomb repulsive forces of the electron on itself and maintain it in equilibrium. Poincaré's counterpressure, however, was not electromagnetic in nature and in fact was completely mysterious.[31]

If the "Poincaré pressure" appears to be *ad hoc* and objectionable, certainly the difficulty which thus arises in treating the electron as having a non-zero radius is not on a par with the objection against its being a dimensionless point. For in the former case the required counterforce is known, calculable: it is in fact equal to the Maxwell stress exerted by the surrounding field. Only the

29. H. A. Lorentz, *Problems of Modern Physics* (New York: Dover, 1967), pp. 125–26.

30. H. Poincaré, "Sur la dynamique de l'électron," *Rend. Palermo,* 21 (1906): 129; cf. W. Pauli, *Theory of Relativity* (New York: Pergamon, 1958), esp. pp. 184–86.

31. Cf. H. Weyl, *Space-Time-Matter* (New York: Dover, 1952), pp. 203–6; Pauli, *Theory of Relativity,* pp. 184–86; A. Sommerfeld, *Electrodynamics* (New York: Academic Press, 1964), pp. 236, 278.

source, the explanation, of this counterpressure is unknown, and the hope could be maintained that it would be explained by some future, more complete theory—either a wholly electromagnetic theory (in which the Maxwell and Lorentz theories would appear as "special cases") or else a theory which would introduce entirely new forces supplementing electromagnetic ones.[32] If later, with the development of quantum theory, objections to the very notion of a radius of the electron appeared, such objections do not militate against the present point that, within the framework of Lorentzian physics, the electron—despite idealized treatments thereof—could not in reality be a dimensionless point, even though it might be possible and convenient to treat it as if it were, in order to deal with certain physical problems.

This point concerning the idealizational status of the notion of a dimensionless charged particle in Lorentzian physics is not affected by the following situation either. Recall that, according to the special theory of relativity, there cannot be such things as rigid bodies in the classical sense. This fact, as Yilmaz points out, has interesting consequences for relativistic discussions of elementary particles.

An elementary particle is, by definition, a material object which takes part in physical phenomena only as a unit. In other words, from the physical point of view it should not be useful to think of any component part to an elementary particle or to analyze it further. In order to describe the state of the motion of an elementary particle, it is sufficient to know only its position, velocity, and rotation as a whole. It is clear that this would imply a rigid structure if the particle had any classically meaningful extension at all. Thus, elementary particles must be pictured as point particles in the theory of relativity.[33]

Thus, whereas Lorentz' theory *precluded* the electron from having a zero radius, the theory of relativity *requires* that it have this characteristic. But Lorentzian electrodynamics is expressible

32. The program of developing a "purely electromagnetic world picture" based on the Maxwell-Lorentz theory was carried on by Gustav Mie, whose views will be discussed shortly.

33. H. Yilmaz, *Introduction to the Theory of Relativity and the Principles of Modern Physics* (New York: Blaisdell, 1965), p. 51.

in relativistic terms, and, indeed, in contributing the Lorentz transformations, it provided an essential ingredient in the development of Einstein's theory. Classical (relativistic) electrodynamics thus appears to contain a contradiction. This state of affairs does not, however, constitute a sufficient reason for rejecting that theory as useless—a conclusion one might be led to draw if one looked upon scientific theories as interpreted axiomatic systems. (For an axiomatic system which contains a contradiction will imply as theorems all well-formed sentences of the "language" in which the system is formulated. Thus, if scientific theories are viewed as interpreted axiomatic systems, one would have difficulty understanding how relativistic electrodynamics managed to distinguish true from false propositions.) The contradiction does, however, lead to considering relativistic electrodynamics to be not a fundamental theory but a theory requiring revision, a theory incapable, in the form in which it gave rise to contradiction, of providing a full account of particles. The contradiction even locates the area of inadequacy of the classical theory: namely, in the domain of the very small; and the realization of this fact might have led scientists, even at that time, to raise a significant question:

Since the occurrence of the physically meaningless infinite self-energy of the elementary particles is related to the fact that such a particle must [because of the impossibility of rigid bodies, according to special relativity] be considered as pointlike, we can conclude that electrodynamics as a logically closed physical system presents internal contradictions when we go to sufficiently small distances. We can pose the question as to the order of magnitude of such distances.[34]

As we have seen, of course, the Lorentz theory, even in prerelativistic form, was already known to be incomplete, in that the stability of the extended electron appeared to require the

_____

34. Landau and Lifshitz, *Classical Theory of Fields*, p. 102. Our treatment of this case illustrates one difference between the philosophy of science and the history of science: for the philosopher is interested not only in what *did* happen but also (among other things) in what *could* have happened—in a precisely specifiable sense of "could" (in this case no new theoretical or mathematical techniques, other than those available at the time, were required for one to have seen the contradiction).

existence of a force which was non-electromagnetic. But such incompleteness alone did not *require* that the fundamental concepts and equations of the Lorentz theory be *altered* or *replaced* —only that they be *supplemented*. In the face of the difficulty about the Poincaré pressure, those concepts and equations *might* have been altered; indeed, this was the aim of Gustav Mie's highly influential work.

The first attempt to set up a theory which could account for the existence of electrically charged elementary particles, was made by Mie. He set himself the task to generalize the field equations and the energy-momentum tensor in the Maxwell-Lorentz theory in such a way that the Coulomb repulsive forces in the interior of the electrical elementary particles are held in equilibrium by other, *equally electrical,* forces, whereas the deviations from ordinary electrodynamics remain undetectable in regions outside the particles.[35]

But Mie had an axe to grind: in line with a "purely electromagnetic world picture (or rather, with the particular electromagnetic world picture which is based on the Maxwell-Lorentz theory)," [36] he wished to develop, along such lines, a theory which would be *absolutely complete*. But the difficulty concerning the Poincaré pressure did not require such unrelenting faith: supplementation, even along non-electromagnetic lines, might suffice. On the other hand, the present difficulty, the contradiction posed by the incorporation of the Lorentz theory into the relativistic framework, shows beyond a doubt that that theory cannot be *fundamental:* it has definite and specifiable limits wherein it cannot be adequate and *must* be replaced (and not merely supplemented), although the equations of the more fundamental theory might

---

35. Pauli, *Theory of Relativity,* pp. 188ff; see also Weyl, *Space-Time-Matter,* pp. 206ff. Along the same lines as Mie's work is the theory advanced by Born and Infeld, which showed how the problems concerning the radius and energy of the electron could be overcome within classical theory of the Maxwell-Lorentz-Mie type. However, the non-linearity of the equations of these theories, together with the fact that they were not incorporated within the highly successful quantum theory, led to their not being widely accepted (M. Born, *Proc. Roy. Soc. London,* A143 [1934]: 410; *idem, Ann. Inst. Henri Poincaré,* 7 [1937]: 425; M. Born and L. Infeld, *Proc. Roy. Soc. London,* A144 [1935]: 425; Schwartz, *Introduction to Special Relativity,* pp. 273–74).

36. Pauli, *Theory of Relativity,* p. 185.

(and, indeed, in light of the success of the Maxwell-Lorentz theory, could be expected to) approximate more and more to those of the Lorentz theory as we pass from the domain of the small to that of the larger and larger.

Special relativity might also be blamed for the inconsistency; but in view of the large measure of independence of that theory from special assumptions about the nature of elementary particles,[37] and also in view of its applicability to domains other than electrodynamics, this location of the blame surely would have appeared unlikely.

Note that one thing that is *not* done is to dismiss the problem by saying that the theory of relativity, or classical electrodynamics, is merely an "idealization" (at least with regard to the treatment of elementary particles), or that the contradiction is merely a characteristic of the "formal structure" of the system. The difficulty is taken seriously and, furthermore, is looked upon as indicating the inadequacy of the theory as an account of nature. Such seriousness surely should be connected with the fact that the theories considered distinguish between the ways certain entities—the entities concerned in the contradiction—cannot be and the ways in which they can or must be. The theories are contradicting one another, not in the idealizations they consider useful (would that be a contradiction in any case?), but in their assertions about the way things are: the idealizations made by the theories (including the idealization of electrons as dimensionless points in the Lorentz theory) are irrelevant. And, in any case, the distinction between idealizations and the way things are is one which, in the cases considered at least, is made within the theories, on scientific grounds; the notion of "idealization" has a definite use in physics. Should we not, then, be wary of extending that notion to physics (physical theories) as a whole—of trying to resolve our perplexities about physics by assimilating physics to

37. Of the two fundamental principles postulated in the special theory of relativity, only the principle of the constancy of the velocity of light is held in common with classical (Maxwell-Lorentz) electrodynamics. No hypotheses are necessary concerning the nature or causes of light or, more generally, of electromagnetic phenomena. In particular, it is unnecessary to assume that electricity or light is particulate in nature.

the status of "idealizations"? For in such extended usage the definite scientific function of idealizations—the working use of the term "idealization"—is not to be found.

Study of the cases of rigid bodies and the electron has led us to consider a new problem, namely, how the non-idealized notions are connected with the notions of "completeness" and "fundamentality" of "theories." No technical meaning of the term "theory" has been presupposed here: certain propositions, ordinarily held to be "parts of" the Lorentz and Einstein theories, have been shown to legislate certain requirements as to the way things must or can or cannot be. In conjunction with other considerations, these requirements in turn lead to the exposure of deficiencies which require that the propositions (and concepts) in question be either supplemented or modified—that the theory in question is, in precisely specifiable respects, either not complete or not fundamental. And on some occasions the steps that need to be taken, or the (or some of the) alternative steps that might be taken, or at least the domain where modifications need to be made can be specified in advance, at least to some degree. (Thus Poincaré calculated the needed but mysterious counterpressure; Landau and Lifshitz—with the benefit of hindsight, to be sure, although a hindsight which *could* have been foresight—locate the limitation of classical relativistic electrodynamics in the domain of the very small.) These are questions that have received little attention in twentieth-century philosophy of science; we shall return to them later.[38]

38. What is of importance in the cases examined here is their relative *in*completeness or *non*-fundamentality. The question naturally arises as to whether these notions imply or presuppose criteria of absolute completeness or fundamentality of theories—whether there could be an absolutely complete (or an absolutely fundamental) theory. (The precise relationships between completeness and fundamentality would also need to be examined.)

It is sometimes alleged that no explanation could ever be truly final (fundamental), because any explanation must always begin with certain postulates, and those postulates could in principle be deduced from more fundamental ones. (The notion of explanation as deduction plays a crucial role here.) Similarly, it is sometimes alleged that no explanation could ever be complete, because there are always phenomena that are not covered by the supposed complete explanation (or, the notion of absolute completeness presupposes the possibility of a definite and final listing of types of phenomena—a list

3. A situation analogous to that regarding the possibility of point particles in the Lorentz electron theory arises within the context of classical mechanics, wherein an infinite gravitational potential would result from the localization of gravitational mass in a dimensionless point. If the occurrence of such an infinite value is ruled out, this could count as an argument to the effect that "mass points" are impossible according to classical mechanics.

Be that as it may, however, Newton himself (or any of his successors over at least the following century, as far as I am aware) did not employ such an argument, which, in the form presented here, had to await the introduction of the notion of potential. Newton's own reason for maintaining that particles are not *really* mass points (as they are considered in his mathematical theory) appears to be based on Rule III of his "Rules of Reasoning in Philosophy": "The qualities of bodies, which admit neither intensification nor remission of degrees, and which are found to belong to all bodies within reach of our experiments, are to be esteemed the universal qualities of all bodies whatsoever." [39] On the basis of this rule, Newton argues that "the extension, hardness, impenetrability, mobility, and inertia of the whole, result from the extension, hardness, impenetrability, mobility, and inertia of the parts; and hence we conclude the least particles of all bodies to be also all extended, and hard and impenetrable, and endowed with their proper inertia." [40] One is tempted here to say that Newton has appealed to "extrascientific" considerations for his ascription of non-zero extension to elementary particles. Yet the status of general principles of inductive inference, such as Newton's Rule III, seems to me to be doubtful:

---

which, it is maintained, cannot be given). The possibility that such arguments, while they have a point, do not tell the whole story about explanation, is suggested by the following considerations. Suppose that we had a theory which over a period of six thousand years was successful in answering all questions that were posed to it. *Despite* the correctness of the above-mentioned logical point, I expect that people would begin to suppose that they had a "complete," and perhaps even a "fundamental," theory.

39. I. Newton, *Mathematical Principles of Natural Philosophy* (*Principia*) (Berkeley: University of California Press, 1946), p. 398.

40. *Ibid.*, p. 399.

scientific considerations have, after all, been relevant to its rejection—namely, considerations issuing primarily from quantum theory.[41]

Whatever the rationale for supposing "mass points" to be idealizations in Newtonian mechanics, however, the rationale for supposing their employment to be both useful and possible is clear. (1) There are certain problems to be solved—problems relating to the positions, velocities, masses, and forces of bodies. (2) Mathematical techniques exist for dealing with such problems if the masses are considered to be concentrated at geometrical points (namely, the geometrical techniques of Newton and, for later scientists, the methods of the calculus). (3) It is, as Newton showed, possible to treat spherically symmetrical bodies as if their masses were concentrated at their centers (and, incidentally, Newton conceived the elementary mass-particles to be spherically symmetrical). And, as for bodies not spherically symmetrical, they could be considered in the same way, provided the distances between their centers was large in comparison to their radii—a condition fulfilled, happily, by the earth-moon system. More generally, bodies could be considered as if their masses were concentrated at their centers of gravity.

These same kinds of considerations are relevant in a wide variety of cases in science which may be (and ordinarily are) classified as "idealizations." This is not to suggest that there are

---

41. It is interesting that Boscovich, on the basis of a similar "principle of induction," argued that elementary particles have *no* extension—that they are point particles:

Taking it for granted, then, that the elements are simple and non-composite, there can be no doubt as to whether they are also non-extended or whether, although simple, they have an extension of the kind that is termed virtual extension by the Scholastics. For there were some, especially among the Peripatetics, who admitted elements that were simple, lacking in all parts, and from their very nature perfectly indivisible; but, for all that, so extended through divisible space that some occupied more room than others; and such that in the position once occupied by one of them, if that one were removed, two or even more others might be placed at the same time.
Since then we never find this virtual extension in magnitudes that fall within the range of our senses, nay rather, in innumerable cases we perceive the contrary; the matter certainly ought to be transferred by the principle of induction, as explained above, to any of the smallest particles of matter as well; so that not even they are admitted to have such virtual extension.

(R. Boscovich, *A Theory of Natural Philosophy* [Cambridge, Mass.: M. I. T. Press, 1966], p. 44, pars. 83–84.)

not other kinds of concepts in science which may be (and are) called "idealizations," the rationale of whose use differs from the cases considered in this section. Nor is it to suggest that there is not more to say about the rationale, the logic, of idealization in the cases that have been considered here: for some purposes it might be useful, for example, to note differences between the cases dealt with above. Thus the impossibility of classical rigid bodies in the light of special relativity is a result of a direct contradiction of that classical notion with a fundamental principle of special relativity; but the impossibility of Lorentzian point particles results only from the rejection of the possibility of an infinite energy (or, if Einstein's principle $E = mc^2$ is used, perhaps from the fact that electrons are "observed" not to have infinite mass). And for certain purposes these differences—passed over in the above account—might well be highly relevant. Again, for certain purposes it might be useful to talk in terms of relative *degrees* of "idealization." Nevertheless, the cases as presented above illustrate the point of crucial importance for *present* purposes, namely, that there are often good *scientific* reasons for distinguishing between the way in which a certain entity is asserted to be (or not to be) and the way in which it is *treated* (although, again for scientific reasons, it could not really be that kind of thing) for the sake of convenience in dealing with certain scientific problems. It is this distinction and the insight it affords into the actual rational working processes of science that now must be examined more closely.

9. *The Logic of Existence Assertions in Physics*

In the preceding section we have seen that in physics there are cases in which a distinction is made, on scientific grounds, between the way (or ways) in which an entity can or cannot exist, and the way (or ways) in which, for the sake of dealing with certain scientific problems, it is possible and convenient to "idealize" that entity. This distinction may now be put in a more general way as follows. On the one hand, we have assertions that certain entities do, or do not, or might, or might not, exist; or, putting the point linguistically, we have terms that can occur in such contexts as ". . . exist(s)," ". . . do (does) not exist," ". . . might

149

exist," ". . . might not exist." (It should be emphasized that
what are of relevance are not the *terms* involved, but rather their
uses; thus, in a problem in which we treat the electron as a point
charge, we may refer to the point charge *itself* by the term "electron." The context of usage, however, will indicate that the term
is in such a case concerned with the idealization and not directly
with electrons as they really are.) There are *clear* cases of such
terms, or of such uses of terms. Sometimes they have to do with
entities that are presumed to exist ("electron"), although they
might not exist (or might not have existed). Others have to do
with (purported) entities that, although they have at some time
been claimed to exist, do not ("ether," "phlogiston"). And,
finally, still others refer to (purported) entities whose existence
is claimed (on presumably good grounds) by some good theorists,
but whose existence or non-existence has not yet been established
("quark"). It should be noted that this class of terms includes
also many terms (uses) which have commonly been classified as
observational—"table," "planet"—as well as terms (uses) usually
classified as theoretical.

On the other hand, we have expressions like "point particle"
(in the Lorentz theory) and "classical rigid body" (from the viewpoint of special relativity), which do not designate (purported)
entities, although they are *related,* in the ways discussed in the
preceding section, to terms (or uses of terms) which do. Thus
their reference to existing things, for example, is indirect. To put
the point in another way, such terms or expressions cannot occur
in the context ". . . exist(s)," *except* in a derivative sense, namely,
that they have to do with "idealizations" of entities that do exist.
And although these terms can occur in contexts like ". . . do
(does) not exist," the sense in which they can so occur is stronger
than, for example, the sense in which we can say "Vulcan does
not exist" or "Nebulium does not exist"; for, in the cases of
Lorentzian point particles or classical rigid bodies (according to
special relativity), it is physically impossible that they should
exist.

The first type of terms or uses may be called "existence terms";
or, inasmuch as, in the cases we have considered, what are alleged
to exist are certain kinds of entities, they may be called "entity

terms." But not all terms in science which refer to something "non-idealized" are naturally classed as entity terms. Many of them are more naturally referred to as having to do with "properties," or with "processes," or with "behavior of entities," for example. Furthermore, there are many borderline cases that are not easily brought under any of these headings. Finally, there are differences between the uses so classified which might lead us, for certain purposes, to distinguish between those cases or to classify them very differently. But all these points only bring out the fact that it is not the terminology of "entities," "idealizations," etc., that is important; what is important is the logic of the scientific usage of the terms so classified. Such expressions as "entity term" must therefore be understood as terms of convenience employed in order to call attention to certain features of the cases discussed—features which, although important and real, nevertheless are not the bases of some ultimate and final classification that excludes all others.

For similar reasons, these classifications should not be considered as providing a new "metascientific" vocabulary—a set of concepts which will serve for unambiguous discussion of *any* scientific work—which can (or even must) be employed in *any* attempt (past, present, or future) to characterize the scientific endeavor. Unless we stretch the meanings of the words beyond utility, the concept of "entity," for example, which is so naturally applied in some cases in science, becomes more and more inapplicable in others.

All these remarks apply also to the second type of uses of terms which, we suggested earlier, may be referred to as "idealization terms." In particular, as was noted at the end of section 8, there are differences between the cases discussed there which might lead us, for some purposes, to distinguish between them. Also those types of cases do not exhaust the kinds that, in science, are to be contrasted with "existence terms." There are many other kinds of cases in physics, not entirely like the cases we have examined and called "idealizations," in which we might feel it more appropriate to talk of, say, "abstractions" (e.g., considering a system of entities as isolated from the rest of the universe), or "approximations" (e.g., calculation only within a certain range of accuracy), or "simplifications" (e.g., considering electronic orbits to be circular rather than elliptical). For, though all these terms—"idealization," "abstraction," "approximation," "simplification"—are used loosely and often interchangeably in talk about science, there are nevertheless significant differences between cases clearly not having to do with things as they really are, which might make distinct employment of those terms useful. (Often, even usually, in science these logically different procedures are combined in attacking a problem, and this fact has encouraged writers to ignore the logical differences between them.)

The relations between "entities" and their "idealizations" may also be different from the cases considered in section 8. For example, it may be that the entities concerned are held not to exist in the way they are treated, not because their existence in such a form would contradict some basic theoretical principle, but rather because such entities have not been found (Vulcan, fifth force of nature), or because the reasons for supposing them to exist have, for one reason or another, been abandoned (ether, nebulium). And yet in some such cases, even after what we might call the "existence claim" of such concepts has been abandoned, there may still remain a *use* for the concepts. Thus, in contrast to the cases of impetus, phlogiston, caloric, and ether, where the conclusion that the (type of) entity did not exist was accompanied by a loss of utility of the concept, the nineteenth-century abandonment of the view that light consists of the transmission of particles, and the adoption of the wave theory, did not preclude the usefulness and possibility of employment of ray optics (which was associated with the particle theory) under certain circumstances.

. . . We are thus led to recognize two kinds of optics. In the first, called "geometric optics," or "ray-optics," light is propagated along rays (straight or curved); it thus behaves much as beams formed of corpuscles might be expected to do. In the second form of optics, called "wave-optics," the wave nature of light becomes conspicuous. Of course the distinction we are here making is artificial. In all truth, there is only one kind of optics, namely, wave-optics; as for ray-optics, it is a mere ideal limiting case never rigorously realized in practice. The present situation is very similar to the one we have met with time and again. Under certain limiting conditions, a theory or a manner of interpreting things, though wrong in the last analysis, is nevertheless so nearly correct in its anticipations that we are often justified in accepting it, even when we recognize that it is a mere approximation. An example was mentioned in connection with classical mechanics: We have every reason to suppose that the theory of relativity is more nearly correct than classical mechanics; and yet, since under the limiting conditions of low velocities and weak gravitational fields, the predictions of the theory of relativity tend to become indistinguishable from those of the classical theory, we are justified in retaining classical mechanics in many practical applications. Likewise, when the energy values are high and the energy transitions are small, we may neglect the refinements of the quantum theory and base our deductions on the classical laws of mechanics and of radiation.

The relationship between wave-optics and the less rigorous ray-optics is of the same type. Whenever the irregularities or inhomogeneities of the medium in which light is transmitted are insignificant over extensions of the order of the wave length of the light, the conclusions derived from wave-optics tend to coincide with those obtained from the application of ray-optics. In such cases, ray-optics may advantageously be applied because of its greater simplicity.[42]

This example is of further interest for at least three reasons. First, it shows how such notions as "ideal," "limiting case," and "approximation" can be used interchangeably in talk about science. Second, the example brings out the fact that entire theories (sets of concepts and propositions), as well as individual concepts, can be spoken of as "idealizations" in the sense that, although it is known, for scientific reasons, that things are not really as they are alleged to be in the theory, it is nevertheless often convenient and possible to treat them in that way. But, again, ray optics is not an "idealization" because *all* scientific theories are "idealizations"; it is an idealization because it is con-

42. A. d'Abro, *The Rise of the New Physics* (New York: Dover, 1951), 1: 278–79. In connection with his remark that "there is only one kind of optics, namely, wave-optics," d'Abro says in a footnote that "in this chapter we are explaining the situation as it appeared to the physicists of the nineteenth century, and we are not taking into consideration the more recent discoveries in the quantum theory."

trasted with another theory which is *not* an idealization. And, finally, the example—and indeed all our examples—brings out the way in which concepts can *change* status—from entity term to idealization term—over the history of science. Such shifts are only to be expected, in view of the fact, brought out in earlier discussions, that the distinction between entities as they are or are not (or can or cannot be) and the ways in which they are treated ("idealized") is based on physical grounds rather than, say, on logical, metaphysical, or linguistic grounds.

Noting, as we have, that there are clear cases in which a distinction is made, on scientific grounds, between existence concepts and idealization concepts does not, of course, constitute an analysis of what is involved in a claim that something "exists." And, one might argue, the history of philosophy has shown that that concept is too opaque to offer any reasonable hope of illuminating the scientific process or any part of it. In reply to this objection, three points must be emphasized. *First*: the examples presented here show that talk about the "existence" (and the same holds for the "real properties") of electrons is not some metaphysician's talk about a subject (physics) which itself offers no assertions about existence; rather, they indicate that the distinction between the way certain things are (or are not) and the way or ways we can and do treat them in certain problem situations is one which is made *within* science, for scientific rather than for metaphysical or otherwise extrascientific reasons. And, in view of this fact, we might paraphrase Kant by saying that the question is not *whether* a realistic interpretation of at least some science is possible, but rather, how we do it—how we manage to make and justify existence-claims, and what the implications of the fact that we do, on occasion, are for the interpretation of science.

Second: it will be recalled that one of the major purposes of Part I of this paper was to show that many—although perhaps not all—of the puzzling features of such statements as "Electrons exist," and much of the apparent gravity of the so-called problem of the ontological status of theoretical entities, can be attributed merely to phrasing the problem, and demanding a solution of it, in terms of the empiricist-positivist distinction between "theoretical" and "observational" terms. If this contention is right, then we need not shy away from taking talk about the existence of electrons seriously just because the question of existence currently *seems* to be so overwhelmingly perplexing and difficult. On the contrary, as was suggested earlier, we may actually be encouraged by the multitude of very serious weaknesses which has been exposed in the theoretical-observational distinction itself. And, if one looks at cases, one finds, as also was noted earlier, that there are at least as many clear cases in which it is natural to use scientific terms in the context ". . . exists," etc., as there are cases in which the term is naturally classified as "theoretical" or "observational."

Third: There are some things that we can say about the role played by existence-claims in physical reasoning. To say that "A exists" implies (among other things, surely) at least the following:

1. A can interact with other things that exist. Particles that exist can interact with other particles that exist, and, derivatively, can have effects on macroscopic objects and be affected by them. "Convenient fictions" or "constructs" or "abstractions" or "idealizations" cannot do this, at least not in any ordinary sense.

This feature of existence-claims brings out an important error in one common positivistic view of science: namely, the interpretation of so-called correspondence rules, co-ordinative definitions, or rules of interpretation. We saw earlier that, modeling so much of their approach to the philosophy of science on mathematical logic, positivists talked about the linkages correlating "theoretical" with "observational" terms as being analogous to the interpretation of a formal system in mathematics and logic. Such linkages in logic clearly are unlike the kinds of connections that can be asserted to hold between existent things (e.g., causal interaction). (And we noted earlier how so many of the puzzling features of statements like "Electrons exist" arise here out of a bad analogy and a bad distinction.) But talk of electrons as existing enables us to consider assertions of linkages between electrons and, for example, scintillations or clicks (to say nothing of positrons) as assertions of causal actions or interactions (i.e., the particles involved cause the scintillations or clicks that we "observe"). Note, incidentally, that what counts as an "interaction" is also specified on scientific grounds.[43]

2. To say that "A exists" implies that A may have properties which are not manifesting themselves, and which have not yet been discovered; and, contrariwise, it is to say that some properties currently so ascribed may be incorrectly so attributed. We may be wrong in saying that a certain property of an entity has a certain quantitative value. Or we may be wrong in thinking that that property is fundamental—it may be, to use Leibniz' colorful phrase, a "well-founded phenomenon," being a manifestation of some deeper reality (e.g., as Wheeler claims that many properties of particles may be explainable as mere manifestations of an underlying "geometrodynamic field"). Or, again—although these kinds of cases are rarer, especially in more sophisticated stages of scientific development—we may be wrong in thinking that the entity has the property at all. Finally, we may be wrong in thinking that we have exhausted all the properties of the entity, and may discover wholly new ones (spin, strangeness). These features are all hard to understand if electrons, for example, are mere "convenient fictions." (Note that what counts as a "property" is also specified on scientific grounds.)

3. To say that "A exists" is to say that A is something about which we can have different and competing theories. From the theoretical work of Ampère and Weber to that of Lorentz, from the experimental work of Faraday on electrolysis to Millikan's oil-drop experiment, there was an accumulation of reasons for holding that electricity comes in discrete units. The notion of the electron thus acquired what amounts to a theory-transcendent status: it was an entity about which theories—theories *of* the electron—were constructed. It is indeed ironic that the term "electron"—often taken as a paradigm case, in the philosophical literature of the positivistic tradition, of a "theoretical" term—should have this status; for the comparability of different, competing theories is now seen to be, not (at least not solely) their

43. My colleague Kenneth Schaffner has given an analysis of the relations between theoretical and observational terms as causal connections in his forthcoming paper "Correspondence Rules."

sharing of a common "observational vocabulary," but rather their being about the same kind of entity. The erstwhile "theoretical term" is now seen to be the source of what is perhaps the most important aspect of the "comparability" of competing theories: for electrons are what those theories are in competition about.

10. *Applications and Extensions of the Analysis*

The forgoing investigations have shown that there is, within at least some cases in science itself, ground for distinguishing between the ways in which entities can or cannot (do or do not) exist and the ways in which, for the sake of dealing with certain problems, it is possible and convenient to treat them, despite the fact that we know, on physical grounds, that they could not really be as they are treated. Thus, the present paper may be said to constitute, in part, a defense of a "realistic" interpretation of at least some scientific concepts.

But the significance of the analyses made in Part II does not lie simply in the support they offer to "scientific realism." For, by looking at science from the perspective of the approach taken in the preceding two sections, we find that new light is thrown on a number of classical problems of interest to the philosopher of science, while others are revealed which hitherto have been slighted. We saw at the end of section 9, for instance, that an unexpected twist has been given to the "comparability problem" by looking at science in terms of the entity-idealization distinction: an important aspect of the comparability of competing theories lies in their dealing with the same entities (formerly called "theoretical") rather than merely in some shared "observational vocabulary."

We have also seen, in our examination of cases in science, something of the rationale by which scientific theories at various stages are considered to be "incomplete" or "non-fundamental." These notions, which have largely been ignored by philosophers of science, have an important bearing on the attempt to analyze the concept of explanation in science. For, what we saw in section 8, in reviewing the fortunes of the Lorentz electron theory, may be outlined as follows: Against the background of a certain body of knowledge (both "theoretical" and "factual"), certain questions arose which required answers. At that stage, the directions in which it was plausible to look for solutions—at least *some* of the possible alternative paths along which it was reasonable to look for solutions—could be discerned, not only with hindsight, but even by the participants in the enterprise themselves. I would suggest that an understanding of what scientific explanation consists in may be gained by filling in the details of this outline: by analyzing the ways in which a background body of knowledge generates such questions, how alternative pathways of research are delineated for answering the problem, and how it is decided when the problem is resolved.[44] Note, incidentally, that—as our examination of cases has already revealed—what is involved here is the notion that there is a rationale, a logic, to the development of science.

Illumination of the notions of "theory" and "observation" ("evidence," "data," "facts"), as well as of the difficulties into which that distinction has fallen, may also be obtained through the present approach. For one thing, the distinction made here cuts across the lines of the old theoretical-observational distinction, for we have found reasons to classify electrons (formerly "theoretical") with tables and rocks. On the other hand, the class of "theoretical terms" now has been broken up into various categories of terms having very different functions: existence terms, idealization terms, and many other (rough) groupings of terms whose functions have only been touched on here. Thus we can see that it was futile to try to find some relatively simple form of relationship between theoretical and observational terms: the class of "theoretical" terms covered many kinds of concepts, having distinct sorts of relationships to one another, and, in particular, in the case of such types of concepts as idealizations, being related only indirectly (through the associated entity terms or concepts) to "observation" or "evidence." It is no wonder that

44. This suggestion will be developed in detail in my "Explanation and Scientific Progress," to be presented at the Boston Colloquium for the Philosophy of Science, and to appear in a forthcoming volume of the Boston Studies in the Philosophy of Science.

both "realistic" and "instrumentalist" interpretations of science faltered with regard to their analyses of some theoretical term or other. For at least those areas of science where such terms as "existence" are appropriate, the problem may now be seen in a different way: to delineate the relationships of those terms (rather, uses) which do not have to do directly with entities as they actually exist, to those terms (or uses) which do; and to analyze the reasons for accepting existence-claims.

Just as the positivistic tradition—as we said in Part I—used the theoretical-observational distinction as an analytic tool for framing certain problems and dealing with certain topics, so the notion that science makes existence-claims, and the contrast between such claims on the one hand and idealizations (and like types of concepts) on the other, now has become a focus, a tool, in the effort to understand science. We can expect difficulties to accumulate regarding this approach, just as they did over the years for the theoretical-observational distinction. And, just as the latter distinction exaggerated or distorted certain problems and features of science while ignoring or slighting others, so also we need not be disappointed if similar limitations are found to exist in this approach. On the contrary, they should be expected and even welcomed, because they might suggest further approaches, which in turn might expose further problems and features of science to be dealt with—just as the positivistic failure to deal with the problem of ontological status in terms of an objection-riddled theoretical-observational distinction made clear the need for a re-examination of that problem independent of the theoretical-observational distinction. More generally, even if such difficulties and limitations are found in the present approach, it can nevertheless have important *heuristic* value if it enables us to phrase certain problems and to discuss certain features of science in new and at least partially illuminating ways which are free of doctrines that have proved seriously defective, and if it brings to light further problems and features of science which have been obscured by previous approaches. And this much, if the arguments of this paper are sound, we have already seen it do.

Viewed in the light of these remarks, the contributions of

the positivistic tradition deserve greater appreciation than we might give it if we considered only the deficiencies of so many of its contentions. For, by looking at science carefully in certain ways, it also raised a great many problems regarding the interpretation of science; its answers to those problems, while perhaps far from being all that one would have wished, still provided considerable illumination and insight; and, finally, its very defects, as this paper contends, pointed the way toward a new approach.[45]

45. These remarks should not be taken as implying that we are forever condemned in the philosophy of science to viewing science only from different and irreconcilable, though perhaps complementary, perspectives—each of which is limited and objectionable, but each of whose limitations and objections are perhaps covered by one or another alternative perspective. There is no reason, at least not in any of the present discussion, why a unified interpretation of science cannot be achieved; but one way of getting at such an interpretation may be to begin with different approaches, as suggested here.

approaches
to
the
sciences
of man

CARL G. HEMPEL

logical positivism and the social sciences

INTRODUCTION

The principal task of philosophy, according to logical positivism, or logical empiricism, is the analysis of the concepts, theories, and methods of the various branches of scientific inquiry, ranging from logic and mathematics through physics, chemistry, and biology to psychology, the social sciences, and historiography. Curiously, however, most of the analytic studies undertaken by logical empiricists have been concerned either with logic and mathematics or with the physical sciences; biology, psychology, and the social and historical disciplines have received much less extensive and detailed attention. This difference is undoubtedly attributable, in large measure, to the professional backgrounds and interests of the most influential among the logical positivists. The majority of them were not "pure philosophers" by training, but had devoted a large part of their academic studies—often including their doctoral work—to logic and mathematics, to physics, or to a combination of these subjects. This is true, for example, of Rudolf Carnap, Herbert Feigl, Philipp Frank, Hans

Some of the research for this essay, and the writing of it, formed part of a program of work supported by the National Science Foundation.

Hahn, Richard von Mises, Hans Reichenbach, Moritz Schlick, Friedrich Waismann, and others. It is hardly surprising, therefore, that these men devoted a great deal of their philosophical effort to the development of logic—partly as a theoretical discipline, partly as a tool for rigorous philosophical analysis—to the philosophy of logic and mathematics, and to the methodology and philosophy of the physical sciences.

Only one among the influential logical empiricists had a specialized knowledge of the social sciences: Otto Neurath (1882–1945). He was an economist and sociologist by training, and many of his writings were devoted specifically to questions concerning the subject matter, the methods, the theories, and the history of the social sciences. Next to him, Carnap has dealt rather extensively, but in less specific detail, with the logic of psychology and the social sciences. Philipp Frank's works include perceptive observations about social and political factors affecting scientific inquiry and about the ideological exploitation of some scientific theories; several of Gustav Bergmann's articles deal specifically with methodological and philosophical issues concerning psychology; and Herbert Feigl has contributed extensively to the analysis of concept formation and theory construction in psychology.[1]

Naturally, one is inclined to adduce here also Sir Karl Popper's work in the philosophy of the social sciences and of history; but, though Popper carried on an intensive and fruitful exchange of ideas with various logical positivists, and, although there were important affinities between his views and theirs,[2] he has con-

1. Frank's observations can be found at various places in his books *Modern Science and Its Philosophy* (Cambridge, Mass.: Harvard University Press, 1949) and *Philosophy of Science* (Englewood Cliffs, N.J.: Prentice-Hall, 1957). Bergmann's contributions include: "The Logic of Psychological Concepts," *Philosophy of Science*, 18 (1951); "Psychoanalysis and Experimental Psychology," *Mind,* 53 (1944); and an article written jointly with the psychologist K. W. Spence, "Operationism and Theory in Psychology," *Psychological Review*, 48 (1941). Feigl's writings will be referred to later.

2. See Carnap's remarks on this point on pp. 31–32 of his autobiography in Paul A. Schilpp, ed., *The Philosophy of Rudolf Carnap* (La Salle, Ill.: Open Court, 1963). Feigl makes a similar point on pp. 641–42 of his engaging and informative essay "The Wiener Kreis in America" (in D. Fleming and B. Bailyn, eds., *Perspectives in American History*, vol. 2: *The Intellectual*

sistently represented himself as an outside critic of the movement, and he cannot, therefore, be reckoned among its proponents.

I will now attempt to survey and appraise the principal conceptions that were developed by logical empiricist writers, especially in the 1930's and 1940's, concerning the nature and status of the social sciences and their relation to other branches of scientific inquiry. I shall begin with Neurath's ideas and then turn to contributions made by Carnap, Feigl, and others.

NEURATH ON THE SOCIAL SCIENCES

Neurath's special fields of interest were economics, political theory, and history, and his bibliography includes many publications on these subjects. But he was also an activist and planner of tremendous energy; he contributed extensively to the organization of the various congresses at which representatives of logical empiricism presented their ideas and debated with their critics; and—with Carnap, Frank, Charles Morris, and others—he played an essential role in founding the Institute for the Unity of Science (now under the directorship of Herbert Feigl) and in planning and organizing the publication of the *International Encyclopedia of Unified Science*. In contrast to his more introverted, cerebrotonic associates in Vienna, such as Schlick, Carnap, and Waismann, Neurath was extroverted, ebullient, and extremely vivacious. He was a heavy but very dynamic and most engaging man, who often signed letters to his friends with a drawing of a cheerful elephant with Neurath's initials branded on his hindquarter, holding a bunch of flowers for the addressee in his trunk.

Neurath had deep social and political interests. His ideas in these matters were of a basically Marxist persuasion; but, as Carnap notes in his recollections on Neurath's role in the Vienna Circle, "he was not a dogmatic Marxist; for him every theory must be further developed by constant criticism and re-examina-

---

Migration: Europe and America, 1930–1960 [Cambridge, Mass., 1968]). Feigl's essay offers a historical account, based to a large extent on his personal experiences, of the development of logical empiricism in Europe and its migration to the United States; it includes interesting information also about several other figures referred to in the present study, among them Carnap and Neurath.

tion."[3] Neurath was keenly aware and wary of the possibilities of social and political misuse of metaphysical and theological ideas; his strong concern with this danger is reflected in some of the more extreme features of his philosophical and methodological views.

Neurath's conception of psychology and the social sciences was basically a sharp, materialistically inspired antithesis to certain idealistic views, much *en vogue* during the earlier decades of this century, which conceived of scientific inquiry as comprising two fundamentally different major branches: the *Geisteswissenschaften* or *Kulturwissenschaften,* and the *Naturwissenschaften.* In this view, the mental or cultural disciplines, in contrast to the natural sciences, are concerned with phenomena in which the human mind or spirit plays an essential role; and, for this reason, the proper modes of ascertaining, describing, and understanding such phenomena differ essentially from the methods of the natural sciences. Thus, observation in the natural sciences is contrasted, by this school of thought, with procedures requiring empathy and insight in the cultural disciplines; and explanation by causes, presumed to be characteristic of the natural sciences, is contrasted with a supposedly quite different procedure in the cultural sciences, namely, the understanding of human actions and of social and historical changes in terms of immaterial reasons or similar "meaningful" connections.

Neurath emphatically rejected the idea of any fundamental differences between the natural sciences on one hand and psychology and the social and historical disciplines on the other; but, unlike Carnap and other logical empiricists, he did so in a rather summary and not very closely reasoned manner. Indeed, Neurath's writings on this subject[4] often seem more like political manifestoes, like programs both for analysis and for action, than

3. In Schilpp, *The Philosophy of Rudolf Carnap,* p. 24. For fuller details see the article "Neurath, Otto," by R. S. Cohen, in *The Encyclopedia of Philosophy* (New York: Macmillan and The Free Press, 1967), 5: 477–79. This article also refers to a forthcoming volume, *Selected Papers of Otto Neurath,* ed. Marie Neurath and R. S. Cohen, which is to include a biographical memoir and a complete list of Neurath's writings.

4. Among them: *Empirische Soziologie* (Vienna: Springer, 1931); *Einheitswissenschaft und Psychologie* (Vienna: Gerold & Co., 1933); *Foundations of*

like carefully reasoned analytic studies. Neurath stresses, in particular, that there is no fundamental difference in subject matter between the natural sciences and the psychological and sociological disciplines, because human individuals and societies are basically nothing other than more or less complex physical systems. Thus he remarks that a living human being may be "more precisely defined" by the expression "heap of cells whose individual cells may exhibit certain large electric potential differences within a very small space, and whose temperature differences between brain and body may display certain oscillations." [5] A state is said to be describable as "a conglomeration of people, streets, houses, prisons, rifles, factories, and so on," and also of "objects of art, buildings, pictures, sculptures, religious books or religious speeches, scientific books and lectures, facial expressions, gestures, love behavior, and so on." [6] And, in Neurath's view, what psychology and sociology are properly concerned with are the behavior patterns of physical systems of these kinds, and the ways in which those patterns change. For the discipline thus envisaged, Neurath coined the name "behavioristics," so as to distinguish it explicitly from behaviorism as a doctrine within psychology; for, while he was in agreement with the general outlook of behaviorists such as J. B. Watson and I. P. Pavlov, he did not wish to endorse all the specific theses of this school of thought.[7]

From the vantage point of behavioristics, what significance could be attributed to the many statements of psychology and the social sciences that are couched in mentalistic terms—statements that speak of thoughts, beliefs, feelings, wants, hopes, fears, purposes, and decisions, for example? Neurath was extremely wary of them and counseled avoidance of mentalistic locutions in

---

the Social Sciences (Chicago: University of Chicago Press, 1944); "Sociology and Physicalism" (translation of an article originally published in *Erkenntnis*, 2 [1931–32]), in A. J. Ayer, ed., *Logical Positivism* (New York: The Free Press, 1959). Passages quoted in this essay from the first two of these works are translated by the present writer.

5. *Einheitswissenschaft und Psychologie*, p. 17.

6. *Empirische Soziologie*, p. 44.

7. See, for example, Neurath, *Foundations of the Social Sciences*, p. 17; *Einheitswissenschaft und Psychologie*, p. 17; *Empirische Soziologie*, pp. 63, 83.

favor of a "physicalistic" terminology, which will be considered shortly. In fact, he drew up, for his own use and as a reminder for others, a list of terms that he thought should be eschewed because they were likely to lead to metaphysical pitfalls and confusions; and, in allusion to a more widely known and more influential list, he called it his *index verborum prohibitorum*.[8] His index of forbidden words included mentalistic terms such as "mind," "mental," "motive," and "meaning," but also others, such as "matter," "cause and effect," and "fact." He objected strongly to saying that statements express facts,[9] and he regarded as metaphysical the early Wittgenstein's ideas about the structure of propositional expressions mirroring the structure of the corresponding facts. I have been told—and the story sounds entirely credible to me—that, at the meetings of the Vienna Circle, in which Wittgenstein was often discussed, Neurath again and again protested that the participants were indulging in metaphysics; and when Schlick became impatient with these frequent interruptions Neurath asked permission simply to call out "M!" each time he thought the debate was becoming metaphysical. But after this had been going on for a while Neurath turned to Schlick once more and proposed: "to minimize my interruptions, let me rather call out 'non-M' whenever you are *not* talking metaphysics." And, while Neurath did not commit himself to all the details of Watson's behaviorism, he would, no doubt, have agreed heartily with Watson's pronouncement on the impact of behavioristic thinking on philosophy—a discipline that had so long been struggling in vain with such intractable issues as the mind-body problem: "With the behavioristic point of view now

8. *Einheitswissenschaft und Psychologie*, p. 12; for further instances of "dangerous terms," see, for example, *Foundations of the Social Sciences*, pp. 4, 5, 18, and p. 55 ("Expressions avoided in this monograph").

9. He insisted, for example, that the test—or, as he called it, the assaying—of a scientific hypothesis should not be conceived of or described as involving a comparison of the hypothesis with relevant "facts," but rather as involving a comparison of the hypothesis statement with certain other statements, namely, "observation statements" or "protocol statements." (*Foundations of the Social Sciences*, pp. 4–5; cf. sec. I of "Sociology and Physicalism" and *Einheitswissenschaft und Psychologie*, p. 29.)

becoming dominant, it is hard to find a place for what has been called philosophy. Philosophy is passing—has all but passed, and unless new issues arise which will give a foundation for a new philosophy, the world has seen its last great philosopher." [10]

Indeed, Neurath put mentalistic terms such as "mind" and "motive" on his *Index* on the grounds that they tended to be construed as standing for immaterial agencies and that this kind of reification gave rise to much stultifying perplexity concerning the relation of those mental agencies to the physical world. Some of his observations on this issue are strikingly suggestive and remind one of ideas that Gilbert Ryle was later to develop much more subtly and fully in his book *The Concept of Mind*.

For example, Neurath argued against conceiving of a man's mind, or of his will or personality, as a homunculus, a "second little man" who plays the role of a machinist controlling the man's behavior.[11] To illustrate the conceptual dangers of such a reification of mentalistic concepts, Neurath uses an analogy concerning the "Gang," that is, the running, of a watch.[12] His version does not lend itself to idiomatic translation, and I will therefore modify it slightly, speaking of the accuracy or precision of a watch instead. Consider a fine watch that keeps time very accurately, neither losing nor gaining more than a minute per month. How does it do that? Well, it's a certified precision chronometer; its close time-keeping is due to its high precision. But that precision surely is not a material component of the watch: however carefully we may examine its works, we won't find it there—in fact, it has no spatial location at all. But how can a non-material, non-spatial agency affect and control a material physical process, the running of the mechanism and the movement of the hands? And what happens to the precision when the clock stops running

10. J. B. Watson, *The Ways of Behaviorism* (New York: Harper and Brothers, 1928), p. 14.

11. *Einheitswissenschaft und Psychologie,* p. 16; see also *Empirische Soziologie,* p. 65.

12. *Einheitswissenschaft und Psychologie,* p. 11; see also "Sociology and Physicalism," p. 299.

and when, eventually, its material components turn into rust and dust? The analogy to the psychophysical problem is clear: how can the mind, a non-material agency that has no spatial location, influence and control the behavior of the human organism, which is a material system with spatial location? And what happens to the mind after the body dies and decays?

It is only one step from here to Ryle's conclusion: The mind, and such mental features as desires and beliefs, must not be viewed as Cartesian ghosts in the body machine any more than the precision of a watch can be regarded as a ghostlike agency. To ascribe high precision or accuracy to a watch is not to say that its running is governed by an immaterial agency; it is rather to attribute to the watch a certain behavioral disposition, namely, the disposition, when properly wound and oiled, to keep time precisely or accurately. Similarly, to ascribe to a person a mental trait, say, intelligence, is to attribute to him a complex disposition to behave, under relevant conditions, in certain characteristic ways commonly described as behaving intelligently.

Neurath himself does not explicitly offer this kind of dispositional construal; indeed, he presents no general schema for a physicalistic interpretation of mentalistic terms. His ideas on this issue, as on many others, are typically stated in bold outlines, in a manner that is colorful and suggestive, but frustratingly vague on points of systematic detail. Broadly speaking, he holds that, insofar as psychological and sociological statements containing mentalistic terms possess objective scientific significance, it is possible to "replace" them by statements couched in "physicalistic terminology," or in "the physicalistic unitary language," which he considered to be adequate for the formulation of all scientific statements. The physicalistic vocabulary is conceived of as including, besides the terms of physics proper, everyday terms for material objects and processes, and, moreover, expressions like "cell aggregate," "stimulus," "amount of cattle," "behavior of chieftains." Thus, in Neurath's science of behavioristics, statements about phenomena of consciousness and about mental processes would be replaced by statements about spatio-temporally localizable occurrences such as macroscopic behavior (including gestures and speech acts) and about physiologically or physicochemically described processes in the brain and in the nervous system.[13]

Now, philosophical programs or theses suggesting the replacement of certain kinds of linguistic expressions by certain others are usually propounded with the claim that the replacement should or does preserve certain important characteristics of the expressions concerned, while eliminating certain undesirable features. The undesirable feature that Neurath proposes to avoid is the use of mentalistic or teleological or otherwise non-physicalistic terminology; about what is to be preserved Neurath is not very explicit. I think he has in mind what might be called the observational content of the replaced statement, as characterized by the "protocol sentences" (observation sentences) to which the statement "leads" or can be "reduced," as he says.[14] This construal seems to accord well with Neurath's conception of science as being primarily concerned with the predicting of new observable occurrences on the basis of given observation statements.

Neurath, then, does not attempt to state general rules for the construction of physicalistic counterparts of sentences containing dangerous or "prohibited" terms; indeed, the very thought of general rules of this kind would probably have been suspect to him. He remarks, for example, that some sociological sentences containing expressions such as "spirit of a nation," "ethos of a religion," or "ethical forces" "can hardly be connected with observation-statements and have to be dropped as parts of metaphysical speculations," whereas we may regard other such sentences as metaphorical and may "transform them into physicalistic statements" because "dropping them would often imply an impoverishment of our argument." [15] It was in this spirit that Neurath acknowledged the great importance of Max Weber's work while objecting to Weber's talk of "rational economic ethos" as a force over and above actual behavior, and to his treatment of protestantism "as a reality that acts upon people." Neurath

---

13. Cf. *Einheitswissenschaft und Psychologie*, pp. 7, 18–19; *Foundations of the Social Sciences*, pp. 2–4; *Empirische Soziologie*, p. 60.

14. *Einheitswissenschaft und Psychologie*, pp. 6, 12–13.

15. *Foundations of the Social Sciences*, p. 4; see also p. 10.

stressed that there could be no question of routinely transforming Weber's pronouncements into scientific (i.e., physicalistically worded) statements: a strictly scientific sociology, he remarks, would have to describe the behavior, the customs, the modes of life and production of the people under study, and then to inquire how new customs arise from the given ones in interaction with other prevailing conditions.[16]

Ultimately, Neurath's program for the elimination of misleading locutions envisaged a reformulation of all of empirical science in a unitary physicalistic language. Neurath held that, in principle, any child could learn to use such a language right from the beginning, without first acquiring the usual natural languages with their metaphysical pitfalls; and he regarded this kind of training as highly desirable.[17] In the same vein, he thought it an important desideratum that a "lexicon of special scientific terminologies" be prepared which would be a valuable tool for stating the findings of psychology, sociology, and other fields in physicalistic terms; he was astonishingly optimistic concerning the possibility of producing such a lexicon and called for a co-operative effort to this effect.[18]

Neurath noted, quite rightly, that in the field of psychology such important doctrines as Gestalt theory, psychoanalytic theory, and behavioristic theories do not permit of comparison or of useful combination with one another, because they use different and ostensibly unrelated terminologies; and he expected that a lexicon making it possible to reformulate the empirical substance of those theories in a unitary physical language would very happily serve to fuse and consolidate what was significant in those doctrines and would at the same time considerably enhance their predictive potential.[19] Some years after suggesting this program, however, Neurath offered a more realistic conception of "Unified Science as Encyclopedic Integration," [20] which no longer

16. *Empirische Soziologie,* p. 57; see also *Foundations of the Social Sciences,* pp. 16–17.

17. *Einheitswissenschaft und Psychologie,* p. 13.

18. *Ibid.,* p. 27.

19. *Ibid.,* pp. 26–28.

20. *International Encyclopedia of Unified Science,* vol. 1, no. 1 (Chicago: University of Chicago Press, 1938), pp. 1–27.

envisaged the physicalistic lexicon; indeed, in order to get the project of the *International Encyclopedia of Unified Science* off the ground, Neurath did not even insist that all contributors should aim at restricting themselves to a physicalistic terminology.

Neurath's conception of the scientific enterprise had strong pragmatic and instrumentalist overtones; *prediction* of empirical phenomena is frequently cited in his writings as the prime objective of the scientific enterprise;[21] theoretical understanding of the world as an aim in itself does not seem to have figured significantly in his view. And he stressed that, also for the sake of effective prediction, it was essential that the various scientific disciplines be organized into one coherent system of unitary science. He was fond of pointing out that in order to predict particular events, such as the outcome of a forest fire or the place where a windblown ten-dollar bill will end up, we often have to combine knowledge drawn from several of the traditionally distinguished branches of empirical science: physics, chemistry, and biology, as well as psychology and sociology; for we will have to take into account the availability, organization, and effectiveness of fire fighters, or, in the other case, the economic status, alacrity, and inhibitions of the persons who happen to notice the ten-dollar bill being blown into the street.

Neurath noted that, in an effort to master conceptually the multitude of social changes, the sociologist must try to formulate general laws that govern those changes and by means of which particular events may then be predicted. His observations concerning such laws are much more sober and realistic than his idea of a physicalistic lexicon of special terminologies in science. Neurath noted that some of the laws established by sociological research may well apply only to rather special social formations and thus may be analogous to certain laws that might be said to apply only to lions or only to ants. And he added that "doubtless there are only few general sociological laws: in general, one has to go back to laws of individual behavior and other things." [22]

21. See, for example, *Empirische Soziologie*, pp. 11, 13; "Sociology and Physicalism," pp. 285, 293.
22. *Empirische Soziologie*, p. 77.

CARL G. HEMPEL

As for the extent to which the behavior of social groups can be derived from that of its constituent individuals, Neurath declared that that was for the sociologists to find out; thus he refrained from making any general claims concerning the realizability of the program of methodological individualism.[23] His views on this issue were shared, I think, by his fellow empiricists.

Speaking of the limitations of prediction in the social sciences, Neurath noted the problems of self-fulfilling and self-stultifying predictions, and already in his *Empirische Soziologie* of 1931 he argued that innovations in science and technology cannot be predicted in very specific detail, on the ground that to make such predictions would be to anticipate the innovations. To be able to predict Einstein's computations, he says, one would have to be Einstein oneself, and, he adds, "here lies an essential limit of all sociological prognoses." [24]

THE ELABORATION OF PHYSICALISM BY CARNAP

Let us now turn to Carnap's views on the character of psychology and the social sciences. Carnap was in substantial agreement with the basic ideas of Neurath's physicalism; but he formulated, defended, and gradually modified those ideas in accordance with his own characteristic style and standards of philosophizing, which are very different from Neurath's. Neurath conveyed his ideas in broad strokes, in vigorous and suggestive, but imprecise and often elusive, language. He cautioned against overestimating the ideal of linguistic precision and held that artificially constructed formal languages, on which Carnap relied extensively in his work, had only limited value for the clarification of philosophical issues. Accordingly, he did not conceive of the unitary physicalistic language of science as having a precise vocabulary and a rigorously specifiable formal structure; to lend emphasis to this point, he referred to the language of empirical science as a "Universal Jargon" which cannot be built up from scratch as a precise system, which "will always be in the making," and which

23. *Ibid.*, pp. 65, 77.
24. *Ibid.*, p. 130; see also *Foundations of the Social Sciences*, pp. 28–30.

174

will always contain certain clusters of "vaguely defined assumptions and assertions." [25] Also, Neurath frequently offered no systematic arguments in support of his ideas; his theses and programs often appear to be prompted by ideological considerations, especially by the desire to pull the terminological rug out from under the pronouncements of idealistic philosophers and theologians.

Carnap, on the other hand, was and has remained a highly rigorous and systematic thinker, insisting on precision and explicitness in the formulation of philosophical ideas, and on careful arguments in support of them. While he, and other members of the Vienna Circle, appreciated Neurath's social, political, and ideological concerns and often shared them, Carnap held that they were logically irrelevant to the problems of physicalism and should therefore be left out of consideration in the philosophical discussion of this subject. [26]

Carnap's own construal and defense of physicalism has gone through several stages, which can be traced here only in outline. A first, prephysicalistic stage is that of *Der logische Aufbau der Welt*, [27] where Carnap argued in considerable detail that all the concepts of empirical science, including those of psychology and the social sciences, can be defined—essentially by iterative use of extensive abstraction—in terms of one basic phenomenalistic concept. The ingeniously designed procedure was to lead from this basis, by definitional steps, first to concepts for sense qualities, then to concepts pertaining to physical objects, and finally to the concepts of psychology and sociology. [28] And Carnap not

25. *Foundations of the Social Sciences,* pp. 2, 3.

26. See Carnap in Schilpp, *The Philosophy of Rudolf Carnap,* pp. 22–24, 51.

27. 1st ed. (Berlin-Schlachtensee: Weltkreisverlag, 1928); 2d ed. (Hamburg: Felix Meiner, 1962). An English translation of the second edition, which also includes a smaller pamphlet originally published in 1928, has appeared under the title *The Logical Structure of the World and Pseudoproblems in Philosophy* (Berkeley and Los Angeles: University of California Press, 1967).

28. For a detailed account and critical appraisal of the procedure, see Chap. V of N. Goodman, *The Structure of Appearance,* 2d ed. (Indianapolis: Bobbs-Merrill, 1966), as well as Goodman's essay "The Significance of *Der Logische*

only set forth a program; he actually formulated detailed definitions for a considerable set of concepts pertaining to the sensory realm. Thus, as Quine has said, Carnap "was the first empiricist who, not content with asserting the reducibility of science to terms of immediate experience, took serious steps toward carrying out the reduction." [29] The construction of the concepts on higher levels, however, was presented only in outline; Carnap later abandoned the view that all those concepts can be introduced by explicit definitions on a phenomenalistic basis.

Already in the *Aufbau* Carnap remarked that a "logical construction of the world" did not require a phenomenalistic basis, but could be achieved on a physical basis as well, that is, that the concepts of empirical science could all be defined in terms of some suitably chosen set of physical concepts; and he briefly suggested several possible choices for such physical definition bases.[30] In the early 1930's, partly under Neurath's influence,[31] Carnap developed this idea in greater detail in the form of the thesis that the language of physics affords a unitary language for all of empirical science, a language in which all the concepts and statements of empirical science can be expressed. At that time he considered a "physicalistic" basis as preferable to a phenomenalistic one, especially because of its intersubjective, public character, that is, because "the events described in this language are in principle observable by all users of the language." [32]

Aufbau der Welt," and Carnap's reply, in Schilpp, *The Philosophy of Rudolf Carnap.* Further reflections by Carnap on the *Aufbau* and on physicalism will be found on pp. 16–17 and 50–53 of the Schilpp volume and in the "Preface to the Second Edition" of *The Logical Structure of the World.*

29. W. V. O. Quine, *From a Logical Point of View,* 2d ed. (Cambridge, Mass.: Harvard University Press, 1961), p. 39.

30. See secs. 59 and 62 of *The Logical Structure of the World.*

31. See, for example, pp. 74–75 of Carnap, *The Unity of Science* (translated with an introduction by M. Black) (London: Kegan Paul, 1934), and Carnap's observations on pp. 50–53 of Schilpp, *The Philosophy of Rudolf Carnap.*

32. Carnap in Schilpp, *The Philosophy of Rudolf Carnap,* p. 52. This stage in the development of Carnap's physicalism is reflected especially in two articles he published in *Erkenntnis* in 1932: "Die physikalische Sprache als Universalsprache der Wissenschaft" and "Psychologie in physikalischer Sprache." Translations of these, with slight revisions, appeared, respectively, in Carnap, *The Unity of Science,* and, under the title "Psychology in Physical Language," in Ayer, *Logical Positivism,* pp. 165–98.

By physical language, Carnap here understands roughly the same thing as Neurath's physicalistic language, namely, the language "in which we speak about physical things in every-day life or in physics." [33] Its vocabulary is taken to include not only the technical terms of physics but also words like "cold," "heat," "liquid," "blue," "taller than," "soluble in," which occur already at the level of what Carnap later called the thing language: "that language which we use in every-day life in speaking about the perceptible things surrounding us." [34]

The principal thesis of physicalism as Carnap construed it at this stage was that the physical language is a universal language, that is, that any sentence of any branch of empirical science can be translated into it "without change of content." [35]

By sentences of empirical science, Carnap here understands only sentences that have empirical meaning, or empirical content, in the sense of what I will call *the wider empiricist criterion of meaning*. This is, strictly speaking, a criterion of meaningfulness; it specifies conditions under which a sentence is empirically

---

33. Carnap, *Philosophy and Logical Syntax* (London: Kegan Paul, 1935), p. 89. Evidently this characterization is not very satisfactory. For plants, animals, and people might well be counted among physical things, especially from the general vantage point of physicalism; and, in this case, biological and psychological terms, which we use in speaking about such things, would qualify as belonging to the physicalistic language, and physicalism would be trivially true. I think that the problem of characterizing with sufficient clarity the notions of physical object, event, and characteristic, and those of physical term and physical law, has constituted a persistent difficulty for physicalism in all stages of its development, although it was not often explicitly recognized as such. One of the exceptions is I. Scheffler's article "The New Dualism: Psychological and Physical Terms," *The Journal of Philosophy*, 47 (1950): 737–52. Scheffler here examines, more specifically, a number of ways in which logical-empiricist writers had sought to differentiate physical from psychological terms; he finds them all inadequate and concludes that the search for a clear general distinction between physical and psychological terms is futile, and that a reconstruction of science must be "based on a unitary approach to all scientific terms" (*ibid.*, p. 752).

34. Carnap, "Testability and Meaning," *Philosophy of Science*, 3 (1936): 419–71, and 4 (1937): 1–40; quotation from 3: 466. See also pp. 52–53 of Carnap, "Logical Foundations of the Unity of Science," in *International Encyclopedia of Unified Science*, vol. 1, no. 1.

35. See, for example, *The Unity of Science*, p. 67; *Philosophy and Logical Syntax*, p. 89; "Psychology in Physical Language," p. 166.

meaningful or has empirical content. This must be distinguished from *the narrower empiricist criterion of meaning,* which purports to characterize "the meaning" or "the content" of a sentence, and which will be considered shortly.

The wider criterion qualifies a sentence as having empirical meaning if, at least "in principle," it is testable by means of observational data, that is, if it "implies," in a suitable sense, observation sentences or "protocol sentences" describing potential observational findings. This criterion of testability was meant to bar from the class of scientific statements untestable metaphysical formulations that might speak of entelechies, *Zeitgeist,* or a historical figure's "manifest destiny": to such "pseudostatements" the thesis of translatability into physical terms was not, of course, meant to apply.[36]

Carnap's explication and justification of the physicalistic thesis also presupposed, however, a narrower, more stringent version of the empiricist meaning criterion: according to it, two sentences that imply the same observation sentences or protocol sentences "have the same content. They say the same thing, and may be translated into one another." [37] Thus, the empirical meaning or content of a sentence here is understood to be determined by the class of its observational implications. Hence, the second meaning criterion implies the first, but not conversely; this is why I referred to them as the narrower and the wider empiricist criterion of meaning.

Carnap's arguments in support of the physicalistic thesis were aimed at showing that for any sentence of empirical science there exists a sentence in the physical language which implies the same protocol sentences and hence has the same content. Thus Carnap reasons that the psychological sentence P_1, "Mr. A is now excited," has the same content as a physical sentence P_2, to the effect that Mr. A's body is in a physical state characterized by rapid pulse and breathing and by a disposition to react, under specifiable physical stimulus conditions, with characteristic kinds of be-

36. See Carnap's explicit exclusion of "pseudostatements" and "pseudoconcepts" in *The Unity of Science,* pp. 70–75.
37. Carnap, "Psychology in Physical Language," p. 166.

havior which can be described in physical terms.[38] And he adds, in effect, that, if P_1 were held to contain a further component not shared with any physical sentence P_2, then that component would lack observational implications and hence empirical content; for any of its observational implications would always be describable in physical terms and thus would be shared with some physical sentence.[39]

Thus, as early as 1932 Carnap anticipated one of Ryle's ideas by arguing that sentences such as "A is excited" or "A has a headache," which attribute psychological characteristics to an individual, are analogous in their logical character to physical sentences like "This object is plastic" or "This wooden support is firm." The latter, Carnap says, are sentences "about a physical property, defined as a disposition to behave (or respond) in a specific manner under specific circumstances (or stimuli)." [40] The psychological terms in question are thus explicitly construed as pertaining to more or less complex behavioral dispositions.

Yet already at this stage Carnap noted that it is a further aim of science to define psychological concepts, not in terms of behavioral dispositions, but in terms of microstructures of the human body with which the dispositions are associated. This would "enable us to replace dispositional concepts by actual properties," just as the characterization of temperature as a disposition to produce certain thermometer readings has been replaced, in kinetic theory, by a microstructural definition in terms of the molecular kinetic energy.[41] Carnap stressed that a sentence S_1, containing psychological terms, and its counterpart S_2 in the physical language often will not be logically equivalent, but only "P-equipollent," that is, derivable from each other only by means of empirical laws. And, indeed, those behavioral symptoms which are generally associated with a given psychological feature will often be determined by empirical investigations leading to empirical laws rather than by an aprioristic reflection upon the

38. *Ibid.*, pp. 170–71, 186–87.
39. *Ibid.*, p. 174.
40. *Ibid.*, p. 170.
41. *Ibid.*, pp. 186–87.

meaning of the psychological terms in question. That every psychological sentence has *some* physical counterpart, however, is guaranteed by the fact that the constituent psychological terms must have some observational, and thus physically describable, criteria of application; otherwise, the psychological sentence would have no content.[42]

In arguing for this physicalistic construal of psychology Carnap considers several likely objections, among them the claim that a purely physicalistic analysis cannot give an adequate account of "meaningful" behavior: that it cannot, for example, distinguish between a mere reflex movement of an arm and a "meaningful" movement such as a beckoning gesture. Carnap replies that whatever meaning can scientifically—and thus testably—be attributed to an arm movement must be fully determined, and hence fully characterizable, by physical features of the moving arm, the rest of the body, and the environment. For, indeed, he reasons, if we were to watch a film of the arm movement, we would be able to ascertain its "meaning" just as well as if we were witnessing the event itself. But the film records only physical phenomena; hence, the physical aspects of the arm movement must be sufficient to determine its beckoning character or whatever other "meaning" can significantly be ascribed to it.[43]

Carnap acknowledges that it is not as yet possible to give explicit characterizations of "meaningful" kinds of behavior in terms of the concepts of physical theory; but he takes the view that expressions such as "assertive nod" or "beckoning gesture" may themselves be regarded as physical terms of a crude sort because, by the argument just outlined, their criteria of application pertain exclusively to physical aspects of behavior.

At the stage we have been considering, then, Carnap maintained that all scientific terms were fully definable in physical terms and all scientific sentences fully translatable into physical ones, with the understanding that the definitions and translations in question were not always based solely on logical or analytic truths, but rested, in some cases, on empirical laws.

42. See *Philosophy and Logical Syntax*, pp. 88–92.
43. "Psychology in Physical Language," p. 182.

In the mid-thirties Carnap began to weaken this claim. Briefly, he argued that "we know the meaning (designation) of a term if we know under what conditions we are permitted to apply it in a concrete case and under what conditions not," [44] and he went on to show that, even within physics, the criteria of application for a term, which in this sense specify its meaning, do not in general provide a full definition for it, at least not when stated in a language using only extensional logical connectives. He argued this particularly for dispositional terms, such as "elastic": the apparently plausible definition

$$x \text{ is elastic} \equiv (x \text{ is stretched and released} \supset x \text{ contracts})$$

would qualify as elastic not only those objects which contract on being stretched and released, but also those which never are stretched or released at all, because, for these, the antecedent of the definiens is false and, hence, the definiens is true. In order to avoid this difficulty, Carnap suggested that sentences specifying criteria of application for dispositional terms be construed as having the form of what he called reduction sentences, which would play the role of partial rather than full definitions. Using obvious abbreviations, the reduction sentence for our example could be written as follows:

$$(R) \quad SR(x) \supset (E(x) \equiv C(x)) .$$

This sentence is logically equivalent to the conjunction of the following two:

$$(R_1) \quad E(x) \supset (SR(x) \supset C(x))$$

and

$$(R_2) \quad (SR(x) \cdot C(x)) \supset E(x) .$$

The first of these states a necessary condition for "$E(x)$"; the second, a different sufficient one; whereas a full definition of a term specifies one condition which is both necessary and sufficient. The reduction sentence R has the character of a partial definition in this sense: it specifies a necessary and sufficient condition of elasticity—namely, contraction—for just those things which are subjected to the stretch-and-release test; in reference to all other

---

44. "Logical Foundations of the Unity of Science," p. 49.

things, no criteria of applicability for the word "elastic" are provided, no "meaning" is given to it. The area of indeterminacy thus left may be reduced by means of further reduction sentences specifying additional criteria of application; but all the criteria available for a scientific term will not, in general, amount to a full definition for it.

Reduction sentences seem to lend themselves well to the formulation of "operational" criteria of application for psychological and sociological terms, as based on specified procedures of testing, rating, or evaluating. And it is clear also that these procedures afford only partial criteria of application. For example, an intelligence test that presupposes literacy on the part of the subject is not applicable to just any subject and thus offers no general definition; an analogous remark applies to a rating scale for socio-economic status whose criteria of application require a count of the electric appliances owned by the family to be rated.

In accordance with these considerations, Carnap's modified physicalistic thesis asserts that any term of empirical science can be linked by means of reduction sentences, but not generally by means of definitions, to the vocabulary of physics, and indeed to a narrow subset of it, namely, observational "thing predicates," that is, terms which stand for directly observable properties or relations of physical bodies. Carnap's argument in support of this claim was briefly to this effect: Any scientific term must refer to a kind of thing or event or state Q whose presence can, under suitable circumstances T, be ascertained on the basis of publicly observable symptoms R, such as instrument readings in physics and behavioral manifestations in the case of psychological or sociological terms. (Otherwise, the term would have no empirical meaning.) Being publicly observable, these symptoms must be describable by means of observational thing predicates; and the resulting criteria of application will be expressible by means of reduction sentences of this kind: "When observable test conditions T are realized, a thing (state, event) of kind Q is present if and only if an observable response of kind R occurs."

As for psychological terms, Carnap did not deny that we often apply them to ourselves "introspectively," without observing our own behavioral symptoms. His claim was merely that, for every such term, there are behavioral criteria which, under suitable conditions, make it possible to determine whether a person is in the kind of psychological condition to which the term refers. For example, the utterances of a person describing his ("introspected") pain or joy or anger are among the potential symptoms for the presence of the states in question; and so are other characteristic kinds of behavior which a person in such a state will display under suitable conditions. Thus, Carnap's theory of reduction sentences enabled him to give a logically subtler expression to the construal of psychological terms as complex bundles of dispositions. And it is of interest to note with Feigl that Carnap's ideas—and, I should add, Feigl's as well—have met with considerable interest among psychologists and have found applications in the work of such investigators as S. Koch; Tolman, Ritchie, and Kalish; and MacCorquodale and Meehl.[45]

Having abandoned the thesis of full physicalistic definability of all scientific terms, Carnap also withdrew the claim of the translatability of all scientific statements into the language of physics.[46] The result, as Feigl notes in his contribution to the present volume, was a considerably attenuated version of physicalism, which asserted only the reducibility of all scientific terms to physical terms, and indeed to a narrow subset of these, namely, the observational thing predicates.[47]

More recently, Carnap has taken the view, closely related to ideas developed by Feigl, that a strictly dispositional construal of psychological terms still is too confining and fails to do justice to their scientific use.[48] For, if a psychological characteristic Q

45. See H. Feigl, "Principles and Problems of Theory Construction in Psychology," in W. Dennis, ed., *Current Trends in Psychological Theory* (Pittsburgh: University of Pittsburgh Press, 1951), pp. 179–213.

46. "Testability and Meaning," p. 467.

47. The most important statements of this stage of Carnap's physicalism are contained in "Testability and Meaning" (especially sec. 15) and in "Logical Foundations of the Unity of Science."

48. See Carnap, "The Methodological Character of Theoretical Concepts," in H. Feigl and M. Scriven, eds., *Minnesota Studies in the Philosophy of Science*, vol. 1 (Minneapolis: University of Minnesota Press, 1956), pp. 38–76. Among Feigl's studies dealing with theoretical concepts and theoretical principles and with their significance in psychology are: "Existential Hypotheses: Realistic *vs.* Phenomenalistic Interpretations," *Philosophy of Science*, 17

is construed as an invariable disposition to show a certain kind of response R under test conditions or stimulus conditions of a specified kind S, then the non-occurrence of R in a case where conditions S are met would establish conclusively the absence of Q in that case. Thus, Carnap illustrates, if "an IQ above 130" is understood strictly as a person's disposition to respond to a certain kind of test with answers scoring above 130, then a subject's failure to score appropriately must count as establishing conclusively that he does not have an IQ above 130; whereas, Carnap argues, psychologists would in fact allow for the possibility that the subject does have that high an IQ, but that depression, fatigue, or other factors interfered with his test performance.

In order to allow for this possibility, Carnap now proposes to assign to the psychological expressions in question the status of theoretical terms. Such terms—whether in physics or in psychology—he construes as being introduced, not simply by definitions or universal reduction sentences providing observational criteria of application, but rather by specifying (*a*) a set of theoretical principles in which they function and (*b*) a set of "correspondence rules" that afford partial observational criteria of application for some of the theoretical terms. The correspondence rules may take the form of reduction sentences, but Carnap does not insist on this particular form; indeed, he mentions even the possibility of correspondence rules of probabilistic-statistical form.[49] In any event he conceives of the meanings of theoretical terms as depending not only on the correspondence rules but also on the theoretical principles in question, with the result that psychological terms thus construed can no longer be held to stand simply for behavioral dispositions. This construal abandons the notion that every psychological term possesses (necessary or sufficient) conditions of application that can be stated in an observational vocabulary. Concomitantly, it gives up two

(1950): 35–62; "Principles and Problems of Theory Construction in Psychology"; and "Physicalism, Unity of Science, and the Foundations of Psychology," in Schilpp, *The Philosophy of Rudolf Carnap*, pp. 227–67.

49. "The Methodological Character of Theoretical Concepts," p. 49; the IQ example is discussed on pp. 71–72.

ideas concerning the significance of scientific terms that are closely related to the empiricist criteria of empirical significance for statements; namely, first, the principle that a term has empirical significance only if it has necessary or sufficient observational conditions of application; and, second, the narrower operationist maxim that the meaning of a term is fully determined by those conditions of application. In order to make sure that his conception of theoretical terms would not sanction the admission of pseudoconcepts and pseudohypotheses, Carnap proposed a new, considerably liberalized "criterion of significance for theoretical terms" and a corresponding "criterion of significance for theoretical sentences," whose somewhat complicated details[50] we need not consider here, however. It suffices to note that the idea of the reducibility of all scientific terms to a "reduction basis" consisting of observational predicates was abandoned.

LINGUISTIC AND ONTOLOGICAL ASPECTS OF PHYSICALISM

This result certainly represents a considerable weakening of one physicalistic claim. But the question whether every scientific term has necessary or sufficient conditions of application expressible in purely observational predicates is hardly the root issue that lent philosophical interest to physicalism. That root issue, I think, lies in questions raised by the old distinctions between the organic and the inorganic, between the mental and the physical, between *Kulturwissenschaft* and *Naturwissenschaft*. Broadly speaking, physicalism was exciting because it promised to shed light on the question whether, as Neurath said, living and thinking organisms, as well as societies and nations, are nothing other than peculiar combinations of physical bodies that exhibit more or less complex kinds of physical features, or whether there is something more to them, something that falls outside the domain of physics. Thus stated, the issues are formulated in what Carnap called the material mode of speech, that is, in sentences that ostensibly concern empirical items such as physical, biological, psychological, and sociological systems and processes. But, quite early in the development of his ideas on physical-

50. *Ibid.*, secs. VI, VII, and VIII.

ism, Carnap argued that these and other philosophic problems expressed in the material mode were not actually concerned with the subject matter of empirical science, but rather with its language, and that the first step toward philosophical clarification should consist in reformulating the issues accordingly—in giving them a "linguistic turn," to use Rorty's apt phrase.[51]

A first step toward a linguistic restatement of the theses just mentioned is suggested by this consideration: the claim that all biological and sociological systems and processes, and all psychological states and events, are just physical systems or occurrences would seem to amount to two theses: (1) any biological, psychological, or sociological characteristic of any system, state, or event can be described by means of purely physical concepts alone; and (2) any phenomenon that can be explained with the help of biological, psychological, or sociological laws or theoretical principles can be explained by physical laws alone.

But, inasmuch as biological, psychological, and social characteristics would be described by means of biological, psychological, and sociological terms, the first thesis might be given this linguistic turn: (1a) All biological, psychological, and sociological terms can be defined by means of physical terms. Similarly, the second thesis might be turned into: (2a) All biological, psychological, and sociological laws can be deduced from purely physical laws.

These two theses, and certain variants of them, have in fact played a central role in the efforts made by logical empiricists to express physicalism as a thesis about the language of science. As for (1a), we saw above that it was part of Carnap's physicalism in an early stage of its development. Let us note that the recent con-

51. For detailed statements of this conception of philosophical problems as concerning linguistic issues, see pt. III of Carnap's *Philosophy and Logical Syntax* and pt. V of his *The Logical Syntax of Language* (New York: Harcourt, Brace and Co., 1937). While Carnap here thought of the philosophically relevant linguistic questions as being strictly syntactic, he later broadened his view; but the details need not be considered here. *The Linguistic Turn* is the title of a collection of articles edited by R. Rorty (Chicago: The University of Chicago Press, 1967) which set forth or criticize various modes of linguistic construal and clarification of philosophical problems.

strual—by Carnap, Feigl, and others—of psychological terms as theoretical terms, some of which may lack observational criteria of application, is quite compatible with the thesis that, nonetheless, all psychological (and similarly sociological, etc.) terms are fully definable by means of physical terms—some of which would then have to belong, however, to the "non-observational," "theoretical," vocabulary of physics. Let us note also that the "definitions" envisaged in (1a) were not conceived of as expressing synonymies; rather, as Carnap has pointed out at an early stage, they would normally be based on empirical laws. This is the case, for example, when a certain hormone, originally characterized in biological terms by reference to the gland secreting it, is later "defined" in physicochemical terms by reference to its molecular structure. In this case the biological term and the corresponding physicochemical expression might be said to be coextensive by law, or nomically coextensive.

A thesis to the effect that psychological terms are thus non-analytically coextensive with physical expressions has been developed in detail by Feigl, whose conception takes explicit account also of the theoretical role of psychological and physical terms. Briefly, Feigl holds that for every psychological predicate there is a corresponding physical—more specifically, a neurophysiological —expression with which it is coextensive by virtue of fundamental theoretical principles, much as the term "temperature" as used "macroscopically" in classical thermodynamics is coextensive, by virtue of theoretical principles, with an expression in the kinetic theory of matter, namely, "(a disjunction of) micro-descriptions in terms of molecular motions." [52] Feigl argues that, when a psychological term is thus theoretically coextensive with a physical expression, the two may be viewed as having the same

52. Feigl, "Physicalism, Unity of Science, and the Foundations of Psychology," p. 256. A much fuller presentation of Feigl's ideas is given in his essay "The 'Mental' and the 'Physical,'" in H. Feigl, M. Scriven, and G. Maxwell, eds., *Minnesota Studies in the Philosophy of Science*, vol. 2 (Minneapolis: University of Minnesota Press, 1958), pp. 370–497; this essay, supplemented by a chapter, "Postscript After Ten Years," has since been republished as a separate monograph (Minneapolis: University of Minnesota Press, 1967).

referent, and he speaks of this identity of the referents as systemic or theoretical identity. In this sense Feigl's "physicalistic identity theory" holds that every kind of psychological state or event is theoretically identifiable with a kind of physical state or event which is describable in neurophysiological terms. Feigl argues that the assumption of the theoretical coextensiveness of all psychological terms with physical expressions, far from being a philosophical a priori truth, is made increasingly plausible by the advances of scientific knowledge in the relevant fields, and that the identification of associated referents recommends itself on methodological and philosophical grounds.

In one of his recent essays Feigl presents this conception in the context of a critical appraisal and restatement of physicalism. He summarizes the basic tenets of his version of physicalism in two theses, which Carnap, in his response to Feigl, endorses in a slightly modified form.[53] The first thesis is to the effect that whatever is subjectively or privately confirmable is also intersubjectively or publicly confirmable, so that anything I can know introspectively to be the case (e.g., that I have a headache) can in principle be ascertained indirectly by others on the basis of publicly observable symptoms or manifestations. This thesis attempts to make a claim similar to, but more cautious than, that expressed by (1a) or by its later variant to the effect that all scientific terms are reducible to physical terms. The second thesis is closely akin to (2a). As stated by Carnap it asserts that "all laws of nature, including those which hold for organisms, human beings, and human societies, are logical consequences of the physical laws, i.e., of those laws which are needed for the explanation of inorganic processes," so that whatever empirical occurrences can be explained at all by means of laws or theories can be explained by means of physical laws and theories alone. Carnap, like Feigl, stresses that these two physicalistic theses are not a priori truths: they reflect, he says, certain very general empirical facts of a kind sometimes referred to as all-pervasive features of

53. See Feigl, "Physicalism, Unity of Science, and the Foundations of Psychology," pp. 241–42, 265–66; Carnap, "Herbert Feigl on Physicalism," in Schilpp, *The Philosophy of Rudolf Carnap*, pp. 882–86.

the world and of the language in which the world can be described.[54]

Clearly, these recent formulations no longer purport to construe physicalism strictly as a set of theses concerning the language of empirical science. In fact, that construal was implicitly abandoned much earlier, by emphasizing that the "translatability" of biological, psychological, or sociological expressions into physical ones depended, in general, on appropriate empirical laws. Thus, the latest statement of physicalism presents again what might be called an ontological aspect.

The ontological reconstrual makes physicalism a rather elusive thesis—more elusive, perhaps, than its formulation might at first suggest. In the second thesis, for example, the notions of physical —or inorganic—process and of physical law give rise to questions. Perhaps it may be assumed that, in regard to processes that can be described in terms of the vocabulary of contemporary science, there would be fairly good agreement as to which of them count as inorganic and which do not; and perhaps a similar consensus might be attainable as to which of the laws expressible in contemporary scientific terms are physical laws and which are not. But suppose that further scientific research were to lead to a well-substantiated, high-level, new theory T that would unite physics, biology, and psychology in the way in which Einstein hoped to unite the theories of gravitation and electromagnetism by a unified field theory. The basic principles or laws of T might then be formulated in terms having no purely and exclusively physical, or biological, or psychological interpretation, but they might permit the derivation of various more specific general statements, some of which we would readily classify as physical laws, others as biological laws, and yet others as psychological ones. The fundamental principles or laws of T would thus explain inorganic as well as other kinds of processes; but would they constitute physical or non-physical laws? Would such a theoretical development strengthen or weaken the second thesis of physicalism?

Feigl takes cognizance of difficulties of this kind, pointing out

54. Carnap, "Herbert Feigl on Physicalism," pp. 882, 883; see also Feigl, "Physicalism, Unity of Science, and the Foundations of Psychology," p. 241.

that the notion of physical explanation has undergone, and will no doubt continue to undergo, radical changes. He therefore construes the claim of the second thesis—that all empirical facts and laws can be given a "physical" explanation—as asserting that those facts and laws can be explained by means of a theory whose terms are partially interpreted in observational terms and whose postulates are conceived "according to the paradigm of modern physical theory"; this qualification is taken to preclude, for example, teleological explanations of the vitalistic variety (even if testable) and interactionist theories of the relation of the mental to the physical.[55] Thus understood, the thesis of the universality of physical explanation is quite vague, as Feigl is the first to acknowledge. Moreover, the thesis would seem to qualify as physical even those explanations which our fictitious unifying theory T would provide for biological and psychological phenomena. Thus, the latest versions of physicalism look pretty pale and innocuous by comparison with the sturdy ontological formulations of materialism and mechanism, which appear to make strong and clear claims about the purely physical character of biological and social systems and events and of mental states and processes. But this throws into relief one of the insights afforded by the evolution of physicalism: those claims are strong and clear in appearance only, as is evidenced by the fact that the steadily refined empiricist efforts to explicate the tenable substance of those theses have yielded formulations that have been increasingly cautious, elusive, and weak.[56]

ON THE METHODOLOGICAL UNITY OF SCIENCE

The unity of science as envisaged by logical empiricism had three major aspects, of which we have so far considered two, sometimes referred to as the unity of language and the unity of laws. In conclusion, at least brief mention should be made of the third aspect, the unity of method. The idea of the methodological

55. Feigl, "Physicalism, Unity of Science, and the Foundations of Psychology," pp. 242–43, 266, 253.

56. The problems here adumbrated are examined more fully in my essay "Reduction: Ontological and Linguistic Facets," in Sidney Morgenbesser, Patrick Suppes, and Morton White, eds., *Philosophy, Science and Method: Essays in Honor of Ernest Nagel* (New York: St. Martin's Press, 1969).

unity of science was developed in opposition to the view that the mental or cultural disciplines are distinguished from the natural sciences by fundamental differences in the methods that are required to ascertain and to explain the facts with which these disciplines are concerned.

The thesis of the methodological unity of science states, first of all, that, notwithstanding many differences in their techniques of investigation, all branches of empirical science test and support their statements in basically the same manner, namely, by deriving from them implications that can be checked intersubjectively and by performing for those implications the appropriate experimental or observational tests. This, the unity of method thesis holds, is true also of psychology and the social and historical disciplines. In response to the claim that the scholar in these fields, in contrast to the natural scientist, often must rely on empathy to establish his assertions, logical-empiricist writers stressed that imaginative identification with a given person often may prove a useful heuristic aid to the investigator who seeks to guess at a hypothesis about that person's beliefs, hopes, fears, and goals. But whether or not a hypothesis thus arrived at is factually sound must be determined by reference to objective evidence: the investigator's empathic experience is logically irrelevant to it. As Feigl puts it, "Quite generally, the significance of intuition, insight, empathetic understanding consists in the power of these processes to *suggest* hypotheses or assumptions, which, however, could *not* be established, i.e. confirmed as scientific statements except by intersubjective methods." [57]

Similarly, the logical-empiricist conception of the unity of science rejects the claim that certain psychological facts can be ascertained only by the method of introspection; it holds instead that for any privately ascertainable kind of state or event there are some publicly observable symptoms which make it possible intersubjectively to confirm the presence of the state or event in question; this, in fact, is the point of the first thesis of physicalism as recently stated by Feigl and Carnap.

57. Feigl, "Physicalism, Unity of Science, and the Foundations of Psychology," p. 258 (italics quoted).

As for basic differences in the methodology of explanation, one of the best-known claims holds that the explanation of human actions in terms of reasons differs fundamentally from the kind of explanation found in the natural sciences, and especially from causal explanation. Here the construal of psychological terms as dispositional or theoretical terms provided the basis for a reply to the effect that explanations of human actions by reference to reasons are strictly analogous to explanations of physical events by reference to dispositional properties or theoretical characteristics of the objects involved. Thus, to illustrate the central idea sketchily, the explanation that Henry passed the cookies because (a) he had been asked to and (b) he was polite, and was thus disposed to comply, is analogous to the explanation that the window pane broke because (a) it was struck by a stone and (b) it was brittle and was thus disposed to shatter under a sharp impact.

While a dispositional construal of psychological terms was explicitly set forth by Carnap in the mid-thirties, I believe it was Ryle who first argued in careful detail that to explain an action by motives or other psychological factors is to subsume it under a "law-like proposition," attributing to the agent a general behavioral disposition characteristic of the motive in question. Thus he says: "The imputation of a motive for a particular action is not a causal inference to an unwitnessed event but the subsumption of an episode proposition under a law-like proposition. It is therefore analogous to the explanation of reactions and actions by reflexes and habits, or to the explanation of the fracture of the glass by reference to its brittleness." [58] To adduce the brittleness of the glass pane in the latter explanation is not to cite a cause for its shattering, but to indicate a law-like proposition expressing the general disposition of the pane to break under impact. This proposition, however, explains the breaking of the pane only in combination with another proposition mentioning the impact of the stone, which plays the role of the cause. Analogously, in Ryle's analysis, to specify a motive for an action is not to cite its cause, but to indicate a law-like proposition concerning a behavioral disposition of the agent; however, "the general fact that

58. Ryle, *The Concept of Mind,* p. 90.

a person is disposed to act in such and such ways in such and such circumstances does not by itself account for his doing a particular thing at a particular moment. . . . As the impact of the stone at 10 P.M. caused the glass to break, so some antecedent of an action causes or occasions the agent to perform it when and where he does so." [59] For example, being asked to pass the cookies might be what caused Henry to do so, in accordance with his politeness, that is, his general disposition to act politely.

This argument seems to me quite effectively to dispose of the claim that explanation by motives or other psychological factors is fundamentally different from the explanation of physical events. But, as was noted earlier, the psychological factors in question cannot generally be construed as behavioral dispositions nor even, in a manner envisaged by Ryle,[60] as large or endless bundles of such dispositions. This becomes clear also when we consider the logic of explaining an action by the reasons that led the agent to perform it. Those reasons will normally have to include the agent's relevant desires and beliefs; and it is readily seen that neither a desire nor a belief by itself can be construed as a disposition to show a characteristic kind of publicly observable (macro- or micro-) behavior under physically characterizable stimulus conditions. For, the behavior in which a given desire (e.g., a desire for food) manifests itself under given stimulus conditions (e.g., when food is placed before the hungry person) will depend essentially on the person's beliefs—for example, on whether he believes that what is put before him is in fact edible, not prohibited by religious or medical considerations, and so forth. Conversely, the behavior in which a given belief manifests itself will depend on the given person's desires (as well as on other beliefs he may entertain, on his moral standards, etc.). Thus, only certain *combinations,* so to speak, of beliefs with desires and possibly with other factors will be associated with more or less specific behavioral dispositions.

Considerations such as these suggest that explaining an action by means of reasons (and similar kinds of psychological explana-

59. *Ibid.,* p. 113.
60. *Ibid.,* p. 44.

tion) is analogous to explaining a physical event by means of theoretically characterized factors (and theoretical principles governing them): such factors also cannot usually be conceived of as general dispositions or as bundles of such.

An interest in exploring the extent of the methodological unity of empirical science is manifested also in further studies, growing out of the logical-empiricist tradition, that examine the form, the force, and the modes of validation of various other kinds of explanation which can be found in the social sciences and in historiography—among them, the functional and the typological analysis of social phenomena and genetic and other types of historical explanation. One of the basic features that all these types of explanation have been held to share with explanation in the natural sciences is the explicit or implicit reliance on general laws or theoretical principles of universal or of probabilistic-statistical form.[61]

CONCLUSION

A fair-minded appraisal of the accomplishments of logical positivism should not focus on the bold and naturally oversimplified devices its adherents wrote upon their banners, but on the quality of the detailed logical and methodological studies carried out under those banners: it should examine the standards of clarity and rigor those studies exemplify, the stimulation they provided for the work of others, and the light they shed on philosophical issues of importance. Thus judged, logical positivism will be found, I think, to have been a strong and fruitful influence in recent systematic philosophy.

61. This is argued, for example, in the articles "The Function of General Laws in History" (1942), "Studies in the Logic of Explanation" (with Paul Oppenheim, 1948), "Typological Methods in the Natural and the Social Sciences" (1952), "The Logic of Functional Analysis" (1959), and "Aspects of Scientific Explanation," all of which are included in my book *Aspects of Scientific Explanation and Other Essays in the Philosophy of Science* (New York: Macmillan [The Free Press], 1965). This book also contains extensive references to further literature on the subject, including various criticisms of the basic idea of a unity of explanatory method.

MICHAEL SCRIVEN

logical positivism and the behavioral sciences

The Vienna Circle or *Wiener Kreis* was a band of cutthroats that went after the fat burghers of Continental metaphysics who had become intolerably inbred and pompously verbose. The *kris* is a Malaysian knife, and the *Wiener Kreis* employed a kind of Occam's Razor called the Verifiability Principle. It performed a tracheotomy that made it possible for philosophy to breathe again, and one cannot rightly object to the imperfections of instruments that save lives . . . at the time that they serve that purpose. Only later, when the populace begins to show signs of worshiping the device of deliverance, is it appropriate to point out that we can go on to better devices, indeed, that to fail to do so is to risk an infection that might prove just as fatal as choking to death on a mess of verbiage.

It really is not very interesting for a literate audience to read once again about the nicks on the blade of the *Wiener Kreis,* because they have been exhibited so well by others, notably by Hempel in the work now published as "Empiricist Criteria of Cognitive Significance: Problems and Changes," in "*Aspects of*

Scientific Explanation.[1] What I shall do is look at the situation in the post-positivist period and see if we really have met or can meet the charges that were brought against pre-positivist philosophy, especially philosophy of the social sciences, in the same way that one might do this with respect to post-Humean philosophy. Russell, in his *History of Western Philosophy,* remarks that it has been a favorite pastime of metaphysicians since Hume to refute him; but, he says, "for my part, I find none of their refutations convincing; nevertheless, I cannot but hope that something less sceptical . . . may be discoverable." We must ask whether the situation is as bad with respect to the logical positivists. Have we really met their objections, or have we merely gone soft?

This surely is a much more important question than that of whether the particular instrument they introduced to remedy the defects, the "empiricist criterion of meaning" (the principle of verification), was itself satisfactory as they formulated it. This is not to say that the logical questions about the possibility of salvation by revision of that formula are not interesting in their own right; on the contrary, they are not only interesting but also valuable in several ways. However, one can sum up the results that seem to emerge from such a discussion quite simply: it is not possible to state a principle that will sharply demarcate meaningful (or "scientifically meaningful") statements from others. One must concede that there is a matter of degree involved; that the borderline between sense and "nonsense," in this sense of "nonsense," is not sharp. But now let us ask instead whether the positivists' specific objections to the philosophy and quasi-science of their time have been or can now be met. In this paper I am concerned only with the social sciences, and I am going to restrict myself still further (for reasons of space and time) to a fairly thorough discussion of only one issue, namely, the analysis of "understanding" (*Verstehen*) in the social sciences, a target of particular interest to the logical positivists. I shall, however, have *something* to say about several other aspects of the methodology

1. (New York: Macmillan [The Free Press], 1965). Reference can also be made to the two dozen other citations in J. Passmore, *One Hundred Years of Philosophy,* 3d ed. (New York: Basic Books, 1966), p. 371n, who curiously omits the Hempel paper.

of the social sciences on which positivism had some bearing.

It is, of course, essential to remember that when we talk about the "logical positivists"—a name apparently due to Feigl—we are not talking about the *original* "positivists," such as Comte (who invented *that* term). The line of descent is clear, from Comte to Mach to Schlick, but there were important changes. In particular, with respect to our topic here, Comte thought that there *was* a special method of the social sciences, the application of the criterion of harmony to our understanding of human nature. But the logical positivists rejected this, or something quite like this (Comte's position is not very clear), for reasons which I shall examine shortly. Hereafter, where I use the term "positivists," however, I am referring to the Vienna Circle and its descendants or disciples from A. J. Ayer to W. C. Salmon.

Impressionistically speaking—and in this area of the history of thought I do not believe we can be very precise—one thinks of the logical positivists as *attacking* nineteenth-century German metaphysics and what they called psychologism in the sciences (which sometimes included Gestalt theory and always included *Verstehen* theory), and as *upholding* the analytic-synthetic distinction, the distinction between the context of discovery and that of verification, the facts-value distinction, operationalism, verificationism, phenomenalism, conventionalism, and formalism (especially in the philosophy of mathematics and in the reconstruction of scientific theories in terms of an uninterpreted calculus and correspondence rules).

The relevance of logical positivism to the behavioral sciences is the result of the influence of these methodological positions on behavioral scientists—and this influence has been enormous, especially with respect to the doctrines of (1) operationalism, (2) the value-free ideal of the behaviorists, and (3) deductivism (i.e., the doctrine that scientific explanation properly consists in deduction of descriptions of, or statements asserting the likelihood of, the phenomenon-to-be-explained from general empirical laws and antecedent conditions).

I shall say only a word about the effect of operationalism, which has been treated by others on many occasions. This is a doctrine whose heart is in the right place, but whose head is in the wrong place. It is good advice to scientists to recommend that they put their claims in testable form, and a very natural extension of this is to suggest that they should make sure that their concepts can be applied in an interjudge-reliable way.[2] The operationalist thought that he saw a nice, neat formula for expressing this recommendation, but unfortunately the formula is considerably too stringent a requirement. It demands that definitions of concepts be expressed as equivalences to sets of operations, but unfortunately there are grave problems about the definition of *operation* and, in particular, grave problems about (1) whether an operational definition of this can be given, (2) what is to count as *one* operation, (3) what is to count as *an* operation. (1) If *operation* cannot be defined operationally, then an important concept in the methodology of science cannot be defined in a way which meets the requirements of operationalism, which certainly appears to restrict its universality and raises the question of whether there may not be other serious exceptions to it. (2) If we measure temperature in one range using a liquid-in-glass thermometer, and in another range using a bolometer, then this would appear to be two different operations, and thus it would be improper to refer to it as the same physical quantity in both cases. In such an instance, operationalism gives a result which is incompatible with standard scientific practice. But, if we interpret these two operations as referring to the *same* concept, it becomes difficult to see how operationalism is true, and especially difficult to see how the claimed master example of operationalism —namely, the introduction of the relativity theory via questioning of the meaning of distant simultaneity—in fact supports the position at all. (3) And, finally, if the notion of an operation is not only not operationally definable, not only plagued by problems of unit identity, but also not very clear itself—as is the case when we try to pin it down—then the rubric becomes somewhat less valuable than appeared at first sight.

Operationalism, which was supposed to have its foundations in physics—although there are grave doubts as to whether it did in

2. This is essentially G. Mandler and W. Kessen's doctrine in *The Language of Psychology* (New York: John Wiley & Sons, 1959).

any way reflect the thinking that led to the introduction of the relativity theory—never had much success there but was far more significant in the area of psychology. Here it all too often became the war cry of an avid empiricism, although for reasons implicit in the above discussion there is nothing about it that intrinsically would require this.

The second major doctrine of the positivist and positivist-associated movements is that of value-free social science. I have discussed this at length elsewhere, most recently (in a forthcoming volume edited by R. Lichtman) in a paper entitled "Value Claims in the Social Sciences." The doctrine now seems to me to be an incredible *gaffe* based on not one but a series of logical mistakes. One of these was the transfer of a distinction which makes sense in a given context—the distinction between the facts in the case and the evaluations that we base on them—into a context-free distinction. But this fallacy is something to which we have become particularly sensitive, and it now seems difficult to imagine that it was plausible. Our sensitivity has been aroused particularly in connection with another position that the positivists at times espoused, the doctrine of reductionism or phenomenalism, which maintained that theoretical statements could be reduced to observation statements and that those of one level of science could be reduced to those of a more fundamental level, culminating in the grand reduction to the observation language of physics. But it has become quite clear that the concept of the observation language makes sense only in a particular context; and the observation language of one epoch in physics, or of one part of physics, is the theoretical language of another. There is no "ultimate observation language" any more than there is an ultimate sense-datum language. Analogously, there is no ultimate factual language. And the more interesting side of this coin is that many statements which in one context clearly would be evaluational are, in another, clearly factual. Obvious examples include judgments of intelligence and of the merit of performances such as those of the runners at the Olympic Games.

Another crucial logical error that had to be made in order that one could recommend the avoidance of value judgments developed as follows: The early advocates of value-free science readily conceded that preferences are factual matters and that the performance of particular entities (e.g., theories or people) with respect to preferred qualities are matters of fact; but somehow they suppose that these could not be combined to yield judgments about the superiority of something for someone without a kind of ineradicable subjectivity coming into the picture. But of course it is simply a fact that certain kinds of medicine are good for certain kinds of disease condition, even if this is also a value judgment. And the underlying "value premise" which involves an assertion that, when such and such needs or wants are fulfilled, good has been done, is itself just a fact about human health, although also a value statement. There is nothing in the least dubious about such assertions by comparison with the other assertions of empirical science that are required for the application of any theory. For example, one cannot explain the elliptical orbits of the planets merely by appealing to facts about the pull of gravitation and the masses of the sun and other planets. One must also have a premise which asserts that only these factors need to be taken into consideration. This kind of "adequacy guarantee" can be supported in astronomy, and the corresponding one can be supported in the social sciences, where it has valuational impact and reference.

Yet a third kind of logical mistake was sometimes involved, that of failing to distinguish moral value statements from value statements in general. There are certainly special difficulties about validating moral claims, but the positivists usually did not make a distinction between these and other value claims. Thus their view, which might be given some semblance of plausibility with respect to morality, became a travesty when completely generalized. I believe that morality can be given an entirely objective foundation, but I concede that doing so is more difficult than supporting a claim about the greater merit of the special theory of relativity by comparison with Newtonian dynamics, or about the greater merit of one kind of tax structure over another. Of course, positivists have often thought that the latter kinds of claim could be construed as instrumental claims, and this, they were quick to point out, could be entirely factual. What they failed to see was that there are no good grounds for thinking that any claims are not instrumental. "Ultimate values" are as elusive as "ultimate facts." Hence, all value claims can be given support or rejected for lack of it.

It was also very common for positivists to suggest that the frequency of disputes about value issues somehow supported their view that these were subjective matters. Yet, in connection with arguments about the existence of God, they were not in the least hesitant to claim that such disputes, which surely are as frequent, were simply signs of poor logical training, poor scientific training, or the interference of emotions with reason.

The final horror in the chamber of bad arguments on the values issue was the suggestion that value claims were not really statements at all, but simply expressions of an attitude with no cognitive content, or with some but only an incidental cognitive component. The emotive theory, with its gradual refinement by Charles L. Stevenson, was the sophisticated version of this idea, and, as is well known, it has been modified to the point where its distinguishability from cognitivism is now in question. To summarize, there is no possibility that the social sciences can be free either of value claims in general or of moral value claims in particular, and the arguments which suggested that, for their own good they should be, were themselves metascientific value claims.

The topic of special interest for us here is the nature of our understanding of people. On this issue the positivists reacted against the school of historians proposing the *"Verstehen* theory," that is, the doctrine that empathic insight was a special and valuable tool in the study of human behavior which was without counterpart in the physical sciences. This view did not die with them, for it is explicit in Collingwood's philosophy of history and implicit in the practice of many other historians.

The positivists argued that empathy was not a reliable tool at all, and that the methods of obtaining knowledge, especially knowledge in history, were just the same as those used in the physical sciences. In particular, understanding was possible only via subsumption under established laws.

I shall argue that empathy is, in principle, a reliable tool for the historian *and* the physical scientist. The methods are thus the same throughout the various fields of knowledge, but are not restricted to those traditionally associated with physics.

This is one of those instructive cases where a little historical research yields big dividends simply because we come to the materials with a fresh eye, one not bloodshot with the battles of that day. Let us consider one of the classical attacks on the empathy theory, under one or another of the latter's aliases.

Here is Edgar Zilsel writing on "Physics and the Problem of Historico-Sociological Laws," a deservedly famous paper:[3]

> On the other hand the method of "understanding" ("insight") which has often been recommended for social science is not sufficient when investigating historical laws. "Understanding" means psychological empathy: psychologically a historical process is "understood" if it is evident or plausible. The main objection to this criterion of the correctness of a historical assertion is that virtually always opposite historical processes are equally plausible. . . . When a city is bombed it is plausible that intimidation and defeatism of the population result. But it is plausible as well that the determination to resist increases. It would not be plausible, on the other hand, if the bombing changed the pronunciation of consonants in the bombed city. Which process actually takes place can not be decided by psychological empathy but by statistical observation only. In the final analysis the method of understanding is equivalent to the attempt to deduce historico-sociological laws from laws of introspective psychology. However, before regularities are established it is premature to attempt to deduce them. In the construction of new empirical sciences the predeductive stage can not be skipped.

Let us consider what Zilsel calls "the main objection to this criterion of the correctness of a historical assertion." To cut through the brush of preliminary analysis let me suggest that he is assuming that an event cannot be explained by appealing to facts from which it could not have been predicted. He is right that from the occurrence of bombing (B) we cannot in general tell whether defeatism (D) or resistance (R) will be the major effect. But this is not of concern to a historian or a social scientist trying to explain or understand an event or series of events. He

3. *Philosophy of Science,* 8 (1941).

knows which particular outcome did occur, for *that is precisely what he has to explain;* his task is only to find the antecedent circumstance that caused this outcome, and to help him he has a record from which he discovers the fact of bombing. He also knows, "empathically" if you like, the simple fact that bombing can very well and often does cause this outcome. There is only one other check required; he must assure himself that no other potential causes are present. If there are none, he can rightly be sure that the bombing was *the* cause. If one or more are present, he must check further to see if the causes co-operated or whether one beat the others to the punch. In simpler cases there is often a certain quality or configuration about the effect which is a sure sign that one particular cause is responsible, and, even without checking that such an antecedent did occur, the historian often is entitled to claim that he *knows* what the cause was. He has seen the key, solved the riddle, diagnosed the condition, and in this kind of case the solution is sometimes so clearly self-identifying that it allows its perceiver to qualify as a knower. "Who is this?" we say, when we are confronted with a picture of some great man as an infant, or hear a few bars from a lesser work, or see a heavily disguised friend, or listen to a strange voice on the telephone at 3 A.M. And then sometimes the answer hits us with eureka-like impact; we spot the giveaway; we *know* the answer. This is like the historian's experience at times, and like the economist's and the psychotherapist's.

There is nothing weaker about our recognition of Sandy through his disguise because of the fact that if the eyes had been blue instead of near-black we would have guessed it was Walter or perhaps not have known whom to guess. Similarly, the fact that we cannot say from $n - 1$ items in a spatio-temporal configuration what the nth will be in no way undercuts the reliability with which we indentify the set of n when all are present. The test of identification is whether we *then* can infer an $(n + 1)$th item which checks out.

So empathy is a fine provider of knowledge; that does not mean it is any *more* reliable than observation or inference, from neither of which it is *entirely* (although it is *typically*) distinct. In the well-trained social scientist or historian it is simply one kind of judgment, and a well-trained man can call by the name of knowledge the judgments of which he is certain.

It appears that Zilsel's argument might well refer only to the search for *laws*. In the traditional positivist view, laws were atemporal universal claims of functional dependency involving no essential reference to particular names, a definition which involves inadequacies by some accounts and redundancies by others. In my view, elaborated elsewhere,[4] that definition is better thought of as an attempt to characterize the most abstract laws of theoretical physics, and is absurdly restrictive as a general account. Just about any non-accidental, relatively simple and useful generalization will be called a law if it is needed badly enough. In particular, laws may be limited in scope by invoking essential reference to particular regions of space-time while weakened in force to express qualitative relative probability; they may be time dependent, and non-predictive, and still be the sweetest sight a scientist ever saw and called a law. The fact that bombing a city will be likely to cause D or R but unlikely to cause a change in the pronunciation of consonants (P) is a fine example of a law —not exactly the pope himself, but a prominent layman or perhaps even a parish priest. This law has no essential time dependency, no particular references—almost no venial sin. Then how do we discover it? By a statistical analysis of bombing studies? No indeed. Just by thinking about the likely effects of B on me, or perhaps instant perception of its likely effects on thou —in short, empathy: estimating our own reactions and their transferability, seeing the inside of events in others' lives.

So Zilsel and the many who agreed with him were wrong in saying that empathy could not yield laws or verify them. They were wrong, not only because they had an overly restrictive concept of law as it is used *and is useful* in the sciences, but also because their argument simply did not entail their conclusion. For they certainly were not going to exclude a putative law on

4. "The Key Property of Physical Laws—Inaccuracy," in *Current Issues in the Philosophy of Science,* ed. H. Feigl and G. Maxwell (New York: Holt, Rinehart & Winston, 1961).

the ground that it involved a compound predicate; hence the empirical law "If B then either R or D" would have qualified under their strictest requirements. And just that law is conceded by Zilsel to be attainable by empathy. It is remarkable that he should then deny the value of empathy in divining laws. Thus their ultimate criterion, regardless of logic, is indeed that an event cannot be understood or explained unless it *alone* is predictable for the putative explanation. Now why was that criterion appealing?

I suspect that there were two reasons, both unsound. The first was some vague feeling that it was equivalent to, or guaranteed, the requirement that laws must have empirical content. But Zilsel's own reference to the improbable consequence undermines this point. For, if P is even logically possible, then the disjunctive prediction "R or D" is falsifiable, hence empirical in content. Thus the "empathizable" law "Whenever B then R or D" is empirical. I suspect that Zilsel never thought of the disjunctive-predicate kind of law, or he would not have overlooked this point. And I suppose that this oversight could be attributed to the context, which is one that focuses our attention on the explanation of a *particular* outcome and therefore—perhaps it seemed plausible to say—on laws which have that outcome as the sole dependent variable. I must add a further point, although it rather smacks of hitting a man when he's down. The reason just mentioned does not support the criterion in the way that Zilsel apparently supposed it would, but it also happens to be intrinsically unsound. That is to say, it is not necessary for historical laws to be empirical in order that they be valuable both for expressing knowledge and for generating understanding. Classical mechanics, the basic law of economics, the ideal gas laws, and many others are not demonstrably empirical, and it is not very important whether they are or not. The functions of laws are to simplify and to summarize, to compress and to extend our explicit knowledge, and even when they express a definitional truth they may be just as informative as Pythagoras' theorem is to a man who knows the definitional truths with which Euclid began. It is tempting simply to state that historical (or existing) laws must be empirical, but that is the kind of temptation which leads you to mystical contemplation of your own marvelous system, whose relation to anyone else's conceptual scheme is lost in mists of wonder. In short, laws in science may or may not be empirical; the only defensible version of this requirement is that they be *informative*—a nasty subjective requirement indeed.

The second reason for this criterion is somewhat more cogent, but still unsound. I believe it is the argument on which Hempel now relies; certainly he has often fallen back on this criterion of "symmetry" between explanation and prediction. Perhaps it is best called the "inferribility requirement." The expansion of the original deductive model of explanation to include inductive (statistical) explanations was accomplished within the framework of this same requirement, and, indeed, it is hard to find any other true and non-trivial requirement with which to identify the model today. For the requirement that propositions contained in the explanation be true is either false or trivial: false if *true* is taken precisely, trivial if *true* means "believed to be near enough right to be relevant." The same applies to the requirement that explanations involve general laws. And the requirement of empirical content in laws is, as we have just indicated, false.

This second reason is the desire to avoid *ad hoc* explanations. If we can invoke B to explain D only when we know that D has already occurred, the suspicion arises that we are simply committing the *post hoc ergo propter hoc* fallacy. Mere succession is not causal sequence. The difference, since Hume's day (according to the positivists), has been the knowledge of a general law that invariably connects the antecedent with the consequent. And an immediate consequence of having that law has been that, given the antecedent, one could predict the consequent. This is a nice, neat solution, but too nice to be good. Without repeating the lengthy and disordered analysis of cause which I have given elsewhere,[5] I can only propose some non-fundamental criticisms. It could hardly be denied that the cause or causes of some phenomena have been discovered. If, for example, it has been found that the cause of a disease X is a particular virus A, then we can

5. "Causes, Connections, and Conditions in History," in W. H. Dray, ed., *Philosophical Analysis and History* (New York: Harper & Row, 1966).

be sure that whenever X occurs it is because of infection with A—that is, A caused X. But there are carriers of A who do not develop X; therefore, we cannot say that the presence of A enables one to infer the (possibly future) occurrence of X. Thus X, when it occurs, is explicable in terms of A; but X is not predictable from A, that is, from that which explains it. This, then, ruins the inferribility thesis. But A is *not* an *ad hoc* explanation. For it is an empirical claim that A and not some other antecedent Q was the cause of X, and we support this claim by showing how A and not Q can lead to the symptoms of X. At the crude level of statistics, this means that infection with A increases the incidence of X in a population when compared with a control population, whereas the introduction of Q leads to no such change. But this crude observation normally can be followed up with a micro-account of the development of the virus' attack on the host which culminates in Q. The story is incomplete in many respects: we do not know what gives the carriers their immunity, or the mechanics of many of the stages we observe under the electron microscope. Those details are the answers to other questions, however. We have found the answer to the question we asked at the beginning of our research, namely, what kind of agent causes X and, in particular, exactly what agent.

Such discoveries are therefore most valuable in identifying the cause of a particular event (or a series of events), but they are not prediction-generating expressions. Once again, informativeness turns out to be a more subtle concept than the positivists supposed.

In recent discussions some positivists have argued that causal explanations of the kinds mentioned above really do implicitly refer to laws in a way which salvages the original thesis. It is true, they say, that the law may not be known, but that there *is* a law connecting the alleged cause with the effect certainly is implicitly asserted, given the explanation. In my view, this claim is simply a result of commitment to determinism, and determinism is false. It is not required by a causal explanation at all. But, even if it were, those who put forth this argument fail to see that they have abandoned precisely the reasons for its plausibility in its original form. As long as one could require the *production* of a true general law connecting cause with effect, one could repudiate the claim that one was confusing succession with causation; the minute that one moves to the view that some law must be present, although it cannot be stated, this refutation of the *ad hoc* nature of the causal claim is no longer possible.

Thus there is a way around the pitfalls of *ad hoc* explanation, lack of informational content, and circularity which does not capitulate to the inferribility model. And there is nothing odd about explanations that appeal to a factor which could have been appealed to equally well if the outcome had been different from what it was, or about explanations that appeal to a factor which is necessarily connected with the outcome that occurs. (Only if the outcome was necessarily connected with the antecedent could it be suggested that the causal explanation was redundant, given the occurrence of the effect.)

What, then, of the *Verstehen* theory? It is a simple, though important, special case of the general procedure of modeling, the special feature being that the model in this case is oneself. But a good electrician experiences the same sense of insight when he hits upon the explanation of a circuit deficiency, and a good theoretical mathematician has corresponding moments of "understanding." The *Verstehen* theorists were right in supposing that there was something special about the behavioral sciences—but it was only that here alone the model of *one's own* behavior can be employed. They were wrong in supposing that this gave them some deeper understanding than could be obtained by the expert wholly imbued with the workings of a mechanical model of the operation of the human fingers, for example. *Verstehen* has its own pitfalls arising from the erroneous transfer of the idiosyncrasies of the observer to the subject of observation, pitfalls which have led to the errors of cultural egocentrism in anthropology and corresponding mistakes in the attempts of clinical psychologists to understand the motivations of hereditarians or minority-group patients. But the positivists were quite wrong in supposing that the *Verstehen* approach could not provide knowledge and that it was essentially different from the procedures of physical scientists in understanding the phenomena of interest to them.

To conclude: there comes a time in the affairs of science and philosophy when nothing is so valuable as hardheadedness. Positivism brought that hardheadedness to philosophy, and perhaps to some parts of science, at a time when it was needed. Hard heads usually have to be thick heads, and it is no surprise to discover in the cool of later years that the issues were not quite so simple as they then appeared. Nevertheless, revolutions are fought by men who lack finesse, and without them we would still be in a rather primitive state. We must pay tribute to the revolutionary while avoiding the mistake of deifying his doctrine.

HILARY PUTNAM

logical positivism and the philosophy of mind

Any discussion of the influence of logical positivism on the field of philosophy of mind will have to include the application of the so-called verifiability theory of meaning to the problems of this field. Also deserving attention, however, is the way in which Carnap and some of his followers have treated psychological terms—including everyday psychological terms such as "pain"—as what in their own special sense they called theoretical terms; they have suggested that the states referred to by those theoretical terms might, in reality, be neurophysiological states of the brain.

The two lines of thought mentioned roughly correspond to two temporal stages in the development of the movement. During the early years (1928–36) attempts were made to apply verificationist ideas in a wholesale and simplistic manner to all the problems of philosophy, including the philosophy of mind. In recent years (1955 to the present) a much more sophisticated analysis has been offered, but it is one heavily weighted with the observational-theoretical dichotomy and with the idea of a "partially interpreted calculus." Feigl's identity theory,[1] while very much an individual doctrine and never the view of the whole school, fits chronologically into the transitional years between the two periods.

These two lines of thought also correspond to decidedly different tendencies warring within the divided logical-positivist soul. Verificationism, I think, may fairly be labeled an "idealist" tendency; for, even if it is not identical with the view that the "hard facts" are just actual and potential experiences, it makes little sense to anyone who does not have some such metaphysical conviction lurking in his heart. The view that mental states are really neurophysiological states is, on the other hand, a classical materialist view. And Feigl's identity theory is an attempt to reconcile the view that all events are physical (a version of materialism) with the view that there are "raw feels" (Feigl's term for sense data) and that each of us has a concept of these "raw feels" which is radically independent of public language. In short, Feigl seeks to keep the private entities of classical empiricism but to incorporate them somehow into the world scheme of classical materialism.

My criticisms of logical positivism are basically two: that verificationism is both wrong in itself and incompatible with the materialism to which the logical-positivist philosophers clearly feel attracted; and that the particular versions of materialism developed by these philosophers are not tenable, even though materialism as a tendency in the philosophy of mind *is* tenable, I believe.

The criticism that verificationism is wrong in itself needs little arguing. It simply is not the case that in any customary sense of the term "meaning" only those linguistic expressions which have a method of verification are meaningful. Indeed, in any customary sense of the phrase "method of verification," it is not linguistic expressions, but rather what linguistic expressions are used to say, that has a method of verification. This latter criticism can

1. Herbert Feigl, "The 'Mental' and the 'Physical,' " in *Minnesota Studies in the Philosophy of Science,* vol. 2, ed. H. Feigl, M. Scriven, and G. Maxwell (Minneapolis, University of Minnesota Press, 1958).

perhaps be turned by saying that a linguistic expression (say, a sentence type) may stand in the triadic relation

$$S \text{ is verifiable as understood by } O \text{ at time } t, \quad (1)$$

and to say "S is verifiable" is simply a harmless abstraction from a particular speaker O (or class of speakers) at a particular time t (or class of times). But, even if we allow this, it still remains the case that there are many, many sentences which are meaningful in the customary sense—that is, which are fully grammatical, occur in standard contexts, do not evoke *linguistic* puzzlement by hearers, are readily paraphrased—but which are not verifiable. One reply that logical positivists sometimes offer to this objection is that their theory of meaning is an *explication,* not a description of usage, and that an explication need not conform exactly to pre-analytic usage. This reply is disingenuous, however. For, in order that it should do what the positivists wanted it to do—rule out metaphysics, normative ethics, etc.—it was necessary that their explication of the term "meaning" *fail* to capture the customary linguistic notion of *meaning.* What we have here is a *persuasive redefinition* and not an explication at all.

The positivists recognized this early and gave up claiming that they explicated the notion of "meaning." Instead, they began to speak of *kinds of meaning.* One kind, they claimed, is "cognitive meaning," and *this* is what they explicated. I shall not discuss this move except to note that (1) I don't know what a *kind* of meaning would be and (2) in practice, being "cognitively meaningful" simply comes to *having a truth value.* Thus, what the positivist really did was to shift from the claim that being meaningful is the same as being verifiable to the quite different claim that having a truth value is the same as being verifiable. But this claim also is untenable. The sentence

There is a gold mountain one mile high and no one knows
that there is a gold mountain one mile high (2)

is, if true, unverifiable. No conceivable experience can show that both conjuncts in (2) are simultaneously true; for any experience that verified the first conjunct would falsify the second, and thus the whole sentence. Yet no one has ever offered the slightest reason for one to think that (2) could not be true in some possible world.

One might meet this difficulty by pointing out that (2) can be falsified, even if it cannot be verified, because any discovery that there is no gold mountain one mile high would falsify (2). But

There is a gold mountain one mile high and absolute goodness exists (3)

is also falsifiable, but not verifiable, and no positivist would want to say that (3) taken as a whole was "cognitively meaningful" (of course, the first conjunct is "cognitively meaningful").

More important than such *outré* examples, perhaps, is the following reflection. Let us assume that the methods of confirmation and disconfirmation which scientists implicitly use are in principle capable of being formalized. Then note the following theorem about inductive logics:[2] given any formalized inductive method (i.e., any formal method for deciding which hypotheses to accept and which hypotheses to reject, or for deciding what quantitative weights are to be assigned to hypotheses, in case one does not like the dichotomy "accept-reject"), there exist hypotheses containing only observation predicates, which, if true, cannot be discovered to be true by the given inductive logic. In short, if human beings are induction machines—which certainly is the

---

2. For inductive logics based on degree of confirmation, this is proved in my paper "'Degree of Confirmation' and Inductive Logic," in *The Philosophy of Rudolf Carnap,* ed. P. A. Schilpp Open Court (La Salle, Ill.: Open Court, 1963), pp. 761–84). In that paper I propose a method M which somewhat mitigates this result, at least for simple universal laws ("effective hypotheses"). However, by extending the result in that paper, it can be shown that there are hypotheses which, if true, cannot be discovered to be true even by M; these hypotheses have mixed quantifiers in the prefix (i.e., they have the form "for every x there is a y such that . . ."). In general one can show that *no* formalized inductive logic has the property that for *every* hypothesis H expressible in observational language, if one's evidence e_n consists of an exhaustive description of the first n objects in the universe as $n = 1, 2, 3 \ldots$, then for some N, if H is true, the logic will assign a "high" value to H on e_n whenever $n > N$. This will be shown in a forthcoming note.

materialist view[3]—then it is not true that, given a meaningful statement, even in "observation language," one could *always* discover the truth value of that statement on the basis of a finite amount of observational material using a fixed induction program. It was with this theorem in mind that I spoke before of an incompatibility between verificationism and materialism (though not, of course, in a strict deductive sense); for, given a classical materialist view of those statements which have a truth value, and given the knowledge that a modern materialist has concerning Turing machines, unsolvable problems, etc., it is easy to see that the class of "cognitively meaningful" sentences does *not* necessarily coincide with the class of sentences whose truth value scientists could in principle discover on the basis of a finite amount of observational material.

As is well known, logical positivists have recently shifted from the criterion "a sentence has a truth-value if and only if it is confirmable (disconfirmable) in principle" to the criterion "a sentence has a truth-value if and only if it is a well-formed formula of an 'empiricist language.' " [4] It is required that the primitives of an empiricist language be either observation terms or linked to observational terms by confirmable theories; but it is required of an arbitrary sentence only that it be built out of the primitives in accordance with the usual formation rules.

This last criterion does not seem plausible to me either, but discussion lies beyond the scope of the present paper.[5] It should be noted that just the "hypotheses" that the logical positivists originally wanted to proscribe—for example, that the world con-

---

3. This materialist view may be summed up by the following extension of Church's thesis to *inductive* logic: no system of inductive logic, that is, no system of exact directions for deciding what hypotheses to accept, or what weight to assign to hypotheses, etc., on the basis of given evidence, a given list of proposed hypotheses, etc., can be employed by a human computer unless it can also be employed by a Turing machine.

4. C. G. Hempel, "Problems and Changes in the Empiricist Criterion of Meaning," in *Logical Positivism*, ed. A. J. Ayer (Glencoe, Ill., 1959).

5. The view of scientific theory that it presupposes is discussed in my paper "What Theories Are Not," in *Logic, Methodology, and Philosophy of Science*, ed. Nagel, Suppes, and Tarski (Stanford, 1961).

sists of nothing but sensations—would appear *not* to be ruled out by such a formulation. This, however, seems to me not to be a defect; I believe that the statement that the world consists only of sensations has a truth value, falsity. Nevertheless, the positivists were right in feeling that this statement was an extremely queer one, although wrong in diagnosing the *nature* of its queerness (what is queer about it is *not* that it is unverifiable but that there cannot be a world consisting *only* of sensations). So we are in a strange position. The positivists called our attention to an interesting problem: what is queer about such statements as "the world consists only of sensations"? But they did not solve the problem. Once we come to see that what is wrong with "the world consists only of sensations," "I have sensations but no other human being does," "the world came into existence five minutes ago," etc., is not *just* unverifiability, and not *primarily* unverifiability, we may be less tempted to take verifiability as a criterion for *either* meaningfulness *or* possessing a truth value.

The application that was made of verificationism to the philosophy of mind was a simple one. The positivists, as is well known, shifted early from phenomenalism to physicalism, that is, they shifted from the view that the events that verify scientific propositions are subjective events (*my* experiences) to the view that they are public events involving "observable things" and "observation predicates." After this shift it became natural for them to reason as follows: "What verifies such a statement as 'John is in pain' is John's behavior. Knowing what a sentence means is closely linked to knowing what verifies that sentence. So knowing what pain means—or, what comes to the same thing, what is meant by such sentences as 'John is in pain,' 'John has a pain in his arm,' etc.— is knowing what *kind of behavior* shows that a person is in pain."

In this way there arose the idea that certain statements of the form "Normally a person who behaves in such-and-such a way has a pain in his arm" are true by virtue of the meaning of the word "pain," or more loosely, that some particular connections between pain and pain behavior are built into the concept of pain, in the sense that no one can be totally ignorant of those connections and have that concept.

I have argued in other papers[6] that this idea is quite mistaken, and I shall not repeat the argument in detail here. Suffice it to say that with a little imagination one can easily imagine worlds in which people feel pain but manifest it in the most extraordinary ways (or do not manifest it at all). Moreover, such people might have the concept of pain by any sane standard, but they certainly would not believe that, for example, normally when someone winces he is in pain (because this would be false in their world). Possessing the concept of pain simply is *not* the same thing as knowing what connections in fact obtain between pain and pain behavior.

How do we know that others are in pain when they are? The positivists' answer to this question depended on two views: (1) to know the meaning of the word "pain" *is* simply to know that when people behave in certain ways they are probably in pain and (2) it is a necessary truth that when people behave in those ways they are probably in pain. Thus, the positivists' failure to answer successfully the question "What is it to have the concept of pain?" involved them in a failure to answer successfully a much more traditional philosophical question, "How do we know what others are feeling?"

I want to suggest that the solution to each of these problems lies elsewhere than where the positivists sought. Let me begin with the problem of other minds. I think that we should neither minimize the difficulty of that problem nor overlook the extent to which that difficulty may stem from the overwhelming difficulty of understanding the procedures of empirical inquiry—especially if we are restricted to armchair reflection.

The first fact that has to be noted in connection with such terms as "pain" is that they *enter into explanations.* Indeed, just how much of the behavior of others *can* we explain at all perspicuously *without* using some psychological term or other? The second fact that has to be noted is that *no other explanation is in*

6. "Dreaming and 'Depth Grammar,'" in *Analytic Philosophy, First Series,* ed. R. J. Butler (Oxford: Blackwell, 1961), and "Brains and Behavior," in *Analytical Philosophy, Second Series,* ed. R. J. Butler (Oxford: Blackwell, 1965).

the field, at least not at the moment. If Othello did not strangle Desdemona because he was jealous, then I do not know why he did. And, if no alternative explanation is available in this single case, how much less do we possess an explanation of behavior which would cover *all* cases at least as well as present-day mentalistic explanation does, and without using a single such notion as pain, jealousy, belief, etc.

So far I have suggested that we are justified in accepting the usual psychological explanation scheme because of its explanatory success and the lack of a real alternative. And, of course, if we are justified in accepting the general scheme (and this means accepting many general principles and many specific explanations), then there is no mystery about how we are justified in accepting or rejecting any given proposed new application of the scheme. But am I, then, saying that the existence of others' pain, jealousy, belief, etc., is an *empirical hypothesis?*

The answer has to be a straightforward "Yes and no." The question, first of all, is not the acceptance of one statement—for example, "Other humans have feelings"—but the acceptance of a whole conceptual system, as Ziff [7] has stressed recently. The acceptance of that conceptual system, or explanatory scheme, is justified, as is the acceptance of many an empirical hypothesis, by the joint facts of explanatory power and no real alternative. But that does not mean that that scheme or system fits the usual paradigm of an "empirical hypothesis."

It would take a long paper to cover all of the differences, for example, that no alternative was *ever* in the field, although different *applications* of the scheme and different proposed *extensions* of the scheme (e.g., psychoanalysis) are very much with us. And, of course, I am not suggesting that the following sequence of events took place—that there was a primitive time at which no one supposed that anyone else had feelings; that some primitive genius suggested the "hypothesis" that others did have feelings; and that this "hypothesis" was accepted because it led to more successful prediction and explanation than did some alternatives.

7. "The Simplicity of Other Minds," *Philosophic Turnings* (Ithaca, N.Y.: Cornell University Press, 1966).

Nevertheless, I *am* suggesting that each of us has an *empirical justification,* in a good sense of the term, for accepting the explanatory scheme we have been talking about.

The most difficult problem is to dispose of such "hypotheses" as the one according to which other human bodies are really moved by a demon[8] whose chief aim is to fool me into thinking falsely that those bodies are the bodies of conscious persons. It is easy to "explain" specific pieces of behavior on the basis of this hypothesis: for example, one could "explain" why Othello strangled Desdemona by saying that the demon caused him to go through those motions because the demon wished me to believe that Othello was experiencing jealousy. And such a "hypothesis" may easily be elaborated so as to lead to predictions—indeed, to *just* the predictions that usual theory leads to, and without explicitly mentioning usual theory. It suffices that wherever usual theory (which is, of course, implicit) states that people who are jealous normally do $X,$ demon theory should state that, when the demon wishes some body to act as if it were the body of a person experiencing jealousy, he normally makes that body do $X.$

The nub of the matter is that, inasmuch as usual theory and demon theory lead to the same predictions, our grounds for preferring usual theory, and for not considering demon theory to be even "in the field," must be a priori ones. And, indeed, it seems that, in large part, the methods of empirical inquiry must be methods for *assigning an a priori preference ordering* (or, better, a *partly a priori* preference ordering) to hypotheses. What these methods are is something we today know little of; it is relatively easy to show that the vague talk about simplicity one commonly hears achieves nothing at all. My own view is that it is only by hard *empirical* research, including research into the construction of *machines that learn,* that we will ever obtain an answer. Philosophical reflection cannot do it—or, at least there is not one shred of evidence to show that it can. But that does not change the fact that we *do* hold demon theory to be so much less plausible a priori than is usual theory that we do not need to consider

8. See Alvin Plantinga's reply to Ziff in the *Journal of Philosophy,* 62 (1965).

it (unless it is modified to lead to *different* predictions than usual theory does). Just as we know that "Chair the on is floor the" is an ungrammatical sentence even without possessing a transformational grammar of English, so we sometimes know which theories are a priori more plausible than others, without possessing an adequate formalization of the methods of empirical inquiry.

I have now argued that we are entitled to believe certain statements which ascribe pain, etc., to other humans, on grounds that are broadly empirical (the explanatory power of usual theory as a whole, and the lack of a real alternative). I have nowhere suggested that this depends on regarding any part of usual theory as "analytic" or, more weakly, as presupposed by the concepts of pain, anger, etc. *That* issue, however, is not too relevant here. For, if *any* part of usual theory is "analytic," it surely is *not* the part that describes how people normally behave when they are in pain, etc., nor the part that says that people who are exhibiting certain kinds of behavior are usually in pain.[9] Perhaps the meaning of the psychological words does impose *some* constraints on usual theory, but, in any case, not *those* constraints.

The issue of verificationism which we raised at the outset seems also to have been bypassed, at least to some extent. It is compatible with the position taken here that every "cognitively meaningful" statement should be capable of incorporation into a scientific theory which, *taken as a whole,* is confirmable (although I believe even that to be false[10]); what is not compatible with the position taken here is that every "cognitively meaningful" statement should be confirmable in isolation, simply by virtue of what it means. (Thus my criticism of the positivist answer to the "How do we know" question bears a certain relation to Quine's criticisms of verificationism.)

9. For a thorough discussion of this issue, see Putnam, "Brains and Behavior."

10. If to be "incorporated" into a theory T means to be a logical consequence of T, then the existence of *observation sentences* that cannot be incorporated into any hypothesis confirmable by a given inductive logic is a consequence of the theorem mentioned in note 2. If it is not even true that every observation sentence has this property, then there seems to be no reason at all for believing that every significant "theoretical sentence" has it.

It is now time to turn to the Positivist answer to the "What do we mean" question. To say what we mean by such a word as "pain" is, in a sense, a silly enterprise. "Pain" is a word we acquire through ostensive teaching (alas!). But we may instead raise a question about what conditions one must fulfill in order to have the concept of pain. It seems to me that three conditions (at least) are essential:

1. When one sincerely reports "I have a pain in my arm," one must in general be reporting a *pain* and not something else.

2. One must have the *reporting use*.

3. One must be able to imagine that others are in pain, and one must possess the linguistic capacity to use such sentences as "There is a pain in John's arm" to express what one believes or imagines.

The first condition, perhaps, has not been mentioned often, because of the traditional view in the philosophy of language that any concept (or intension) *determines* its referent. What I am suggesting is that any empirical evidence which might tend to show that certain people are not in what *we* call "pain" when they are in what *they* call "pain" would also tend to show that they had a different concept; but there need not be any way of showing that they have a different concept *other* than by showing that what is behind their reports is not *pain*. The fact that we can permissibly use the concept of pain in explicating the concept of having the concept of pain seems to have been overlooked.

The second condition involves the difficulty that the reporting use of "pain" involves uttering pain utterances partly *because* one is in pain; yet reporting pain by means of a grammatical report is somehow very different from a mere cry. The fact is that a complex causal interaction is involved here which includes both pain and linguistic habits, and today we can give neither a theory nor a perspicuous description of that interaction. Still, we can recognize it well enough when it takes place.

The third condition is, of course, a classical one. It has been dismissed in recent times on the ground that knowing the so-called picture meaning of such sentences as "John has a pain in his arm" is *irrelevant:* what one needs to know is the "cognitive meaning," that is, the method of verification. I am suggesting that, on the contrary, the picture meaning *is* part of the meaning of *pain,* in any customary sense of *meaning,* and that the method of verification is not.

Let me turn now to late positivist doctrine and, in particular, to the doctrine that psychological terms are theoretical terms.[11] Crudely, what this amounts to is the following: the terms "pain," "anger," etc., are implicitly defined by a theory, that is, by a body of beliefs which has testable consequences involving behavior. What we mean by these terms is those states of organisms $P_1, P_2, \ldots, P_n$ such that $T(P_1, P_2, \ldots, P_n)$, where $T(P_1, P_2, \ldots, P_n)$ is what usual theory (in a suitable formalization) becomes when we regard the psychological terms $P_1, P_2, \ldots, P_n$ as mere *second-order variables.* Note that in this view the psychological terms have to be *simultaneously* implicitly defined; they cannot be individually defined. Also, the logic of such implicit definition is complex: Carnap has proposed to invoke the somewhat esoteric Hilbert ϵ-symbol in order to formalize it.[12] However, the general content of the doctrine is clear enough; it is also clearly false, for *no* particular body of connections between behavior and pain, anger, etc., nor, a fortiori, any theory which implies such connections, is presupposed by the meaning of pain, anger, etc.

We have here a confusion of two ideas. There is the idea that our grounds for accepting the conceptual scheme of psychology— be it scientific psychology or common-sense mentalistic psychology —are broadly empirical in nature and not completely unlike the grounds for accepting a scientific theory; this, I have urged, is correct. Then there is the idea that the terms occurring in a theory have no meaning apart from the theory; and this is a false doctrine, not just in the case of psychology, but in general. Moreover, it is a doctrine which arises from the positivists' lack of interest in the customary notion of meaning. (Linguistics is

11. Rudolf Carnap, "The Methodological Character of Theoretical Concepts," in *Minnesota Studies in the Philosophy of Science,* vol. 1, ed. H. Feigl and M. Scriven (Minneapolis: University of Minnesota Press, 1956).
12. Rudolf Carnap, "On the Use of Hilbert's ϵ-operator in Scientific Theories," in *Essays on the Foundations of Mathematics,* ed. A. Robinson (Jerusalem, 1961), pp. 156–63.

the science the positivists have cared least about.) Of course, the positivists might reply that we ought to *change* our customary notions of meaning and truth to fit their rational reconstruction. I do not believe that any good reasons exist for making such a change; but I shall not discuss this here.

The claim that pain might really be a brain state is easily defended in Carnap's view: we have only to note that "pain," "anger," etc., mean P_1, P_2, etc., where P_1, P_2, . . . , P_n are many states which bear certain causal relations to one another and to behavior, namely, the relations specified by $T(P_1, . . . , P_n)$. Inasmuch as it is trivial that there may be brain states which are so related to one another and to behavior, it follows that "pain," "anger," etc., may refer to brain states. Unfortunately, this argument rests on two false premises: the premise concerning the meaning of theoretical terms which has just been criticized, and the premise that "pain," "anger," etc., are theoretical terms in the positivistic sense. This latter premise is false because these terms have a reporting use and thus would not be implicitly defined *merely* by a theory, even if it were true that theoretical terms are characteristically so defined.

We come, therefore, to the problem of the positivists' relation to materialism. Perhaps the safest statement of materialism is this: that a whole human being is simply a physical system with a certain complex functional organization. This version of materialism is certainly tenable and probably correct, I believe. The difficulty is that, in itself, this version of materialism says nothing about such specific mental states as pain and anger; and, from Hobbes to Carnap, materialists have come to grief when they have tried to fill this lacuna. The difficulty appears to have been a certain limitation of imagination. If a whole human being is just a physical system, then pain, anger, etc., must be physical states, for—what else could they be?

I have proposed elsewhere the view that there is a special kind of state, the *functional* state, the notion of which comes from cybernetics and automata theory, which is a natural candidate for a modern materialist theory of mental states. I stress that this suggestion—the suggestion that mental states are, in reality, functional states of certain naturally evolved "systems"—is not meant to be part of the meaning of mental words. I have already urged in this paper that very little indeed is "part of the meaning" of mental words. What I have in mind is an empirical identification on all fours with the claim that heat is average kinetic energy.

Some materialists may prefer the tentative identification of mental states with brain states. Difficulties will arise, however, as soon as we begin to make cross-specific comparisons. The neurophysiological counterpart of pain may well be one thing in a man and another in, say, an octopus. Even if one decides to say "Well and good. Then *pain* is one thing in a man and a different thing in an octopus," one will be left with the problem of explicating the higher-order property of *being a pain;* and *this* property, I now suggest, will not be a physicochemical one, but a functional one, that is, a role in the "organization" of a "system." If any version of materialism is to be defended—be it a brain-state theory or a functional-state theory—the defense will have to involve a study of the logic of theoretical identification, and especially the theoretical identification of *properties*. It cannot be defended merely by reference to the idea of scientific theories as "partially interpreted calculi."

The upshot of this discussion is not as wholly critical as it might seem at first. The greatest weakness of positivism, in the philosophy of mind as elsewhere, is that it tries to make the notion of meaning bear too heavy a burden. This is always a bad tendency in analytic philosophy, but it is fatal in a school which begins by scrapping the customary notion of meaning anyway, and which has seriously examined every science *except* linguistics. However, the school also has real merits. It has emphasized the importance of considering whole theories and not just isolated propositions, which is an important insight. It has stressed the importance of the fact that psychological concepts are used in *explanations*, whereas that fact has often been ignored, or its significance (in connection with the "other minds" issue) minimized. It has pioneered the studies of the logic of theory confirmation and the logic of empirical identification; I have been urging that these are two topics on which we desperately need more knowledge in the philosophy of mind. Above all, it has stressed the intellectual integrity of science and the importance of science as a way of trying to determine the nature of all things —including man's mind. It is these tendencies of logical positivism which I should like to see continued. I believe that the tendency to *philosophically reinterpret* science, which has always been a characteristic of empiricism, far from being a stimulus to the sound methodological work that empiricism, and, in the present century, logical positivism, have inspired, has been the main source of error in these movements. Science does not need positivistic interpretation; but, in the spirit of the best positivist work, it very much needs an analysis of its methods.

editors'
epilogue

STEPHEN F. BARKER

logical positivism and the philosophy of mathematics

More than most other movements in recent philosophy, logical
positivism constituted a "school" of thought. As a result of their
extensive collaborative discussions over a period of years, the
logical positivists came to share not only a common spirit and
orientation in their approach to philosophical problems but also
a distinctive set of explicit basic doctrines (these doctrines they
derived more from Wittgenstein than from any other single
source). In their stream of published articles and books they
reiterated these distinctive doctrines so often and in so much the
same terms that it has come to make reasonable sense to speak
of "the logical-positivist position" here. Let us start by considering these doctrines; this will lead us toward the main topic of
this essay, the logical positivists' philosophy of mathematics.
Their general conception of mathematics will be considered, and
after that the difference between their view of arithmetic and
their view of geometry will be discussed.

STEPHEN F. BARKER

One basic preliminary doctrine of the logical positivists was that there are sharp distinctions to be drawn between the analytic and the synthetic and between the a priori and the empirical. They held that every proposition (often they said every sentence) is either analytic or synthetic (either its truth or falsity is determined by considerations of logical consistency alone, or it has factual content). And they held that whenever someone knows something his knowledge is either a priori or empirical (either not requiring evidence drawn from sense experience, or dependent upon such evidence). The view that these distinctions are sharp and clear had of course been maintained by many earlier philosophers, especially by Kant and also by Hume. It had been actively denied by absolute idealists and by pragmatists, whom, however, the logical positivists tended to dismiss as woolly thinkers innocent of logic. The logical positivists felt satisfied that brief characterizations of these distinctions are sufficient to establish them[1] and thus to clear the way for the stating of more exciting doctrines that employ these distinctions.

To us today, made warier by Quine's strictures,[2] it may seem evident that the logical positivists were uncritical in so readily taking for granted that the a priori–empirical and analytic-synthetic distinctions are sharp and clear. As early as 1936 Quine had incisively voiced his skepticism about the analytic-synthetic distinction,[3] and in later years his attack upon it gathered momentum. Quine objected that those who made much of the analytic-synthetic distinction had not succeeded in showing that the distinction in the end amounts to any more than just a differ-

1. Carnap's writings do contain extensive discussions of the concept of analyticity in formalized languages. However, he also used the concept of analyticity in philosophical discussion of sentences drawn from natural language and did not feel any need for extensive clarification or defense of such usage.

2. W. V. Quine, "Two Dogmas of Empiricism," *Philosophical Review*, 60; this essay is reprinted in Quine's *From a Logical Point of View*, 2d ed. (Cambridge, Mass., 1961). See also his *Word and Object* (New York, 1960).

3. W. V. Quine, "Truth by Convention," in *Philosophical Essays for A. N. Whitehead*, ed. O. H. Lee (New York, 1936); this essay is now reprinted in Quine's *The Ways of Paradox* (New York, 1966).

ence in the degree of tenacity with which sentences are maintained in the face of recalcitrant sense experience. If, in the end, analytic sentences are in general merely those whose truth or falsity we rather tenaciously maintain, while synthetic sentences are those less tenaciously maintained, then the analytic-synthetic distinction is of little philosophical importance—it cannot be used in philosophy as the logical positivists intended. In effect, Quine was equally attacking the a priori–empirical distinction: he did not distinguish between the one distinction and the other —being skeptical of both, he did not believe it was incumbent on him to do so.

In several respects, the logical positivists' glib view of the analytic-synthetic distinction left them wide open to attack. For one thing, they spoke of *sentences* as the items that are analytic or synthetic, and often operated with examples as though they thought that certain sentences in our language are inherently analytic and others inherently synthetic. They could have made their case less implausible had they emphasized that often a sentence when understood in one way is used to say something analytic and when understood in another way, to say something synthetic. For another thing, they showed little recognition of the "open texture" of language (the ineradicable vagueness of actual language that Wittgenstein and Waismann came to stress), and in their treatment of examples they proceeded as though they were entitled to be confident that every assertion is either definitely analytic or definitely synthetic. Their distinction could have been made to seem less implausible had it been frankly admitted that often the established meanings of terms in a sentence are open-textured in such a way that what is being said by one who uses the sentence, understanding the terms in their normal senses, is neither definitely analytic nor definitely synthetic. For example, when its terms are taken in their standard senses, does the sentence "A person knows something only when his belief is based on evidence" express something analytic or something synthetic? It is doubtful that there is any definitely correct answer here, for our standard sense of the word "knows" seems open and indefinite with respect to this.

However, even though it may be the case that in our language such examples are numerous, and even though the philosophically most important examples generally are of this type, still it does not necessarily follow that the analytic-synthetic distinction is rendered worthless. For perhaps it is of philosophical value to have the notions of the analytic and the synthetic as polar opposites, comparison with which can illuminate the status even of assertions that do not belong at either pole. Thus, if we are interested in understanding the concept of knowledge, it may be helpful to ask how close to being analytic the assertion is that knowledge never occurs without evidence; that is, to what extent does a person's not having *evidence* for a proposition tend in and of itself to establish that he does not *know* whether the proposition is true? If the concept of knowledge is hazy, we shall get a hazy answer; but the notions of the analytic and synthetic may aid us in carrying out such conceptual inquiries. It should be granted that the question "Is it analytic or synthetic?" is a bad question if it is asked with the presupposition that there must always exist a definite yes-or-no answer. Yet it may often be a rather good question to ask if we ask it in a spirit of inquiry and are ready to be satisfied should the answer turn out to be that, fundamentally, there are various conflicting tendencies present in our established uses of the key words in the example, tendencies in different directions which do not add up to any definite yes or no.

The general question of the legitimacy of the analytic-synthetic distinction is far too large to be treated here, however. Suffice it to say that the logical positivists overrated the clarity and sharpness of this distinction, just as elsewhere in their philosophy they overrated their distinctions between the cognitively meaningful and the cognitively meaningless, and between observational language and theoretical language. Nevertheless, it can be argued that the analytic-synthetic distinction is of philosophical value when properly qualified. For the sake of argument let us suppose that this is so—and let us pass on to notice the further doctrines —ones more exciting to them—that the logical positivists stated in terms of this distinction.

Foremost among these is the doctrine that there is no a priori knowledge of synthetic propositions. In holding this, the logical positivists were agreeing with Hume but disagreeing with Kant and with rationalism generally. They believed it to be of the greatest philosophical importance to demolish the rationalistic idea that the human mind has a power of a priori insight into synthetic matters of fact. Claims to possess such knowledge they regarded as dogmatic, mystical, and antiscientific. Therefore, they made it a cornerstone of their philosophical position that there is no synthetic a priori knowledge. This doctrine has the effect of conflating the a priori with the analytic and the synthetic with the empirical: a priori knowledge they held to be possible only of analytic truths; and it was thought that the truth or falsity of synthetic propositions could be known only empirically. However, it is worth noting that this conflation is best construed not as a claim that the term "analytic" is arbitrarily defined as "knowable a priori" but rather as a claim that reflection shows that whatever falls under the concept of the a priori must also fall under the concept of the analytic. To regard the doctrine that there is no synthetic a priori knowledge as important is to presume that two separate distinctions have been made, that between the a priori and the empirical and that between the analytic and the synthetic—so that it can be *discovered* that only analytic propositions are knowable a priori. If there had been only one distinction to begin with, that is, if the term "analytic" were arbitrarily defined at the outset as a synonym for "knowable a priori," then the thesis that there is no non-analytic a priori knowledge would be an utterly uninteresting truism and would not serve to express the philosophical view that the human mind lacks the power of rational insight into reality. Alas, the logical positivists were not careful about this point (their view of the nature of a priori knowledge made it difficult for them to recognize the possibility of conceptual discoveries), and as a result their arguments against alleged examples of synthetic a priori knowledge often were rather question-begging.

Passing on now to doctrines that are distinctive of logical positivism, let us mention in turn their special view of the character of synthetic propositions and that of the character of analytic propositions. With regard to synthetic propositions the verifiability principle, that controversial scourge of metaphysics, was their novel and distinctive doctrine. Its most infamous yet most suggestive formulation was "The meaning of a sentence is the method of its verification" (this seems to have been proposed to the Vienna Circle by Wittgenstein). In this formulation the principle means both that a sentence purporting to express a synthetic proposition is "cognitively meaningful" if and only if it is verifiable, and that its verifiable implications are what constitute its meaning—what you must consider if you want to grasp what it means.

With regard to analytic propositions, they also held a novel and distinctive doctrine, a linguistic theory of the analytic. Their view of the nature of the analytic contrasts with the rationalistic type of view that Frege had maintained. He had held that in grasping the laws of logic (which for him were the basic analytic truths) the mind through its rational power is apprehending non-empirical necessary truths about reality.[4] Such a view of the analytic was too much in the same spirit as the idea of the synthetic a priori to be to the taste of the logical positivists. Therefore they enthusiastically welcomed and embraced Wittgenstein's liberating teaching in the *Tractatus Logico-Philosophicus* that all logical laws, and indeed all analytic truths, are tautologies, which do not *say* anything but merely *show* the structure of language.[5] Schlick had independently emphasized the "empty" and "formal" character of deductive inference, a notion akin to Wittgenstein's though less radical.[6] In the *Tractatus* Wittgenstein had used the term "tautology" in a narrow truth-functional sense and had required that all other analytic truths be reducible to truth-functional tautologies in order that their dependency merely upon linguistic conventions be assured. The logical positivists, however, felt no hesitation about extending the linguistic theory to cover all analytic propositions as such, irrespective of whether or not they are reducible to truth-

4. G. Frege, *Die Grundlagen der Arithmetic* (Breslau, 1884), translated into English as *The Foundations of Arithmetic* (Oxford, 1950); see especially sec. 105.
5. *Tractatus Logico-Philosophicus* (London, 1922).
6. Moritz Schlick, *Allgemeine Erkenntnislehre*, 2d ed. (Vienna, 1925).

functional tautologies (in this they may have been following oral suggestions of Wittgenstein). In their view, then, analytic truths are necessarily and incontrovertibly true, for by knowing the conventions of our language we can tell a priori that no empirical evidence could possibly overturn these truths. However, they gain this assured status at the expense of content, for they are essentially verbal and are true merely because they express linguistic conventions. As the logical positivists often put it, analytic assertions are *empty* and *without content;* they do not *describe* anything, they do not *convey information,* they do not *state facts,* they are not *about objects;* sometimes it was even said that they are merely *about language.*[7] Such affirmations did little to clarify matters, although they did have the air of making the theory decisive.[8] Moreover, the logical positivists believed that the conventions of language are alterable by us at will, and that this meant that by changing our linguistic conventions we could make what are now analytic truths into falsehoods. Thus analytic truth was regarded as a matter of human fiat, not as eternal and unalterable.

In addition to these doctrines concerning the synthetic and analytic, the logical positivists also had other common doctrines, such as the idea of the unity of science. But the verifiability principle concerning the synthetic, and the linguistic theory concerning the analytic, constitute the central core of what defines the logical-positivist movement as a distinct school of philosophy. It was as a consequence of these central doctrines that Carnap came to draw a distinction between what he called "factual science" and what he called "formal science."[9] In studying a factual science, it was held, we are seeking to obtain empirical knowledge concerning the truth of synthetic sentences; such

7. Hans Hahn, "Logic, Mathematics and Knowledge of Nature," in *Logical Positivism,* ed. A. J. Ayer (Glencoe, Ill., 1959).

8. Is every analytic truth true by virtue of its *logical form,* that is, reducible to a logical truth by putting synonyms for synonyms? The logical positivists were equivocal in their discussions of this point; sometimes they affirmed it, sometimes they seemed to deny it. Arthur Pap's *Semantics and Necessary Truth* (New Haven, 1958) contains discussion of this issue.

9. Rudolf Carnap, "Formal and Factual Science," in H. Feigl and M. Brodbeck, eds., *Readings in the Philosophy of Science* (New York, 1953).

knowledge must be based on observation and experiment. In studying a formal science it was held that we are seeking to obtain a priori knowledge concerning the truth of analytic sentences; here all appeals to observation and experiment are unnecessary, for nothing is required beyond determining what linguistic conventions are to be assumed and investigating their consequences. The other essays in this volume mainly treat implications for the philosophy of science of the logical positivists' views about "factual science." This essay will try to fill out the picture by offering a critical account of some aspects of the way in which the logical positivists erected a philosophy of mathematics upon the foundation of their basic doctrines concerning the analytic.

MATHEMATICS AS TRUE BY CONVENTION

It was in the philosophy of mathematics that philosophers of the past had believed they could find their strongest support for the idea of the synthetic a priori. Kant, that archproponent of synthetic a priori knowledge, had held that the very clearest and most indisputable examples of synthetic a priori knowledge are to be found in mathematics. His examples are theses of arithmetic, such as "5 + 7 = 12," and theses of Euclidean geometry, such as "Two straight lines cannot enclose an area." Kant's position was that these clearly are not analytic, yet clearly their truth can be known a priori; and he believed that, if we recognize that we do possess synthetic a priori knowledge in mathematics, then we shall feel less reluctant to concede that we also possess such knowledge concerning the fundamental principles of natural science, concerning the moral law, and elsewhere. If only Hume had paid more careful attention to the nature of mathematics, Kant suggests, he would not have allowed his empiricism to lure his philosophy to shipwreck on the shores of skepticism.[10]

Some of the logical positivists themselves had at first felt the attraction of the older scheme of ideas and had flirted with the synthetic a priori in mathematics.[11] But, as the distinctive logical-

10. Immanuel Kant, *Prolegomena to Any Future Metaphysics* (1783), sec. 4.
11. Rudolf Carnap, *Der Raum,* published as supplementary volume 56 of *Kantstudien* (Berlin, 1922).

positivist viewpoint in philosophy crystallized, the idea of the synthetic a priori became its especial *bête noir* and there remained no room for sympathy with the older view of mathematics. A new philosophy of mathematics was called for which would comport with the linguistic theory of the analytic and with the verifiability of the synthetic. So far as these central doctrines went, it would have been possible for the logical positivists either to classify mathematics along with physics as a type of factual science or to classify it along with logic as a type of formal science. This was never an open question for them, however; a combination of powerful reasons compelled them from the start to reject the former alternative insofar as mathematics proper is concerned. The logical positivists themselves were well acquainted with mathematics and with mathematical logic and were keenly aware of the similarity in style and method. They were skilled and enthusiastic advocates of the new logic and regarded the "logistic thesis" of Frege and of Whitehead and Russell (the thesis that mathematics is reducible to logic) as a triumphant achievement of modern thought.[12] For them, there never was any question but that mathematics must be classified as a formal science.

The result was a general view of mathematics which assigned to it a strictly a priori character and affirmed the necessity of all mathematical truths. At the same time, it was stressed that these truths are analytic, not synthetic, and that this makes them true merely because of the conventions of our linguistic symbolism. Hence they are utterly empty of all factual information, without content, purely verbal. What kind of analytic truths belong to pure mathematics, to mathematics proper? The logical positivists did not always give the same answer to this question. But usually

---

12. There is, however, an ambivalence in their attitude toward the logistic thesis. Although they cite it with high regard, they do not make clear how they regard its philosophical importance. Do they believe that the reduction of arithmetic to logic provides the sole justification for the claim that the laws of arithmetic are analytic, or do they believe that even propositions which are not reducible to logical truths can be analytically true? Their high regard for the logistic thesis suggests the former, but their handling of many other examples suggests the latter.

they spoke as though pure mathematics is to be regarded as having for its analytic truths those truths expressed by such sentences as "$5 + 7 = 12$" and "$x + y = y + x$"—sentences which can be regarded as expressing truths that simply reflect the meanings of the symbols involved. And if it is asked why such truths should be considered important when they have been declared to be utterly empty and uninformative, then the answer is twofold. One point is that, although all sentences of pure mathematics are "empty" and "without content" in that they convey no empirical information about the world, nevertheless, in all but the most elementary cases mathematical propositions are not trivial in the sense of expressing only what everyone is fully aware of; far from it, for it often turns out that unexpected theorems hold. Moreover, the practical scientific value of mathematics results from the power that mathematics has to show us how from a factual statement expressed in one way we can mathematically extract unexpected consequences that were logically "contained in" it. Even the crude example "$5 + 7 = 12$" shows us how from a factual statement like "There are five sheep and seven others" we can extract the consequence "There are twelve sheep"—a kind of consequence which, especially in more complex cases, may be unforeseen and valuable. Thus Hempel spoke of mathematics as a "logical juice extractor." [13]

This philosophy of mathematics maintained that mathematical truth is dependent upon linguistic convention. Now, it is human decision which institutes certain conventions rather than others, and any existing convention could have been otherwise. It was therefore thought to follow as a clear consequence that mathematical truths are not eternal and immutable, but are alterable by human fiat. No doubt some linguistic conventions are more convenient than others, and very inconvenient conventions would be hard to live with (e.g., any scheme of conventions which would allow every well-formed formula of a mathematical system to be a theorem, was regarded by the logical positivists as highly inconvenient). But there is no higher standard than convenience, no

---

13. Carl G. Hempel, "On the Nature of Mathematical Truth," in *Readings in Philosophical Analysis*, ed. H. Feigl and W. Sellars (New York, 1949).

standard that can dictate or strictly require the choice of one scheme of linguistic conventions in preference to another.

This viewpoint found its fullest expression in Carnap's famous "Principle of Tolerance": it is not our business to set up prohibitions, he declared, but to arrive at conventions; "in logic, there are no morals." [14] By this he meant that there is no such thing as correctness for linguistic conventions; no set of conventions is more correct than any other. Now, a sentence that is analytic with respect to one set of linguistic conventions need not be so with respect to another; no sentence can inherently be an analytic truth, it can be one only relative to specified conventions. Important consequences for the philosophy of mathematics were held to follow from this. Carnap believed that his viewpoint resolved the philosophical controversies that had arisen concerning mathematical method. One such controversy was that between those who accepted and those who denied the legitimacy of the law of the excluded middle, of impredicative definitions, of the axiom of choice, and of other non-constructive conceptions. The resolution of the controversy consisted in dismissing it as a pseudoproblem, an essentially verbal dispute that had been mistaken for a real dispute. Brouwer and the other intuitionists advocated a set of linguistic conventions for mathematics according to which the law of the excluded middle is not analytic; their opponents recommend a scheme of conventions according to which it is. The parties to the dispute imagined that they were disagreeing about some real question, but actually, according to Carnap, it is only a matter of how one chooses to speak; neither language is more correct than the other.

The logical positivists' philosophy of mathematics not only proposed a novel account of the nature of mathematical truth; it also put forward this brisk technique for dissolution of all the outstanding controversies in the field of the philosophy of mathematics. For the future, Carnap held, philosophy should recognize as its proper study the investigation of the "logical syntax of language" (later he was to include also semantics); the task of the

14. Rudolf Carnap, *The Logical Syntax of Language* (London, 1937), p. 51.

philosopher will be no more and no less than simply to investigate the consequences of adopting various schemes of conventions.

All this, of course, had a brisk air of doing away with metaphysical nonsense. Yet there are flaws in the picture. One difficulty with the logical positivists' approach is that, instead of really dissolving the problems of the philosophy of mathematics, they merely turn away from them. For example, Carnap tells us that, if the conventions of a language allow indirect proofs and impredicative definitions, then mathematical theorems derivable only by these means will be analytic in that language; while, if the conventions of another language do not sanction such derivations, no such sentences will be analytic in that language. This is all very well; but should it satisfy someone who had been perplexed about the legitimacy of indirect proofs and impredicative definitions? Surely if there was serious perplexity it was not perplexity about whether there could be some scheme of linguistic conventions according to which formal transformations corresponding to these methods would be permitted. Surely any serious perplexity would be about whether or not our actual conventions are of this kind—the actual conventions that obtain in our discourse about numbers (especially the conventions governing use there of the phrases "it follows that" and "it is provable that"). The logical positivists had little sympathy for this kind of perplexity. Ordinary conventions are vague, they would have said; make your conventions precise and your questions (e.g., about the legitimacy of indirect proof) will answer themselves. But this is an evasion: the original perplexity concerned what our existing conventions permit, and it cannot be resolved merely by telling what would be permitted under different schemes of conventions. The perplexity arose because conflicting tendencies in our existing conventions make it difficult to see what these conventions do or do not permit. Perhaps it will turn out that our present conventions are indeed too hazy either definitely to permit or to forbid, say, indirect proofs in mathematics. But, if this is so, some effort should be made to establish it. The way to deal with the original perplexity is to examine existing conventions and *show* to what extent they are capable or incapable of yielding a definite verdict concerning the controversial methods. In his later writings, to be sure, Carnap did explicitly recognize that this task, which he called "clarifying the explicandum," can be a legitimate undertaking; but, like other logical positivists, he has engaged in it very little and has always seemed to suppose that the task of constructing new conventions is what is important.

Connected with this weakness in the logical positivists' treatment of controversies in the philosophy of mathematics are peculiarities in their conception of the task of philosophy itself. Carnap wrote that the proper study of philosophy is solely to investigate the different results (concerning what sentences are analytic, what sentences are derivable from what others, etc.) to which different schemes of linguistic conventions logically would lead. This makes it sound as though the paradigm of a philosophical task is to find out whether some given scheme of linguistic conventions C *really* would lead to results R. Yet, at the same time, Carnap maintained, as did other logical positivists, that all rules of logic hold only by linguistic convention and that it is metaphysical arrogance to suppose that some logical conventions are more correct than others. But then we are prohibited from supposing that from a given scheme of conventions C results R are *really* the ones that logically follow. Could we say that under specified logical conventions C' the scheme of conventions C really would yield results R? No, this too would be metaphysical arrogance. Could we say that under logical conventions C'' logical conventions C' make C yield R? No, it is as bad as before, and no progress can be made. The logical-positivist approach renders it impossible to formulate coherently any question for investigation here. The trouble arises because the logical positivist wants to put all conventions on an equal footing—as though the existing conventions governing the language in which one is now speaking did not give whatever sense there is to the notion of one thing really following logically from another. Characteristic of the positivistic approach are this lack of concern for the existing conventions under which one speaks and this unsatisfactory striving for a viewpoint from which we could discuss all linguistic conventions without being governed by any.

A further difficulty about the logical positivists' approach concerns their notion of truth by convention. They want to hold that analytic truths, in mathematics and elsewhere, hold solely by virtue of linguistic conventions; yet their idea of this embodies two conflicting tendencies. On the one hand, they maintain that analytic truths, because they hold merely by virtue of the meanings of the terms in which they are expressed, are strictly necessary truths, expressing what could not be otherwise. According to this line of thought, if it is analytic that $5 + 7 = 12$, then necessarily five things plus seven others always make twelve, and nothing could possibly alter this. On the other hand, they maintain that analytic truths, because they reflect linguistic conventions that human beings could alter at will, are alterable into falsehoods by human fiat. According to this line of thought, if we wanted to change the conventions, we could make it no longer true that $5 + 7 = 12$; and in general this suggests that it is we who make numbers what they are and that mathematical truth is a human creation. These two lines of thought are inconsistent. Someone who asserts that $5 + 7 = 12$ cannot be affirming something that is both a strictly necessary truth (hence eternally immutable in its truth) and also alterable into a falsehood at our pleasure. Necessary truth is incompatible with such alterability. The difficulty here arises from an ambiguity: it is *what the speaker said* (the proposition he affirmed) that is necessarily true, but it is the *sentence* (the sequence of words or symbols) he used in saying it whose associated truth value can be altered by human fiat. The logical positivists cultivated this ambiguity by speaking of sentences as the items that are analytic, and their philosophical view of the mutability of analytic truth enshrines the ambiguity. But, if we distinguish between sentences and the propositions they express, then the doctrine that analytic truth is alterable loses its plausibility. Insofar as someone who asserts that $5 + 7 = 12$ is making an assertion which is analytic, what he says is necessarily and immutably true; we could, of course, alter the conventions of our language so that the sequence of symbols "$5 + 7 = 12$" would no longer be appropriate for expressing the assertion he was making—but to do this is not to alter the truth of what he said.[15] To criticize logical positivism in this way is not to deny that the distinction between propositions and sentences expressing them might under scrutiny turn out to be much more complex and obscure than this oversimplified discussion has brought out. Also, it is not to rule out the possibility that there may be some subtler sense in which "the mathematician creates essence." [16] The criticism is merely that the logical positivists did not put forward any considerations which suffice to establish that an analytic truth could be made false—for example, that five and seven could be made to have a sum other than twelve.

So much for some difficulties associated with the conventionalistic aspect of the logical-positivist view of mathematics. What can be said in a more positive way about their account of mathematics as analytic? Surely their efforts to extrude the synthetic a priori from mathematics constituted a philosophically liberating forward step, as did their wish to explain our knowledge of mathematics as resting upon linguistic conventions. The philosophical thesis that mathematics is analytic in the sense that our knowledge of mathematical laws rests in the end solely upon our insight into the language that we use, whatever its defects and obscurities, is a better general thesis about mathematics than earlier philosophers had offered. It is at its best as an account of the simplest principles of arithmetic, where indeed it seems appropriate to say that anyone who doubts or questions them must be failing to understand them in their normally intended sense. And, if we accept this philosophical account of the status of the simplest principles concerning numbers as such, then the same kind of status must be accorded also to all other mathematical principles deducible from these by series of simple analytic steps.

However, there is much in mathematics that this account fails to help us with, especially such controversial matters as the axiom

15. For further discussion of related points, see Peter Achinstein, "Rudolf Carnap," *Review of Metaphysics,* 19.

16. As suggested by Ludwig Wittgenstein, *Remarks on the Foundations of Mathematics* (Oxford, 1956).

of choice and the use of indirect proof. Is the axiom of choice analytic? Is it analytic that indirect proofs are valid in number theory? Carnap says we could have conventions under which the answer would be yes and conventions under which the answer would be no—but that does not help us to see whether or not the questions have answers under the prevailing conventions that do govern our counting and calculating. The original heroic thesis that every bit of mathematics *is* analytic tends here to be transformed into the more weasly claim that any bit of mathematics *could become* analytic. It is a pity that the logical positivists never tried to make their doctrine more informative by attempting to say just how much of mathematics they would regard as consisting of theorems that are analytic under established prevailing conventions, and how much they would regard merely as capable of being made analytic by the institution of new conventions.

THE CONTRAST BETWEEN ARITHMETIC AND GEOMETRY

So far we have been discussing aspects of the logical positivists' view of pure mathematics, their preferred examples of which were usually drawn from arithmetic. Let us now consider their philosophical view of geometry.

Philosophers of past centuries commonly have held that both arithmetical propositions, which centrally involve the concept of number, and geometrical propositions, which centrally involve the concepts of point, line, and figure, properly belong to mathematics. They have held that there is a fundamental similarity between the status of arithmetic and the status of geometry, so that substantially the same kind of philosophical account is to be given of our knowledge of each field. Whatever kind of truth it is that, for any integer x, $x + 0 = x$, and whatever way it is in which we know this, they have held that this is the same type of truth and is known in the same way as is the truth that two straight lines cannot enclose an area. Thus, rationalists such as Descartes regarded arithmetical propositions and geometrical propositions as alike in providing equally clear examples of necessary truths that we apprehend through the mind's power of rational insight into reality. Hume regarded propositions of both kinds as alike in providing equally clear examples of our knowledge of the relations of ideas. Kant suggested that they are alike in that geometrical knowledge and arithmetical knowledge both rest upon the mind's synthetic a priori acquaintance with its own forms of sensibility.[17] Mill held that the principles of both arithmetic and geometry are inductive generalizations—and, although his view was unusual, it still agreed with tradition to the extent of viewing geometry and arithmetic in the same light.

Among the logical positivists this situation of equality is altered, and their view of geometry differs substantially from their view of arithmetic. The status of geometry interested them greatly because they believed that traditional views of geometry, and traditional philosophy in general, had been excitingly undermined by the development of non-Euclidean geometries and by the theory of relativity. Their new viewpoint concerning geometry was evolved in various of their publications of the 1920's, of which Reichenbach's *Philosophy of Space and Time*[18] is the most memorable. By the 1930's their view had hardened into a rather set line, often reiterated, which later was summed up especially clearly in Hempel's paper "Geometry and Empirical Science." [19] Let us consider how their view of geometry differed from their view of arithmetic.

One way of describing matters is to say that the logical positivists assigned a different status to arithmetical propositions about numbers as such than they did to geometrical propositions about points, lines, and figures as such. They viewed the former as analytic and expressive merely of linguistic conventions. Thus they held that the reason why it is true, for every integer x, that $x + 0 = x$, is because denial of this would be inconsistent with the conventions that govern the symbolism of our language, whereas typical propositions of geometry, for instance, the Eu-

17. Kant seldom considered arithmetical propositions and had no view of them which was as settled as was his view of geometrical propositions, however.

18. Hans Reichenbach, *Philosophie der Raum-Zeit-Lehre* (Berlin-Leipzig, 1928), translated as *The Philosophy of Space and Time* (New York, 1958).

19. Carl G. Hempel, "Geometry and Empirical Science," in Feigl and Sellars, *Readings in Philosophical Analysis* (New York, 1949).

clidean proposition that two straight lines cannot enclose an area, were regarded by the logical positivists as empirical propositions expressing contingent hypotheses about the world. Such hypotheses must be tested by observation and experiment; and this is the case with the theses both of Euclidean and of non-Euclidean geometry, they held. When experimental tests are carried out, as was done in connection with the theory of relativity, we find that the axioms of Euclidean geometry are not all true, but that the axioms of a form of Riemannian geometry are all true. Thus the logical positivists differ from the philosophical tradition insofar as arithmetical propositions are classified by them in one way (as a priori and analytic) while typical propositions of geometry are classified in a different way (as synthetic and empirical). For them, the question "Does the physical world conform to Euclidean geometry?" is a serious factual question, whereas the question "Does the physical world conform to the laws of standard arithmetic?" is to be dismissed as trivial.

However, this traditional way of characterizing the logical positivists' position is not wholly satisfactory, for it leaves out their general view of what pure mathematics is, and it might be supposed that an appeal to this would restore the similarity of status between arithmetic and geometry. In their general account of the nature of mathematics the logical positivists did aim to have one single position: that mathematics proper is pure mathematics, a formal science. And they held that both arithmetic and geometry can be studied as pure mathematics; to this extent they did accord the same status to arithmetic and to geometry. Yet, even when this is insisted upon, there remains for logical positivism a significant difference between arithmetic and geometry. Just how we are to characterize this difference will depend upon what "pure mathematics" is understood to be.

Often the logical positivists spoke as though by "pure mathematics" they meant simply a priori knowledge of analytic propositions concerning matters mathematical. If this is what "pure mathematics" is, then there will be two distinct senses in which an inquiry may be said to belong to pure mathematics: either because it gains a priori knowledge of analytic propositions about mathematical entities (such as sets, or numbers, or points, lines, and figures), or because it gains a priori knowledge of analytic propositions concerning deductive relationships within systems of sentences, deductive relationships of sufficient complexity to interest mathematicians. Thus the difference for logical positivism between the philosophical status of arithmetic and that of geometry can be brought out by saying that these two fields differ with regard to the senses in which they belong to pure mathematics. The logical positivists regard arithmetic as pure mathematics in both senses: its axioms and theorems are analytic and thus knowable a priori; and the deductive relationships among its axioms and theorems are describable in analytic propositions that are knowable a priori also. In contrast, geometry for the logical positivists is pure mathematics only in the latter sense; they hold that an a priori "pure" investigation of the deductive links between axioms and theorems in systems of geometry can be conducted, but that the axioms and theorems themselves are not items of a priori knowledge. Viewed in this way, there remains a real difference for logical positivism between arithmetic and geometry.

However, sometimes logical positivists spoke as though by "pure mathematics" they meant a study more austere than this, a study which is to concern itself solely with the properties of formal deductive systems whose non-logical words and symbols are to be left entirely uninterpreted. The axioms and theorems, then, do not say anything true or false but are, at most, mere logical skeletons of sentences. If "pure mathematics" is to be understood in this sense, then the difference for logical positivism between arithmetic and geometry must be characterized in yet another way. Arithmetic and geometry both can be studied merely as uninterpreted deductive systems (as can large parts of physics and at least fragments of almost any subject), and so both can be viewed as branches of "pure mathematics" in this sense. But the logical positivists' position implies that there will remain a difference between arithmetic and geometry, a difference concerning what happens when these uninterpreted systems are provided with interpretations.

Assume that to study arithmetic as pure mathematics is to study merely what derivations of uninterpreted theorem-formulas

STEPHEN F. BARKER

from uninterpreted axiom-formulas can be carried out in accord with specified logical rules. Nevertheless, the arithmetical symbols occurring in those uninterpreted formulas are familiar symbols that also occur meaningfully in ordinary scientific discourse (in engineering, for instance). The logical positivists seem to suppose that the uninterpreted system of arithmetic has a primary intended type of interpretation for its formulas. This type of interpretation, even if it does not play any role in the formal deductive investigations that constitute "pure arithmetic," still is especially associated with the formal system, for it comprises the standard conventions prevailing in ordinary scientific discourse with regard to the meanings of the arithmetical symbols ("+" is to be interpreted as symbolizing addition, "0" as naming zero, etc.), the conventions that are employed for normal applications of the formalism of arithmetic. And this kind of prevailing interpretation is such that under it the formulas of pure arithmetic become arithmetical truths: the abstract formula "$x + y = y + x$" under this interpretation comes to express the analytic truth that for any integers x and y the sum of x and y is identical with the sum of y and x, and so on. To be sure, the logical positivists cannot have meant to deny that it is also possible to interpret the formalism of arithmetic so that its formulas become empirical hypotheses about the outcomes of physical experiments. For example, it is possible to interpret "+" so that "$x + y = y + x$" comes to express the empirical hypothesis that, whenever two weights x and y are set on the pans of a balance, it makes no difference whether x or y is set down first—the joint weight of x and y-added-later is equivalent to the joint weight of y and x-added-later, as regards the range of other weights that each can balance. The formulas of arithmetic could be interpreted in the latter way; but the logical positivists clearly believed that such an interpretation would be sharply at odds with our prevailing standard conventions concerning the meanings of arithmetical symbols. If these symbols are interpreted in standard fashion, the formulas of arithmetic have to become analytic truths, not empirical ones, they held—and they sharply criticized J. S. Mill's view of arithmetical laws as inductive generalizations.

Is there any primary intended type of interpretation for the abstract formal systems of "pure geometry"? The logical positivists spoke as though any worth-while interpretation of the abstract formulas of geometry must turn those formulas into empirical hypotheses—and to say this is to rule out certain types of interpretations, for instance, those which would make the formulas into true analytic propositions (the Skolem-Lowenheim theorem assures us that any consistent set of logical formulas, such as the axioms of a pure geometry would be, always does come out true under some interpretations in the domain of the natural numbers). It would seem that they regarded geometrical terms like "straight line" as not being governed by any rigid set of prevailing conventions, yet they did regard prevailing conventions as limiting the range of worth-while interpretations of these terms. According to prevailing conventions, the term "straight line" must mean some kind of even pathway through physical space; this rules out many kinds of interpretations but leaves leeway for a variety of others. Within the limits imposed by prevailing conventions, the term "straight" as applied to lines may be interpreted as meaning the path which a ray of light will travel, or the path along which a measuring rod would have to be laid down the fewest times to reach from one place to another, or the path along which a taut cord tends to lie as the tension on it increases without limit. Such being the case, the abstract formal systems of "pure geometry" do not have primary intended interpretations but do have a range of possible interpretations that are primarily associated with them. And the logical positivists' view seems to be that any interpretation of this kind— that is, any interpretation which does not conflict with prevailing conventions concerning the meanings of geometrical terms—must be such that under it the uninterpreted axioms and theorems of pure geometry are turned into empirical hypotheses.

The difference between the status of arithmetic and that of geometry for logical positivism has now been characterized in several ways. The existence of this difference, however it is characterized, is a striking and rather puzzling feature of the logical positivists' philosophy of mathematics. We have seen that they were committed to regarding arithmetic as analytic; that is, they believed that there is a standard, prevailing interpretation of the formulas of arithmetic under which they become analytic truths. Why then did they come to believe, contrary to philosophical tradition, that geometrical propositions are different—that is, why did they think that a geometry cannot become a body of a priori truths under some interpretation that would be consonant with the ordinary scientific meanings of geometrical terms?

Prima facie it would seem that nothing stands in the way of such an interpretation of Euclidean geometry. Let us understand the geometrical terms in ordinary, straightforward ways: let the term "line" apply to any continuous, breadthless pathway through the universe; let "point" apply to any precise location in the universe; and let us understand the crucial term "straight" in such a way that lines count as straight only if two of them alone cannot enclose an area, only if, when three of them form a closed figure, its angle sum always equals two right angles, and so forth. Along these lines we can have an interpretation of geometry under which the axioms and theorems of Euclidean geometry become analytically true—true because they merely express aspects of the meanings assigned to the terms.[20] Moreover, this type of interpretation does not seem to be at odds with ordinary prevailing usage: indeed, it seems to be rather more in accordance with ordinary usage than is the type of interpretation which the logical positivists regard as alone worthy of consideration. The fact that this is so is suggested by the following imaginary experiment. Suppose that a vast three-sided figure is laid out, its sides being determined by one or another of the operational methods which the logical positivists emphasize (as paths of light rays, as paths along which measuring rods need be laid down the fewest times, etc.). Now, suppose that the sum of the angles of this three-sided figure turns out to be greater than two right angles and that this outcome is found to be associated with an unevenness of the gravitational field within the region where the figure is laid out—perhaps massive galaxies are close to one side

20. This kind of interpretation would seem to be what Henri Poincaré had in mind; see his *Science and Hypothesis* (New York, 1955). A recent advocate of it is R. D. Bradley, "Geometry and Necessary Truth," *Philosophical Review*, 73.

while there is little matter on the other side. How shall the results of this experiment be described? The logical positivists would say that the experiment shows that triangles do not always have an angle sum equal to two right angles, and hence that Euclidean geometry is not strictly true. But surely a plain man, even a plain scientist, would find it at least as much in tune with previously established linguistic practices to say instead that the experiment shows that light rays do not always travel in straight lines, or that measuring rods can sometimes shrink—and that uneven gravitational fields are responsible for this. This suggests that the interpretation which makes Euclidean geometry into a body of analytic truths is at least as much and perhaps more in accord with ordinary usage than are the types of interpretations favored by the logical positivists, which would turn it into a body of empirical falsehoods.

It seems curious that the logical positivists should have insisted that an interpreted geometry be a body of empirical hypotheses. Elsewhere in philosophy they insist that anyone is free to use terms as he chooses; the "Principle of Tolerance" purports to proscribe proscriptions. Yet here in their philosophy of geometry the logical positivists seem to be proscribing a type of interpretation of geometrical terms which not only is a possible type of interpretation but which actually seems closest to traditionally prevailing usage. How can their attitude be explained? They seem to have been led to their position by a combination of influences and arguments of varying degrees of soundness.

The existence of non-Euclidean geometries probably was one factor influencing the logical positivists' stand. Non-Euclidean geometries had come to be recognized as systems that are consistent in their logical form and that are just as worthy of mathematical study as is Euclidean geometry. Often it has been supposed—and sometimes by logical positivists—that, if various different geometries are equally consistent, then no one of them can have axioms that are all necessarily true. And from this it has been thought to follow that it must be an empirical question, which type of geometry has true axioms; an empirical question, whether the world is Euclidean or non-Euclidean in its spatial character. There is a confusion of thought here, however. Merely because non-Euclidean geometry is formally consistent—that is, because the logical form of its axioms is such that some ways of interpreting its primitive terms can succeed in making its axioms come out true—it does not follow that Euclidean geometry cannot be necessarily true—that is, have some interpretation of its primitive terms under which its axioms all come out necessarily true. Indeed, any system whose logical structure is such as to admit of interpretations under which its axioms all become empirical truths must also admit of interpretations under which its axioms all become necessary truths. Thus the mere existence of non-Euclidean geometries as formally consistent systems is not by itself a good reason for concluding that interpreted geometries have to become bodies of empirical propositions; but it is one reason that probably influenced the logical positivists to think so.

Another factor that probably influenced them was the feeling they seem often to have had that a word or symbol has been fully interpreted only if an explicit definition has been provided (i.e., the definiens is a phrase exactly synonymous with the definiendum), and that (outside the realms of logic and arithmetic) the only scientifically respectable way of assigning meaning to a term is by specifying an observational or operational criterion.[21] This conjunction of attitudes would have predisposed the logical positivists either to overlook or to disapprove of the type of interpretation under which Euclidean geometry can become a body of analytic truths. Suppose we interpret the term "straight" as applied to lines to mean "path of a light ray through media of uniform refractive index"; then we have given an explicit definition, and in doing so have indicated an operational criterion for detecting straightness of lines. Or suppose we interpret "straight" to mean "path along which a measuring rod, manipulated in the standard manner, need be laid down the fewest times to get from any point on the path to any other"; again we have an explicit definition, and it is one which indicates an operational criterion for detecting straightness. Such assignments of meaning live up

21. The doctrines of reduction sentences and of theoretical terms were attempts to extend the mantle of scientific respectability to terms whose meanings did not seem to conform to the requirements of full interpretation.

to the logical positivists' conception of what an interpretation should be. But the interpretations of "straight" that both provide explicit definitions and indicate operational procedures all do seem (when combined with straightforward interpretations of the other geometrical terms) to turn geometry into a body of empirical hypotheses. In contrast, the type of interpretation of "straight" suggested above, which (when combined with straightforward interpretations of the other geometrical terms) would turn Euclidean geometry into analytic truths, does not meet the two requirements. It does not afford any explicit definition of "straight," for "straight" is not to be synonymous with "kind of line, no two of which can enclose an area," or with "kind of line such that a closed figure formed by three of them must have an angle sum equal to two right angles," and so on. Nor does this type of interpretation indicate some one operational criterion for detecting straightness. Instead, it suggests a variety of empirical tests (if two lines enclose an area, then both are not straight; if a closed three-sided figure has an angle sum not equal to two right angles, then not all its sides are straight; etc.), no one of which provides a criterion of straightness which is both necessary and sufficient. The logical positivists might therefore have considered that this interpretation is at best only a "partial interpretation," and that it does not suffice to turn the axioms and theorems of uninterpreted geometry into truths or falsehoods. However, such an attitude seems unreasonable. The idea that a sentence has no truth value, unless for each of its extralogical terms a definition can be stated affording non-trivial necessary and sufficient operational criteria of applicability, is an implausible one. It suggests that a person who is not able to state definitions of the terms he uses does not attach full-blooded meanings to them, whereas, actually, a person who finds it impossible to define some of his terms (perhaps because his language is not rich in synonymous words and phrases) can still show that he does attach definite meanings to his terms. He can show this by applying his terms to instances in a steady, reliable way, and by displaying in his usage a coherent pattern of opinions concerning what assertions employing these terms are analytic. Thus the logical positivists' conclusion that interpreted geometry must be empirical is not effectively supported by the line of thought just discussed; yet it is likely that this line of thought was a factor impelling them toward their conclusion.

Other and perhaps sounder types of considerations which the logical positivists regarded as supporting their view of geometry as empirical came from physics. Their great admiration for Einstein and their wish to accord his work as much philosophical significance as possible must have predisposed them to describe his findings as involving the refutation of Euclidean geometry. But, more important, there were certain arguments concerning the interrelation of geometry and physics which some of them believed supported their view.

One argument invoked the notion of systematic simplicity for science. It was urged that science ought always to seek the simplest over-all system of ideas for explaining phenomena, and that in deciding whether to retain Euclidean geometry in light of the findings of recent physics we ought to consider whether such a move will result in a simpler over-all system. The argument, then, was that, if Euclidean geometry is retained, physics must be made more complicated so as to contain queer hypotheses to the effect that gravitational fields bend light rays and shrink measuring rods (these hypotheses were stigmatized as *ad hoc*—although this vague term of opprobrium was never defined and so adds little to the argument). If Riemannian geometry is used, no such hypotheses are needed, for light rays will travel in straight lines (the only thing queer will be that two straight lines can enclose an area, etc.). The argument is that a simpler over-all explanatory scheme is attained by rejecting Euclidean geometry in favor of Riemannian.

The notion of simplicity involved here is certainly not a very precise one, nor is it very clear what it is about a physics based on Riemannian geometry that is supposed to make it simpler than a physics based on Euclidean geometry. But, setting that aside, the most interesting feature of this argument is the way in which, in order to reach its conclusion, it suppresses the distinction between the analytic and the synthetic which the logical positivists elsewhere insisted upon. If we adhere to the idea of a sharp distinction between the analytic and the synthetic, we would have to say that, although simplicity is a consideration both in the choice among competing analytic claims and in the choice among competing synthetic claims, there are two very different senses of simplicity involved here. Reichenbach, who rejected the above argument concerning geometry, called these two senses of simplicity *descriptive* simplicity and *inductive* simplicity.[22] By descriptive simplicity he meant the simplicity of a scheme of descriptive conventions. In this sense, the conventions upon which the centigrade scale of temperature is based may be said to be simpler than those embodied in the Fahrenheit scale, and so one might say that the analytic truths about centigrade temperature are simpler than are the analytic truths about Fahrenheit temperature. The simpler truths are not truer here, they merely are more convenient. By inductive simplicity Reichenbach meant the kind of simplicity which is relevant to a choice between two factual hypotheses when we believe that the simpler explanation of given data is more likely to be true than is a more complex explanation. In this sense, we might say that the hypothesis that smoking causes lung cancer is a simpler explanation of the known statistics than is the hypothesis that some special genetic factor causes both a predisposition toward smoking and a predisposition toward lung cancer; here this would mean that the simpler hypothesis is more probably true, irrespective of whether it is convenient. Thus the two senses of simplicity are quite different: the sense of simplicity that concerns analytic truths has to do only with convenience, while the sense of simplicity that concerns synthetic truths has to do only with truth, not with convenience. Returning now to the question of geometry, we can say that, if the sharp distinction between the analytic and the synthetic is maintained, then, if Euclidean geometry is so interpreted as to be analytically true, it will follow that only considerations of descriptive, not of inductive, simplicity are relevant to whether or not it should be adopted. And, if the hypotheses of physics are regarded as synthetic, then only con-

---

22. Reichenbach first made this distinction in his *Axiomatik der Relativistischen Raum-Zeit-Lehre* (Brunswick, 1924); see also his *Experience and Prediction* (Chicago, 1938), pp. 374–76.

siderations of inductive, not of descriptive, simplicity are relevant to whether or not they should be adopted. So the argument appealing to simplicity, by which some logical positivists have sought to support their conclusion concerning geometry, cannot be a sound argument unless the analytic-synthetic distinction, that vital starting point of logical positivism, is itself abandoned.

Reichenbach, who rejected this simplicity argument, offered a different argument involving the appeal to physics. He argued that, if Euclidean geometry is regarded as true, then physics can be made consistent with modern discoveries only if the laws of physics take on a form that he held to be unattractive and indeed unacceptable.[23] In such a physics, what Reichenbach called "the principle of normal causality," that is, a continuous spreading from cause to effect in a finite time, or *action by contact,* would not be a universal principle. Instead, such a physics, based on Euclidean geometry, would have to hold that what Reichenbach called *causal anomalies* can occur; for example, under some circumstances light would have to be described as traversing an infinite distance in a finite time. Reichenbach said that he regarded this argument as supplying the strongest refutation of the necessary truth of the conception of Euclidean geometry.

This argument is a striking one, and it is striking that Reichenbach should have used it. We do not need to enter into any discussion of whether or not Reichenbach was correct in holding that retention of Euclidean geometry must result in rejection of "the principle of normal causality" in order to see that the argument is extraordinarily incompatible with the basic doctrines of logical positivism. What is the status of this "principle of normal causality"? Is it analytic or synthetic, and a priori or empirical? If we suppose that Reichenbach is in effect rejecting these distinctions in this case, that in itself is a remarkable departure from the basic doctrine of logical positivism. If he did not intend to reject these distinctions with regard to his causal principle, then its status would appear to be synthetic yet a priori—syn-

23. Reichenbach, *Philosophy of Space and Time,* p. 67; see also his "The Philosophical Significance of the Theory of Relativity," in *Albert Einstein: Philosopher-Scientist,* ed. P. A. Schilpp (Evanston, Ill., 1949).

thetic because the idea of instantaneous action at a distance (often associated with the law of gravitation in classical physics) does not seem to be self-contradictory at all, a priori because Reichenbach is not maintaining his principle as a result of empirical confirmation. If the attack on the a priori truth of the axioms of Euclidean geometry is to have for its strongest argument an appeal to synthetic a priori knowledge concerning causality, then it is an understatement to observe that logical positivism cannot be said to have succeeded in this attack.

All in all, the various arguments that seem to have impelled logical positivists toward their conclusion about the difference between geometry and arithmetic do not seem to add up to a convincing case. Undoubtedly there are philosophically significant differences of some kind between these two areas of mathematics, but the standard logical-positivist account of the matter is insufficient; where its reasoning becomes most suggestive, it departs most radically from the central tenets of logical positivism. Nevertheless, we owe a great debt to the logical positivists for their vigorous treatment of these issues in the philosophy of mathematics, where philosophical understanding comes not only through the formulation of doctrines that ultimately prove to be sound but also through the advocacy of stimulating and knowledgeable ideas of all kinds.[24]

24. For important recent discussion of the philosophy of geometry, see Adolf Grünbaum's *Philosophical Problems of Space and Time* (New York, 1963), his *Geometry and Chronometry in Philosophical Perspective* (Minneapolis, 1968), and Hilary Putnam's "An Examination of Grünbaum's Philosophy of Geometry," in B. Baumrin, ed., *Philosophy of Science: The Delaware Seminar* (New York, 1963).

PETER ACHINSTEIN

approaches to the philosophy of science

A CONTEMPORARY POSITIVIST APPROACH

Logical positivism, as Professor Feigl stresses in his paper in this volume, has seen many changes, both major and minor, in the past forty years. There is still lively controversy among those working in its tradition. Revisions in the early tenets of positivism have yielded a doctrine that is considerably more sophisticated, one that is not refutable by simple objections to the original verification principle. The doctrine I shall consider here is one to which I believe positivistic writers, such as Feigl, Carnap, and Hempel, tend to subscribe at the present time, at least in broad outline, although to be sure there would be some departures from this and some differences over the way details are to be filled in. It is also a doctrine important tenets of which are defended by philosophers such as Nagel, Braithwaite, and Hutten, even though they would not want to classify themselves as positivists, having developed their positions more or less independently of this movement. My plan in the present section is to offer a brief

In this essay I have used material from my book, Concepts of Science *(Baltimore, 1968), that is especially relevant to the present subject, and I thank* The Johns Hopkins Press *for permission to do so.*

characterization of this current positivist position and then, selecting one or two concepts analyzed by it, to suggest some difficulties with these analyses; afterward I shall present a few general observations on the viewpoint as a whole.

To understand the present approach, consider *explication,* an idea introduced by Carnap.[1] According to this idea, it is the philosopher's job to explicate concepts, that is, to replace them with ones that, although somewhat similar, are more precise, simpler, and more fruitful than those presently employed. While in many contexts the present concepts create no difficulties, in certain "critical contexts" their use "involves confusions or even inconsistencies" and leads to unanswerable questions and paradoxes.[2] Accordingly, like inefficient tools, they must be replaced.

Take the concept of a *theory.* As ordinarily employed, even in science, the positivist will say, this concept is used to apply to any assemblage of propositions, whether or not it has order, empirical significance, or explanatory value. The positivist invites us to replace such a concept with that of a *hypothetico-deductive system.* Here order is introduced by explicitly indicating which propositions are to be treated as axioms, which as theorems, and how the latter are to be derived from the former. The theory is formulated by using "theoretical" and "observational" terms from an agreed-upon vocabulary, and is empirically significant, since each term is either observational or related to observational terms via "correspondence rules." Finally, because of its deductive order, as well as its empirical content, a theory, in the present sense, will have explanatory value. For these reasons the explicated concept is to be preferred over the "pre-analytic" one, and the scientist is enjoined to construct theories in the explicated sense.

For example, the kinetic theory of gases contains an assemblage of propositions including these: Gases contain an enormous number of tiny molecules in rapid motion; the molecules are subject

---

1. Rudolf Carnap, *Logical Foundations of Probability,* 2d ed. (Chicago, 1962), chap. 1; *The Philosophy of Rudolf Carnap,* ed. Paul Arthur Schilpp (La Salle, Ill., 1963).

2. *The Philosophy of Rudolf Carnap,* p. 935.

to the conservation laws of classical mechanics; they collide elastically with each other; the absolute temperature of the gas is a function of the mean kinetic energy of the molecules. To reconstruct the theory the positivist would begin with a vocabulary of terms that he separates into "theoretical" and "observational." The theoretical list might include "molecule," "mass of a molecule," "mean kinetic energy of molecules," and so forth. On the observational list we might find "pressure of a gas," "temperature of a gas," "volume of a gas," and so on. Choosing some of the propositions as axioms, the positivist will show how others can be derived as theorems. Among the purely theoretical axioms might be $p = \frac{1}{2}mn\bar{v}^2$, where p is the pressure of all the molecules on the walls of the container, m is the mass of a molecule, n is the number of molecules per unit volume, and $\bar{v}^2$ is the mean square velocity of the molecules. Among the correspondence rules might be $\frac{1}{2}m\bar{v}^2 = constant \times T$, where $\frac{1}{2}m\bar{v}^2$ is the mean kinetic energy of the molecules and T is the absolute temperature of the gas. The observational theorems include $PV = constant \times T$, where P, V, and T are the pressure, volume, and temperature of the gas, respectively. In such a reconstruction the positivist can show exactly what assumptions the theory is making and how these are related to and tested by observations.

Consider another concept, that of a *model*. Scientists, the positivist may say, use the term "model" in conflicting and confusing ways. They may call any of the following a model of a gas: a tinkertoy representation of molecules comprising a gas; propositions attributing mechanical properties to molecules; propositions attributing mechanical properties to billiard balls; an analogy between molecules and billiard balls; and perhaps others. How much better it would be to replace such a confusing concept with one more consistent and more fruitful. The suggestion of the positivists is to focus on *formal similarities* present in all such cases. They propose to use the term "model," with reference to a theory, to mean any set of statements with the same formal structure (the same "calculus") as that of the theory. So, with respect to kinetic theory, a model of a gas would be a set of statements which describes, say, billiard balls in a box and which has the same formal structure as the statements comprising the kinetic theory. Thus the "pre-analytic" amorphous idea of a model is supplanted by a unitary, precise concept.

For example, the following might constitute part of a calculus for the kinetic theory (that part expressing principles of classical mechanics for molecules treated as mass points):

1. For p and q in set P and for t in set T, $f(p,q,t) = -f(q,p,t)$.

2. For p and q in P and for t in T, $s(p,t) \times f(p,q,t) = -s(q,t) \times f(q,p,t)$.

3. $m(p)D^2 s_p(t) = \sum_{q \varepsilon p} f(p,q,t) + g(p,t)$.

In the kinetic theory, P is a class of molecules in a gas, T is a class of elapsed times, $s(p,t)$ is the position of molecule p at time t, $m(p)$ is the mass of p, $f(p,q,t)$ is the force that p exerts on q at time t, and $g(p,t)$ is the resultant external force acting on p at time t. We obtain a model for this theory by reinterpreting some or all of these terms. We might let p be a class of perfectly elastic billiard balls in a box and we might let the remaining terms have the same interpretations as before. Formula (1) would then read: The force exerted by billiard ball p on billiard ball q at time t is equal in magnitude and opposite in direction to that exerted by q on p at time t. The set of formulas so reinterpreted would be a model for the kinetic theory. According to the positivists, the advantage of constructing such a model is to allow the scientist to think about the formal structure of the theory by considering something more familiar in which this formal structure is embedded. Thinking of billiard balls in lieu of molecules may lead to a better understanding of the theory. It may also lead to a further development of it, suggesting to the physicist certain hypotheses about molecules which are not yet incorporated into his theory, for example, hypotheses about molecular rotation.

Here, then, are two examples of a contemporary positivist approach to the philosophy of science. The aim is to replace a given concept, such as that of a theory or model, with one that is more precise and reflects some of the important aspects of the original concept while ridding it of impurities.

Appealing though the precision and organization of such an approach might be, it does, I believe, face serious difficulties. Let us turn first to some particular explications. Consider the positivists' concept of a theory, and the condition of empirical significance which they require theories to satisfy. According to their view, the theoretical terms in a theory will be empirically significant because correspondence rules within the theory will relate them to observational terms. For example, in the kinetic theory the theoretical term "mean kinetic energy of the molecules" will be significant because it is related, via a correspondence rule, to the observational term "temperature of the gas." A correspondence rule is generally understood to be a sentence, of whatever form, which contains both theoretical and observational terms. Carnap defines it as a "mixed sentence" containing essential occurrences of at least one theoretical term and one observational one.[3] Now, a principle of empirical significance for theoretical terms which seems implicit in many positivist writings is this: A theoretical term in a theory T is empirically significant if and only if there is within T a correspondence rule for that term. Such a principle, however, renders any term in any theory empirically significant, whether or not correspondence rules have been explicitly stated for it. To see why, consider any theory whatever, and from it choose any axiom or theorem T which contains a theoretical term M. T logically implies $O \supset T$, where O is any sentence all of whose terms are observational. But $O \supset T$ is a correspondence rule for M, being a "mixed sentence" containing both M and observational terms.[4] So, according to the above principle, M is empirically significant. This argument can be repeated for every theoretical term in any theory, no matter what axioms the theory contains. Such a criterion would also guarantee significance for any term in speculative metaphysics, a discipline which positivists have always claimed lacks empirical significance. We need only think of a metaphysical theory as a set of sentences containing theoretical (metaphysical) terms. In accordance with the previous principle, any term in any meta-

---

3. *Ibid.*, p. 959.

4. The correspondence rule in question can also be made universal in form, as required, e.g., by Grover Maxwell in "Criteria of Meaning and of Demarcation," *Mind, Matter, and Method,* ed. P. Feyerabend and G. Maxwell (Minneapolis, 1966), p. 322. All that one must do is take the prenex normal form of $O \supset T$, where T begins with one or more universal quantifiers.

physical axiom T is significant because T implies the correspondence rule $O \supset T$, where O is any observational sentence you please.

In reply, the positivist might wish to modify his principle of significance by suggesting more stringent formulations. Elsewhere I have considered such formulations, showing that none escape the general type of difficulty indicated above.[5] Either the theory by itself—no matter what its content—guarantees empirical significance for all its terms, or it does so when trivial modifications are introduced which in no way tie the theoretical notions to observations.

There is a second problem besetting the positivist account of theories. This account, I maintain, renders the task of constructing theories trivial. Suppose, for example, that we want to construct a theory explaining why gases behave in accordance with a set of well-confirmed laws L that employ only observational terms. In order to produce a theory in a completely trivial way, it suffices to construct any set of sentences T using only theoretical terms and to add $T \supset L$ as a correspondence rule. The latter serves to confer empirical significance upon the terms in T, and because the empirical laws follow deductively from this theory they can be said to be explained by the theory on the deductive model of explanation which positivists accept. Moreover, the theory can be constructed so as to satisfy other requirements that positivists specify. For example, it can be entirely general; it can satisfy criteria of simplicity, such as that of postulating only a few entities and using simple mathematical techniques. The theory also can be trivially constructed so that laws not yet tested are derivable from it. For example, we can take some other theory T' (satisfying the other criteria), all of whose consequences have not been tested, and construct the following grand theory: $T \cdot T \supset T' \cdot T \supset L$. This will yield laws not yet tested and will also provide a more comprehensive theory into which to incorporate T'.

My third criticism concerns the ideal of axiomatization, something central to the positivist conception of a theory. According

5. Peter Achinstein, *Concepts of Science* (Baltimore, 1968), chap. 3.

to this conception, to present a theory axiomatically, it is sufficient as well as necessary to list as axioms all those assumptions that proponents of the theory make which are not derived from others, theorems that follow from these, and proofs of the theorems with logical and mathematical inferences rendered explicit; this will be done using terms from some initially agreed-upon vocabulary. Undoubtedly there are certain advantages in so presenting a theory. For example, in non-axiomatic presentations it may be unclear what is being assumed and what is being taken as proved from assumptions, as well as how the theorems are supposed to follow; and assumptions may be implicitly made which, if explicitly formulated, would be recognized as implausible or even inconsistent with others. Moreover, in an axiomatic presentation, organization is provided for the terms in the theory, since all are specified in advance and connections among them are explicitly indicated by definitions or postulates of the theory.

On the other hand, axiomatic presentations have potential disadvantages. For example, because they include as axioms *all* the assumptions actually needed for the theory, they make it difficult to discern which ones are especially central to that theory, which introduce its distinctive and characteristic ideas, as contrasted with other less central ones which may be needed only for the solution of special problems or which may have been appropriated from other theories or formulated *ad hoc* simply to cope with these problems. Again, to present a theory simply by introducing axioms, theorems, and proofs is to ignore motivating considerations: What kinds of problems was the theory meant to solve? Why were these rather than other assumptions made? What are the weaknesses of alternative theories? By ignoring such issues an axiomatic presentation can make the assumptions of the theory seem perfectly arbitrary. Also, requiring a theory to be presented using terms in an initially agreed-upon vocabulary can have a stifling effect. It may prevent the theory from being applied in areas not discovered or even envisaged at the time the vocabulary was formulated; it may prevent the introduction of alternative and equally enlightening formulations of principles which use different "vocabularies."

This is not to deny that for some purposes an axiomatic presentation is useful. The point is that there are many ways a theory can be presented. Some presentations will emphasize motivation; others will be concerned mainly with development of the central principles for the analysis of special systems; some may stress more the kinds of experiments relevant to that theory's confirmation. In some of these cases only the most important assumptions of the theory will be formulated, few if any theorems will be derived, and terms will not be restricted to some initially specified vocabulary. Even so, more information may be supplied than that given in a presentation which simply states assumptions, theorems, and proofs.

James Clerk Maxwell, who made important contributions to the kinetic theory in the nineteenth century, offers contrasting presentations of this theory. In his paper "Illustrations of the Dynamical Theory of Gases," Maxwell spends very little time stating the distinctive assumptions of the theory; the bulk of his effort is devoted to a quantitative development of the theory which shows how the assumption that gases are composed of minute particles can be used to solve problems such as determining the probability of a molecule's reaching a given distance before striking another, finding the mean path of molecules in a mixture of two gases, discovering the average number of particles whose velocities lie between given limits, and so forth.[6] This presentation can be contrasted with one that Maxwell offers in his paper entitled "Molecules."[7] Here the presentation is much more elementary and qualitative; less time is devoted to the development of the theory and more to elucidating some of the basic concepts; motivating considerations, as well as examples and analogies, are given. In neither paper is the presentation axiomatic. Yet each succeeds in presenting the theory to the audience for which it is designed: the first to one with considerable knowledge of physics, the second to a less sophisticated audience.

No presentation, axiomatic or otherwise, can satisfy all intellectual needs that might be felt. Positivists, however, seem to be

6. *The Scientific Papers of James Clerk Maxwell,* ed. W. D. Niven (New York, 1965), I, 377–409.

7. *Ibid.,* II, 361–78.

saying that, because a theory (in their explicated sense) is just a set of axioms, theorems, and proofs, there is only one true and intellectually satisfying type of presentation in science. This is not to deny that indications of motivation, centrality of assumptions, alternative formulations, and examples could be added to an axiomatic presentation. But positivists tend to ignore these or treat them as excess baggage, considering them to be useful merely as heuristic devices for the slow thinker; in general, their examples of axiomatizations omit such considerations. I fail to see how one could come to have a genuine grasp of a theory simply by gazing upon axioms, theorems, and proofs.

There are other difficulties with the positivist concept of a theory, for example, difficulties with the theoretical-observational distinction presupposed.[8] However, it is time to say something about the second concept mentioned earlier, the model in science. Positivists explicate this as "another interpretation of a theory's calculus," claiming that a formal similarity between model and theory is the essence of a model. Models, positivists say, are useful because they aid in understanding the concepts of a theory and also because they provide a basis for extending a theory. The question is whether or not models *in the positivists' sense* can perform these functions. Certainly an analogy between molecules in a gas and billiard balls in a box may aid one's understanding of the concept of a molecule as well as provide a basis for extending kinetic theory by considering problems of rotation, and mean free path. But these advantages do not accrue simply from formulating and contemplating a set of statements having the same formal structure, the same calculus, as that of kinetic theory. At best, statements bearing only a formal similarity to those of kinetic theory may help one to understand the formal features of concepts in kinetic theory, but they will be of no help in understanding the semantical ones. And it is the latter which are usually problematic. We want to understand what it means to talk about invisible molecules in a gas, what familiar and observable items these molecules are like. Simply to provide a set of statements with the same formal structure as those describing

8. See *Concepts of Science*, chaps. 5–6.

molecules is not to promote this sort of understanding. Nor will it provide a basis for extending the theory. The mere fact that statements in a set S_2 have the same logical form as those in a set S_1 provides no rational basis for adding postulates of any kind to S_1, even if the formal correlates in S_2 are known to be true.

Finally, it is doubtful that the positivists' concept of a model adequately captures even one feature of the scientist's concept. A scientist may draw an analogy between X and Y when the principles involved (if any) are non-mathematical or are not subject to the formal axiomatization required by the positivists' account—for example, analogies in biology between parts of birds and parts of fish. Or, analogies may be drawn between X and Y despite the fact that relevant laws governing X and Y, although mathematically expressible, have different forms. There is an analogy between a Bohr hydrogen atom and a planetary system containing one planet, even though relevant energy and momentum equations, which determine the character of the orbit, have different forms in each. Most important, in the typical case the analogy turns not on formal similarities, or at least not only on these, but on physical ones, that is, on similarities between the *designata* of terms in principles governing X and Y. The similarities generating the analogy between gases containing molecules and boxes containing billiard balls are physical ones between geometrical and mechanical properties exhibited by both systems; they cannot be discerned simply by contemplating uninterpreted formulas.

I have noted two examples of current positivistic explications, and now I want to make a more general point regarding the present approach. The contemporary positivist begins by trying to replace concepts, or, as some say, by "rationally reconstructing" them. Why? Because he assumes that the concepts presently in use are not adequate. But he refuses to offer any detailed characterization of these concepts, and usually fails to indicate, or at least to say very much about, the dangers of continuing to use them. We are never informed by the positivist what concept of a theory he seeks to replace, that is, what way or ways scientists (or others) use the term "theory," what conditions generally obtain when something is classified as a theory. Not every statement or set of statements is so classified; indeed, there seems to be a good deal of agreement on what is and is not classifiable as a theory. But, inasmuch as we are offered no analysis of this concept, how do we know it needs replacement? Again, since positivists refuse to provide any general characterization of the types of items called models in science, why should we assume that the scientific concept or concepts of a model ought to be replaced or altered? Moreover, if we do not know what problems beset the concepts already in use, how do we know that the positivists' explications avoid these problems? How do we know that the positivist concept of a theory or a model is superior to present ones? The positivist merely assumes that the present concepts are inadequate and that his explications are superior. Finally, I have tried to suggest a few of the problems that will arise if, irrespective of whether or not present concepts are inadequate, positivistic replacements are adopted.

A CONTEMPORARY ANTI-POSITIVIST APPROACH

I turn now to an approach taken by a number of contemporary philosophers with strong anti-positivistic sentiments. Among those who might be mentioned are Hanson, Toulmin, and Feyerabend. I do not claim that there is unanimity within the group, but certain common theses, especially as regards aims and methods, do appear in their writings and perhaps justify treating them together.

One is the aim of examining concepts actually employed in the sciences rather than replacing them with others. Thus the positivists' use of symbolic logic is criticized as requiring too rigid a mold for scientific concepts. A further reason for rejecting the positivist approach is because of its lack of concern with actual scientific cases. Indeed—and this is another common theme—the anti-positivists advocate a case-history approach to problems in the philosophy of science: To characterize a concept in science see how it functions by analyzing a particular case in science where it is employed. As Hanson puts it, use the case as "the lens through which these perennial philosophical problems will be viewed." [9] Hanson considers the concept of a theory by studying Kepler's theory of the elliptical orbit of the planet Mars and the manner in which it was developed. Feyerabend discusses the medieval impetus theory, trying to show how its concepts are incommensurable with those of Newtonian mechanics.[10] Toulmin, in his investigations of the concept of a theory, selects geometrical optics as his paradigm.[11]

In addition to the case-study approach, philosophers in this group, especially Hanson and Toulmin, tend to rely heavily on the use of analogies. When characterizing the concept of a theory Hanson employs an analogy between the facts a theory is supposed to explain and drawings used by psychologists which consist of assemblages of lines whose meanings produce puzzlement. A theory explains a set of facts much as an interpretation of the lines in the drawing organizes them into a coherent, intelligible pattern. Toulmin draws an analogy between a theory, which allows inferences to be drawn from one set of facts to another, and a map, which allows one to determine information about spatial relationships between cities. Much of Toulmin's discussion proceeds by exploring this analogy. Hanson's treatment of scientific terminology involves analogies, for example, between terms like "temperature" and "wavelength," whose meanings depend upon the theory in which they appear, and terms like "trump," "checkmate," or "double fault," whose meanings depend upon the game in which they are employed.[12]

Why use analogies? For one thing, they are convenient expository devices. But there may also be a theoretical reason, namely, a rejection of the idea that informative, non-trivial necessary and sufficient conditions can be given for general concepts of concern to the philosopher of science.[13] It might be

9. N. R. Hanson, *Patterns of Discovery* (Cambridge, 1958), p. 2.

10. P. K. Feyerabend, "Explanation, Reduction, and Empiricism," in *Minnesota Studies in the Philosophy of Science*, vol. 3, ed. H. Feigl and G. Maxwell (Minneapolis, 1962).

11. Stephen Toulmin, *The Philosophy of Science* (London, 1953), chaps. 2–3.

12. Hanson, *Patterns of Discovery*, p. 61.

13. See, e.g., Stephen Toulmin, *Foresight and Understanding* (Bloomington, Ind., 1961), chap. 2.

claimed, for example, that there is no feature or set of features common to scientific theories, but only a "family resemblance" among them. Accordingly, it is futile to try to formulate necessary and sufficient conditions for theories; the method of analogy, whose purpose is to indicate only what theories are *like,* is one important way of characterizing the "family resemblance." In drawing analogies it need not be supposed that all theories are like the analogue in all respects, but only that for any theory there will be certain respects in which it will resemble the analogue, these respects varying to some extent from theory to theory. By using an analogy between X and Y you don't have to pinpoint a set of characteristics to be attributed to X's. You can characterize X's by indicating various ways in which they resemble Y's, as well as the different degrees of resemblance that are possible. The method provides a looser kind of characterization which befits the concepts in question.

Apart from a concern with actual science, the appeal to case histories, and, at least with Hanson and Toulmin, reliance on analogies, are there any more specific doctrines shared by these philosophers? What comes closest is the doctrine of "theory dependence," the idea that terms used in connection with a scientific theory depend for their meaning upon that theory and suffer a change in meaning when the theory is altered or replaced. Hanson speaks of terms such as "pressure," "volume," "wound," "poison," and "pendulum" as being theory-laden.[14] Toulmin, introducing a related idea, speaks of "ideals of natural order," very basic presuppositions by reference to which concepts in a science are to be understood and explanations are to be given.[15] But the doctrine takes its most explicit, radical, and interesting form in the writings of Feyerabend, who claims that *all* terms utilized in a theory are theory-laden, including terms used to describe observations supporting the theory.[16] Even though the same term is used in two different theories, its meaning in one

---

14. *Patterns of Discovery,* p. 61.
15. *Foresight and Understanding,* chaps. 3–4.
16. Feyerabend, "Explanation, Reduction, and Empiricism"; see also *idem,* "Problems of Empiricism," in *Beyond the Edge of Certainty,* ed. R. G. Colodny (Englewood Cliffs, N.J., 1965), pp. 145–260.

will not be the same as its meaning in the other, because the principles upon which its meaning depends will be different in each; the two theories will be "incommensurable." This, of course, is to deny a fundamental assumption of contemporary positivism, namely, that there can and indeed must be terms—to wit, observational terms—whose meanings are independent of the theory and remain constant from theory to theory.

Here, then, are some of the central ideas of this anti-positivist group. As in the case of positivism, I think there are serious difficulties in the present approach. Let me begin with Feyerabend's version of the doctrine of theory dependence. If it were true, no two theories could contradict each other. For example, when Bohr in explaining his theory of the atom wrote "The energy radiation from an atomic system does not take place in the continuous way assumed in the ordinary electrodynamics, but . . . on the contrary, takes place in distinctly separated emissions," he could not really have been denying or contradicting the "classical" theory of the electron.[17] For, according to the doctrine of theory dependence, terms such as "energy radiation" and "atomic system" mean one thing for Bohr and something else for the "classical" theorist; nor could other terms in these theories be used to express the disagreement, inasmuch as all pairs of terms from different theories express "incommensurable" concepts. Not only would disagreement between theories be impossible, according to this doctrine, but so would any agreement. Bohr and his "classical" opponent could not even agree on a description of the facts to be explained by their respective theories, because the words in their descriptions would have different meanings. In what sense, then, could the theories proposed be (as Feyerabend calls them) alternatives?

Again, when it is claimed that the meaning of a term in a theory depends completely upon the theory, the suggestion is that, in effect, the principles say what the term means. If this were so, the principles would be analytic, that is, defensible solely by appeal to the meanings of their constituent terms. Bohr's principle that

17. Niels Bohr, "On the Constitution of Atoms and Molecules," *Philosophical Magazine,* 26 (1913): 4.

the electron's angular momentum is quantized could be defended by appeal to the fact that in this theory the terms "electron" and "angular momentum" mean just those things such that the electron's angular momentum is quantized. To this it might be replied that, although the principles of the theory would be analytic, the claim that there exist entities satisfying these principles would be empirical, and this is all that is necessary to make the theory empirical. But, even if we grant the latter claim, the empirical character of theories would not be demonstrated. For, according to the present doctrine, since all terms used in connection with a theory, including all terms used to report observations, presuppose the theory, no observations could be described which would refute the theory or even tend to make it implausible. Nor could any other theory T' be used to refute T, because the concepts of T and T' are "incommensurable." Even independently of language, observations could not be made that would refute the theory, since observations themselves presuppose a theory; they are theory dependent. If observations are made presupposing T, T could not be refuted, whereas, if they are made presupposing T', again T could not be refuted, because T' and T are not, and cannot be, conflicting theories. In short, given the present doctrine, an empirical character could not be attributed even to the existence claims of a theory.

The problems here stem from a failure to consider the concept of meaning. Feyerabend has little to say on this subject. He merely assumes that meanings always depend on theories, and cites a few examples which, he thinks, illustrate this. But, unless some explanation of meaning is forthcoming, the previous consequences of the present doctrine should cast doubt on the concept of meaning which it presupposes. Moreover, I would claim that there are other examples from science which violate this thesis; even some of those which Feyerabend cites are not wholly convincing.[18]

I turn now to another specific doctrine, although it is not one

---

18. For a positive view of meaning which attempts to show that not all scientific terms depend upon a theory for their meaning, see my *Concepts of Science*.

shared, even in various forms, by all anti-positivists in the group. It concerns the concept of a theory and is proposed by Hanson. Hanson rejects the positivist hypothetico-deductive account of theories on the ground that, contrary to what the latter suggests, scientists do not begin with hypotheses and then deduce the observed data. They begin with the observed data and seek hypotheses to explain them. Having employed the analogy between a theory's explanation of the data and the interpretation of lines in a drawing, Hanson goes on to characterize a theory as something that organizes initially puzzling observed data into an intelligible, conceptual pattern so that these data will be "explicable as a matter of course." He writes: "What is it to supply a theory? It is to offer an intelligible, systematic, conceptual pattern for the observed data. The value of this pattern lies in its capacity to unite phenomena which, without the theory, are either surprising, anomalous, or wholly unnoticed." [19]

This "conceptualization" doctrine is extremely suggestive and is documented by illuminating explorations into the history of science. Yet the doctrine strikes me as being too liberal in one respect and too restrictive in another. Suppose A and B are walking in the woods and B observes something moving on a distant tree which he finds very puzzling. Once this is called to his attention, A informs B that it is a bear climbing a tree, even though all that is visible from the present vantage point are the bear's paws clinging to the tree.[20] Here A has organized what B observes into "an intelligible, systematic, conceptual pattern" whose value (for B, and presumably others) "lies in its capacity to unite phenomena" that would otherwise be "surprising, anomalous, or wholly unnoticed." Yet surely A is not, at least not in the type of example I have in mind, supplying some *theory* that he has. For he knows that it is a bear, or at least could come to know this in a simple and direct way. And (I would claim), if A knows the truth of T or could immediately and directly come to know it, T cannot be classified as a theory that A has,

19. Hanson, *Patterns of Discovery*, p. 121.
20. The example is Hanson's very own and is used where he is explaining what it means to see the pattern in the phenomena; *ibid.*, p. 12.

as the concept of theory is used within as well as outside science.[21]

The reason I take the "conceptualization" doctrine to be too restrictive is that it makes two assumptions that I find questionable: (1) the supplier of a theory always begins with observed phenomena that are puzzling, and (2) the primary or even sole aim of the theory is to explicate these phenomena. Indeed, in a different passage from the work cited above, Hanson claims that the following inference pattern, which, following Peirce, he calls "retroduction," characterizes what transpires when a theory in science is proposed:

> Some surprising phenomenon *P* is observed.
> *P* would be explicable as a matter of course if *H* were true.
> Hence there is reason to think that *H* is true.

I would not deny that for some theories assumptions (1) and (2) hold. But in many cases matters are less simple. The supplier of a theory may begin by considering something that is not surprising, not a phenomenon, and not even observed; it may not be his sole or primary aim to explicate puzzling observed phenomena. Niels Bohr, in developing his theory of the atom, began by considering not observed phenomena but rather the structure of the hydrogen atom postulated by Rutherford's model, the various problems such a model posed, the possibility of introducing Planck's radiation law into this model, and so on. To be sure, his theory does provide an understanding of certain observed phenomena, such as the production of discrete lines in the spectrum of hydrogen. But this was not the item (at least not the only one) with which Bohr began, nor was it the only or even primary one for which he believed his theory would provide understanding. For example, his theory was designed to explain the stability of the atom, why atoms have fixed frequencies of radiation, the Balmer formula relating the wave lengths of the lines in the hydrogen spectrum, and so forth. If any one thing is to be identified as what Bohr was attempting to explicate, I should describe it simply as the structure of the atom (some-

---

21. This concept will be discussed more fully in the third section of this paper.

thing that is neither a phenomenon nor observed). Moreover (although this is not so with Bohr), a scientist might propose a theory, even though he would at that moment be unable to supply actual explanations of anything observed, phenomenon or otherwise. What will suffice, I think, is that such explanations be possible and forthcoming when the theory is sufficiently worked out. In short, a scientist may treat his theory as a *potential* explainer with respect to what is, or will be, observed.

I have considered two specific doctrines, one on the meaning of scientific terms, another on the concept of a theory. Now I want to turn attention from specific doctrines to two techniques or methods of analysis. I have in mind the extensive use of a case history from the sciences and the use of an analogy. Undeniably, these techniques are often valuable in the philosophy of science. What I want to stress are some of their potential dangers, which anti-positivists tend to ignore, for these may be responsible for difficulties in specific doctrines.

An obvious advantage of using a case history is that one remains faithful to actual science, something positivists, for example, often ignore. But one potential danger is that of generalizing prematurely from the case treated, considering it to be like any other that might have been chosen. Hanson, in his chapter on theories, presents his analysis almost entirely by reference to Kepler's theory of the elliptical orbit of Mars. His presentation does indeed show that Kepler was motivated in large part by Brahe's observations. "Kepler," Hanson writes, "did not *begin* with the hypothesis that Mars' orbit was elliptical and then deduce statements confirmed by Brahe's observations. These latter observations were given, and they set the problem—they were Johann Kepler's starting point. He struggled back from these, first to one hypothesis, then to another, then to another, and ultimately to the hypothesis of the elliptical orbit." [22] But why assume that all theories develop in this way? Why assume that the "retroductive" inference pattern fits other cases snugly? Why suppose that in general the scientist begins his thinking by pondering simply the observed phenomena, and that in general his aim

22. Hanson, *Patterns of Discovery*, p. 72.

can best be described as that of organizing the results of observations? With Kepler, Hanson has chosen an example of a theory motivated largely by, and developed in close contact with, observations. But in other cases, as with Bohr, the relationship between theory and observation is less immediate, so that to apply the "retroductive" inference pattern to the reasoning involved, or to suggest that the sole or even primary aim in supplying the theory is to make sense of observations, would oversimplify the picture.

Analogies, like case histories, carry potential dangers. One is that of thinking that the items between which the analogy is drawn are identical or resemble each other more than they really do. It is illuminating to draw an analogy between the way in which a theory may explain observed data and the way in which the interpretation or explanation of seemingly disorganized lines in a drawing may make the latter cohere into an intelligible pattern. The danger lies in thinking as follows: given the fact that whenever someone has thus organized the lines he has provided an interpretation or explanation of the drawing, it must follow that whenever someone has organized observed data, making them "explicable as a matter of course," he has supplied a theory. Earlier I tried to show that providing such organization is neither a necessary nor a sufficient condition for supplying a theory.

Another potential danger with analogies is the temptation to rely heavily upon them in such a way as to leave key concepts invoked when noting the respects in which X resembles Y (e.g., the concept of "conceptual organization" in the case of a theory) unanalyzed. Excessive reliance on analogy may also tempt one to avoid offering a general characterization of the concept, at least any very careful one, independently of the analogy. As noted earlier, anti-positivists may hold that for general concepts such as "theory," "model," "explanation," and "law" no tidy set of logically necessary and sufficient conditions can be formulated. Any condition one might be tempted to propose will have exceptions. But why suppose that the only types of conditions for such concepts are logically necessary and sufficient ones? Might it not be possible to formulate conditions that are relevant and quite central to being a theory, even though they

277

are not logically necessary? Such conditions would be ones the satisfaction of which tends to count in favor of classifying something as a theory, even though no one of them is absolutely required.[23] In the next section I will suggest what these conditions might be. But now, by way of summary, let me state briefly the kind of objections I have been raising to the present approach.

Although many insights can be found in the doctrines of the philosophers under discussion, the tendency, I think, is to attribute one striking feature to a concept: for example, to describe all scientific terms as theory dependent, or to construe all theories as organizers of puzzling observations. The result is a bold and admittedly interesting thesis which unfortunately tends to oversimplify the situation by assuming that all cases are alike and which may presuppose some crucial concept that is left unanalyzed (e.g., "meaning"). The difficulty may arise because of too much concern with scientific examples and too little with formulating in depth what the examples are supposed to show. It may also arise when too heavy a reliance is placed on some analogy and not enough attention is paid to characterizing the differences between the concept and its analogue or to indicating what the analogy is supposed to demonstrate. To say this much about a doctrine, however, is not necessarily to reject it completely, for it may be illuminating with respect to certain types of cases, or at least suggestive of how such cases might be treated once key concepts are analyzed. This, I think, can be said about Feyerabend's doctrine of theory dependence as well as about Hanson's view of theories as conceptual organizers of puzzling observations. There are some terms whose meanings depend heavily upon a theory in which they are employed; there are some theories which were developed primarily to explain puzzling observed phenomena. And noting this may lead to a better understanding of one important type of term or theory in science.

AN ALTERNATIVE APPROACH

What I shall now say is meant to apply to the study of some,

23. For a discussion of this conception of relevance, see my *Concepts of Science,* chap. 1.

though by no means all, concepts of concern to philosophers of science. The concepts I have in mind are general ones employed in many sciences, for example, "theory," "model," "law," "explanation." My aim is to consider concepts actually in use in the sciences, rather than to replace them with others, and to formulate conditions for their application. These need not be necessary and sufficient conditions, for, as the concept is employed, there may be none. It may suffice to indicate a set of conditions, each of which is relevant and especially central, although none is necessary; something might be correctly classifiable under the concept even if it failed to satisfy one or more of these conditions.

The anti-positivist I have described is also concerned with concepts actually in use. He tends to proceed by ascribing one striking feature to a concept which he regards as particularly illuminating. However, the feature he notes usually holds only for certain types of cases, more often than not leaves some notion unclear, and neglects other central aspects of the concept. The contemporary positivist, on the other hand, is concerned to provide a complete set of conditions for concepts. However, in doing so he replaces concepts in use with others. His claim is that there is no uniformity in science when terms such as "theory," "model," "law," and "explanation" are employed and that the concepts involved are inadequate. Possibly he is right. It may be that what one scientist calls a theory on one occasion he will call something else on another. Or it may be that, although there is some uniformity, use of the term is based on presuppositions that are contradictory, or unsatisfactory for some other reason. But we will never know until we consider how the term is actually employed. If we fail to do this, we will never know whether or not some "explicated" concept might alleviate difficulties (if any) with the present one. In short, don't think about replacing a concept or about making it more "exact" until you first try to determine what it is.

How is *that* to be done? One way to begin is by listing items actually identified as theories, models, laws, or explanations in science (or in some particular science). Of course there will be some disagreements among scientists as to classification, and cases where just about every scientist is unsure of how to classify something. But I suggest that examination of papers, textbooks, histories, and so forth, does reveal considerable uniformity in classification. If quite different kinds of things are identified under the same concept, before seeing whether general conditions can be formulated, it may be useful to divide the cases into types.

Take the concept of a model. What types of items are actually so classified in science? Let me narrow the question further by confining it to physics.[24] At the simplest level the term is used to refer to items such as a tinkertoy representation of a molecule, models of the solar system, atoms, or gases found in science museums, a rolling-ball model of radio signals, nineteenth-century mechanical devices built to represent the structure of the ether, and so on. In such cases the term "model" refers to a three-dimensional physical representation of an object which is such that, by considering it, one is supposed to be able to ascertain facts about the object it represents. I shall call these *representational models*. They may be larger or smaller than the original, and they may represent the original either by reproducing those characteristics of importance to the scientist (with scale changes) or by serving as an analogue for the original with respect to the characteristics of interest. In the latter case, properties of the model are not the same as those of the original but are analogous to them in certain respects. For example, James Clerk Maxwell represented the electric field by describing an imaginary incompressible fluid flowing through tubes of variable section. Analogous properties are electrostatic force and the velocity of the imaginary fluid (both quantities vary inversely as the square of the distance from respective sources), as well as potential of the electric field and pressure of the fluid (both vary inversely as the first power of the distance).

Whether the properties of the model are reproductions or analogues of properties in the original, to refer to a model in the present sense is to refer to an object distinct from that of which it is a model. This is not so in the case of a second group of

24. I do, however, believe that the distinctions about to be drawn hold for other sciences as well.

conceptions called models in physics. I have in mind the billiard-ball model of a gas, Bohr's model of the atom, the corpuscular model of light, the shell model of the atomic nucleus, the free-electron model of metals, the hard-sphere model of a fluid. Here physicists are referring not to an object Y distinct from the object of which it is a model, X, but to a set of assumptions about X. For example, the billiard-ball model is a set of assumptions according to which molecules in a gas exert only contact forces on one another, travel in straight lines except at the instant of collision, are small in size compared to average intermolecular distances, and so on. The shell model assumes that particles in the atomic nucleus are arranged in shells and move in orbits with quantized angular momentum in a nuclear field due to all the other particles in the nucleus. What kinds of assumptions would tend to be called models? Why are some assumptions called theories, some just models, and some both? Here one needs to plunge deeper into the subject by examining these examples and seeing how physicists treat them in contrast to assumptions they classify as theories. In other writings I have described charac-teristics of these types of models;[25] let me here mention three of them.

First, models of this type, which I call *theoretical models,* describe an object or system by attributing to it what might be called an inner structure, composition, or mechanism, reference to which is intended to explain various properties exhibited by that object or system (properties that might be considered macro-scopic relative to those of the inner structure). So, for example, the billiard-ball model ascribes a molecular structure to gases to explain various relationships between the pressure, volume, temperature, entropy, etc., of gases. Second, theoretical models are treated as simplified approximations useful for certain pur-poses. The billiard-ball model assumes that the only intermolec-ular forces are contact forces and thus ignores non-contact attrac-tive and repulsive forces. It offers a simplified representation of a gas useful for allowing a number of important relationships to

25. *Concepts of Science,* chap. 7; "Theoretical Models," *British Journal for the Philosophy of Science,* 16 (1965): 102–20.

be derived, for presenting some intuitive idea of the structure of gases, and even for suggesting how kinetic theory might be developed further. Third, a theoretical model is proposed within the broader framework of some more basic theory or theories. By this I mean that the scientist appropriates certain principles of some more general theory or theories and applies them, along with various new assumptions, to X, where "X" designates some relatively restricted class of objects. In the billiard-ball model Newton's laws of motion are applied to molecules in a gas, and various new and specific assumptions about these molecules are made.

There is a third use of the term "model." Sometimes by a model of an X a physicist means assumptions about X, but ones which do not say what X is, even approximately. Instead they say what X could be like if it were to satisfy a certain set of conditions initially stated. Poincaré constructed a model of a non-Euclidean world by describing an imaginary sphere about which he made various assumptions; for example, that the temperature is greatest at the center and gradually decreases as one moves toward the circumference, where it is absolute zero, that bodies contract as they move toward the circumference, and, as they move, are instantly in thermal equilibrium with their new environment. In the world described by Poincaré, postulates of Lobachevskian geometry are satisfied. However, Poincaré does not claim that there is a Lobachevskian world or even that, if there is, it is like the one he describes. His point is to show what a world could be like if it were to satisfy postulates of Lobachevsky's geometry. Conceptions of this type, which say only what X could be like if it were to satisfy certain conditions, I call *imaginary models*. They may be used to show that certain suppositions which might otherwise be thought self-contradictory, for example, postulates of a non-Euclidean geometry, are at least consistent. And they may promote more understanding of such principles by imagining a physical application for them.

By considering, to begin with, conceptions actually classified as models in science, we may be led to divide them into various types. Above I distinguished three types, and I would claim that these are the principal ones employed, at least in physics. There are other uses of the term "model" in fields such as mathematical logic and formal semantics, and some philosophers of science, notably contemporary positivists, claim that *model* understood in one of the latter ways can be applied to conceptions classified as models in physics. This claim, I would argue, is unjustifiable.[26] Also, positivists and others tend to use the term "model" interchangeably with "analogy." Insofar as this is merely a terminological convention which they wish to introduce, I have no quarrel. But those who use the terms interchangeably offer the same analysis for items that are quite different. Positivists classify together as models not only all the conceptions discussed above but also, for example, the analogy, drawn by Kelvin, between electrostatic attraction and the conduction of heat, or the analogy between a gas and a container of billiard balls; they describe each of these as "another interpretation of a theory's calculus." Analogies, I should claim, are essentially different from models. To refer to an analogy between X and Y is to refer either to certain types of similarities between unlike items X and Y or to a noting of such similarities; to refer to Y as a model of X, on the other hand, is to refer either to some physical system representing X or to certain types of assumptions which attribute properties to X.

Suppose, then, after considering uses of the term "model," we distinguish and characterize various types. Is there more to be done? A natural question is this: Why are these classified together? Is there any characteristic common to all of them? I think perhaps there is, although it is not sufficient for being a model and it must be described in a fairly abstract and loose way. In each of the cases noted the model can be described as (or as containing) (1) a representation of X; but (2) one which is not literal or not faithful in all respects, or not complete, and which may represent X in some "indirect" manner; and (3) one which utilizes something more or less familiar, known, understood, readily grasped, or easily experimented upon. A representational model represents X by utilizing something Y that is distinct from X, where Y has some features similar to or identical with certain

26. See *Concepts of Science*, chap. 8.

ones in X and is familiar or more readily grasped. A theoretical model represents X, but only approximately and not completely, by bringing it under, or at least utilizing parts of, some more basic theory or theories which are familiar and understood. An imaginary model represents X, not by describing what is the case (even approximately), but by imagining how X could satisfy certain conditions, where the conditions or the description of X is more or less familiar and understood.

The "common element" I have described is not a sufficient condition, since it can be found in items other than models, for example, diagrams and oversimplified accounts. And it is fairly loose, requiring the term "representation" to cover both physical objects and propositions, and requiring the use of alternation in conditions (2) and (3) so that all cases will be covered. Perhaps it is by reference to these conditions, loose though they be, that we can understand why the conceptions I have distinguished tend to be classified together. But the more important task, I think, is that of describing characteristics of each of the various types of models, something I attempted, albeit briefly, above. Another task is to determine whether and to what extent such distinctions and characterizations are applicable to conceptions called models in sciences other than physics, for example, in economics or psychology. This remains to be done, although I will not embark on it here.

With "model" we have a concept more or less peculiar to science. True, the term is often used outside the sciences to mean (among other things) what I mean by "representational model." But the other uses I distinguished are different from ordinary ones. With "theory," to which I now turn, we have a concept the sciences cannot claim for their very own. Let me indicate how I would proceed in this case. To begin with, if we make a list of items actually called theories, we will, I think, recognize the need for the following distinction. The term "theory" is used in a narrower sense (as in "Bohr's theory of the atom," "Newton's theory of mechanics") to refer to a more or less specific set of propositions. It is also used in a broader sense (as in "physical theory," "nuclear theory") to refer to a field or subject matter, which may contain not only theories (in the narrower sense) but also methods of analyzing or structuring situations, applications to various systems, methods for solving problems, concepts, and so forth. Of course the latter may all be included when a theory (in the narrower sense) is presented. But to use *theory* in the latter sense is to view all of these simply or primarily as part of a set of propositions; to use *theory* in the broader sense is to view them not simply or primarily in this way but more or less independently. In what follows I shall speak only of the narrower "propositional" sense, for this has been of most concern to philosophers of science.

Let me begin by asking what it means to say that someone has a theory T. My aim is to formulate conditions that are relevant and especially central for this, even though they may not be logically necessary. The fact that one of them fails to obtain may count to some extent against saying that someone has a theory, without necessarily precluding it. My assumption is that these conditions obtain for theories inside and outside science and therefore that further conditions would need to be formulated for the concept (or concepts) of a scientific theory. An answer to the question I am now raising would obviously provide a basis for characterizing the latter concept. In what follows I shall briefly state those conditions which typically obtain, I believe, when someone, call him A, has a theory T.[27] Afterward, by reference to these conditions, I will say what it is to be a theory.

1. A does not know that T is true, although he believes it is. Moreover, he cannot immediately and readily come to know the truth of T, or could not at the inception of his belief in T. A may think he knows that T is true, but *we* say he has a theory T when we impute to A a lack of knowledge concerning the truth of T. If A later comes to know the truth of T, it is no longer appropriate to say that he has a *theory* T (or that he has T as a theory) unless we doubt that he knows the truth of T. Thus, one of the reasons we are willing to say that Bohr had the theory that the angular momentum of the electron in the atom, as well

27. Various qualifications and further explanations can be found in *Concepts of Science*, chap. 4.

as the energy radiated or absorbed by the atom, is quantized is because he did not know, and could not immediately and readily come to know, that this was so. And one of the reasons why the proposition "There is a green chair in the room next to mine" is not a theory I have is because I know it to be true, and, even if I did not, I could readily come to know it in a simple and direct way.

2. A does not know, nor does he believe, that T is false; moreover, he cannot immediately and readily come to know that T is false, or could not at the inception of his belief in T. If A later came to know or to believe that T is false, we would no longer say that he has the theory T. One of the reasons we are willing to say that Kepler (at one time) had the theory that the orbit of Mars is a perfect circle is that he did not at the time know or believe it to be false and indeed thought it to be true. And one of the reasons we are willing to say that after a time Kepler no longer had that theory is that he came to disbelieve it because it yielded consequences seriously at odds with observations.

3. A believes that T provides, or will eventually provide, some (or a better) understanding of something, and that this is, or will be, one of the main functions of T. By providing an understanding I mean something quite broad that can be done, for example, by explaining, interpreting, removing a puzzle, showing why something is not surprising, indicating a cause or causes, supplying reasons, analyzing something into simpler, more familiar, or more integrated components. Moreover, those things which are explained, interpreted, and so on, may be items of many different kinds, not just "surprising phenomena that have been observed" (Hanson).

4. T consists of propositions purporting to assert what is the case. Normally, when we speak of A's theory we are referring to those propositions treated by A as *assumptions* (i.e., as not being derived from others in his theory), as *central* to his theory (i.e., as expressing the most important ideas of his theory), and as *distinctive* of it (i.e., as serving to identify it as that particular theory and distinguish it from others). But A's theory may have associated with it (as presuppositions, ancillary assumptions, con-

sequences) propositions not in the set of central and distinctive assumptions. In referring to Bohr's theory of the atom one usually has in mind his two assumptions regarding quantization of the angular momentum of the electron in the atom and quantization of energy radiated or absorbed by the atom. But Bohr uses other propositions, such as Newton's second law of motion, Coulomb's law, and the principle of conservation of mechanical energy, in order to obtain his results.

5. A does not know of any more fundamental (theory) T' from which he knows that the set of central and distinctive assumptions of T can be simply and directly derived, where A satisfies all the other conditions with respect to T'. In formulating his principle of conservation of momentum and the principle of inertia for the center of mass of a system of bodies, Newton was not formulating a theory that he had, but only certain propositions that follow, and that he knew followed, simply and directly, from such a theory.

6. A believes that each of the assumptions in the set regarded as distinctive and central will be helpful, together with others associated with the theory, in providing an understanding of those items for which A believes his theory may provide an understanding. In short, A believes in a joint effort on the part of his central and distinctive assumptions. This condition expresses a weak "working together" requirement. If A is committed to Malthus' theory of population, to Einstein's special theory of relativity, and to Freud's theory of the unconscious, he does not have a theory consisting of the conjunction of these (unless in some extreme case he actually believes that their conjunction is helpful in promoting an understanding of something).

Here, then, are six conditions relevant for having a theory. Can we use them to say what it is to be a theory? Can we say, for example, that for T to be a theory it is necessary and sufficient that there be some A who has T? This is too restrictive, for it prevents us from classifying as theories T's which no one still has, for example, the phlogiston theory. So we might say that for T to be a theory it is necessary and sufficient that some A either have or have had T. But again we are in trouble, for sometimes we classify T as a theory if it is plausible to imagine someone as having it, even though no one ever did or will. The problem stems from the fact that what can be classified as a theory depends in part upon the context of classification. In certain contexts, for example, that of a historian of science, what will count as a theory may be T's that leading scientists actually have had throughout the ages. In other contexts what will count as a theory may be T's that leading scientists of today have. And in some contexts what will count may be T's that are now had or that it might be plausible to imagine someone as having, be he scientist or not.

What we must say, therefore, is this: T is classifiable as a theory, within a given context of classification, if and only if there is (or, depending on the context, was or might plausibly have been imagined to be) some (person, scientist, leading scientist) A who satisfies all or most of the six conditions with respect to T. Putting this briefly, and roughly: T is a theory, relative to the context of classification, if and only if it is a set of propositions which (depending on the context) is (was, might have been, etc.) not known to be true or false, but which is believed to be true, potentially explanatory, relatively fundamental, and somewhat integrated. Finally, then, given that some A satisfies the six conditions with respect to some T, we are not automatically entitled to classify T as a theory. What we can say is that, if an A does satisfy (all or most of) these conditions, then he has what in appropriate contexts will count as a theory. And, if he has what in some context counts as a theory, then he satisfies (all or most of) the conditions.

This analysis can be contrasted with that supplied by positivists and by Hanson. Each of the latter omits contextual considerations relevant in deciding whether to count something as a theory. Moreover, according to positivists, it would seem that for A to have a theory would simply be for A to have formulated or to be willing to formulate axioms, theorems, and proofs. If so, questions about A's knowledge of the truth or falsity of T would be irrelevant. Furthermore, on the positivist account, there is no requirement that A not have any more fundamental theory T' from which he knows that T could readily be derived: in short, any subset of propositions in (or implied by) A's theory would itself be a theory for A. Nor is there any "working together" requirement; thus, any unrelated propositions that A might string together could count as a theory. Hanson's conception also ignores several of the conditions I formulated. For example, it makes no requirement that the supplier of a theory not know its truth or falsity. Nor does it take into account the "non-derivability" and "working together" conditions.

In this discussion my assumption has been that the concept of a theory is the same inside as well as outside the sciences. My approach has been to suggest conditions that are relevant and especially central for this concept. Obviously, important questions remain: Can conditions also be formulated that are central for classifying a theory as a *scientific* one? Do such conditions change from era to era and even from science to science, or are they quite general? Can something be said on a subject of special concern to positivists, namely, the "structure" of scientific theories? What elements in a scientific theory might it be useful to distinguish, and how are they related? I deal with the issue of structure elsewhere by considering various ways that theories in science are, or can be, presented.[28] This issue, as well as that of what makes a theory scientific, should be of fundamental concern to philosophers of science, and both, I suggest, become tractable once we agree on some analysis of the concept of theory.

Let me summarize the main points of the approach I have been suggesting. With respect to certain general concepts employed in the sciences, for example, "model," "theory," "law," and "explanation," the question I would raise is this: What concept or concepts are actually in use? It may not be possible to characterize these concepts by citing conditions that are logically necessary and sufficient, for such conditions may not exist. But it may be possible to formulate conditions that are relevant and especially central, and, if so, this would constitute an answer to the question I seek to raise. The present approach, then, combines certain features of positivist and anti-positivist aims. Like the positivists, I seek to formulate general conditions for concepts under discussion, although, unlike them, I do not demand necessary

28. *Ibid.*

and sufficient conditions. Like the anti-positivists discussed earlier, my concern is not to replace concepts in use in the sciences but to discover what they are. However, my primary aim is to formulate conditions for the concepts, and I regard analogies and case histories as important only insofar as they facilitate such formulations. For an analysis of concepts they are not ends in themselves, nor do they provide a sure-fire method for obtaining results. Where the concept in question is used primarily in the sciences, one procedure is to cite many cases actually classified under it and, if these are diverse, to distinguish various types. This is what I did in the case of models, and it is also the general procedure I would suggest for laws. If there is reason to think the concept is the same both inside and outside science, as with "theory" or "explanation," then it may prove simpler to begin by considering non-scientific examples.[29] In any case, the aim should be to formulate general conditions that are relevant and quite central for the concepts actually employed or, failing this, to distinguish several such concepts and formulate conditions for each.

What, then, about "explication"? Can it be useful in the philosophy of science? [30] I can conceive of a purpose that might be served by *considering* a concept which is somewhat different from the one actually employed, namely, as a way of describing the latter by setting up an idealized version and then trying to indicate how the concept in use differs. In discussing the concept of "definition" in science, I have found it useful to construct several idealized models and to show the various respects in which the actual concept is different.[31] But in the philosophy of science is there ever any point in *replacing* one concept with another? Consider two situations.

1. A term might be used by some scientist or group in such a way that standard cases to which it does and does not apply cannot be cited or clearly described, or in such a way that such

29. For an account of explanation, see my "Explanation," *American Philosophical Quarterly*, Monograph Series, no. 3.

30. For a discussion of explication, see my "Rudolf Carnap," *Review of Metaphysics*, I, no. 19 (1966) : 517–49, and II, no. 19 (1966) : 758–79.

31. *Concepts of Science*, chap. I.

cases seem to shift in unpredictable ways. If so, the concept in question would be at least somewhat confused, and a philosopher of science might do well to "explicate" it by constructing one or several clearer and more consistent concepts, suggesting that any of these is what the scientist might want to mean when he uses the term, since what he now means is unclear, involves inconsistencies, and so on.

2. A term might be used by a scientist or group in such a way that, although standard cases to which it is and is not applicable can be cited or described, there are certain actual or at least hypothetical borderline cases where it is unclear whether or not the term is applicable; and we may find some scientists tempted to apply it, others not, and many not knowing what to do. But this, it seems to me, is so for concepts generally, and simply reflects the fact that none are defined for all conceivable contexts. Even concepts that positivists treat as the clearest and most basic ones—primitive concepts such as "red," "warm," "hard," expressed by terms in their "observational" vocabulary—are subject to this fate. To be sure, it is possible to sharpen a concept by reducing the number of its borderline cases; and this is sometimes useful. But neither clarity nor consistency demands elimination of all conceivable cases of this type, something I would claim to be impossible anyway.

It must be conceded that general concepts actually in use which are of concern to philosophers of science, concepts such as "model," "theory," "law," and "explanation," are subject to condition (2). But for me, "explication," in the sense of replacement, would be valuable only if it could be shown that these concepts are also subject to condition (1). Philosophers who demand "explication" surely have not demonstrated this, and, in suggesting analyses of concepts such as "model" and "theory," I am, of course, committed to rejecting such a demand.

index

Designed by James Wageman

Composed in Baskerville, with Sans Serif Light and Medium display, by The Colonial Press Inc.

Printed offset on 60 lb. P&S "R" and bound in Interlaken ALl-975 by The Colonial Press Inc.